THINK GOOD AND IT WILL BE GOOD

THINK GOOD

AND IT WILL BE

GOOD

SPIRITUALLY-BASED THERAPY INSPIRED BY
VIKTOR FRANKL AND JEWISH WISDOM

Rabbi Daniel Schonbuch, M.A., L.M.F.T.

Cover design by Glen M. Edelstein
Book design by Glen M. Edelstein

Printed in the United States of America

First Printing, 2017
ISBN 13: 978-0-692-85879-0

CONTENTS

This book is dedicated to my dear grandfather,
Mr. Jack Aron z"l, who taught me the pathway to
being happy and sharing it with others.

SECTION I

DISCLAIMER

Think Good and It Will Be Good presents a refreshing approach for treating depression, anxiety, and addiction. It offers practical advice and spiritually-based strategies to supplement therapy and maintain positive changes.

It is important to note, however, that *Think Good and It Will Be Good* is not a replacement for consulting a physician or licensed therapist who can diagnose and treat emotional disorders. If you feel you are suffering from depression, anxiety, or addiction, please visit a licensed professional, or if it's an emergency, call 911.

Introduction

WHEN THERAPY IS NOT ENOUGH

What happens when therapy doesn't work? Over the last few years, I have had the privilege to work with many brave clients for whom the traditional therapeutic methods have brought some improvement in their condition, but not the total relief they hoped for. Searching for new methods of healing for my clients, I discovered I was not the only therapist to recognize this problem.

"Evidence continues to accumulate that many people who have anxiety and depression suffer bouts of it all their lives, even after a good response to therapy," writes noted psychologist Dr. Margaret Wehrenberg.

Working with clients over thirty years, Wehrenberg found that depression and anxiety were chronic problems that required a comprehensive approach to address ongoing emotional distress, similar to addiction treatment protocols. In addiction recovery, clients are not left alone to simply meet once-a-week with a therapist for a brief 45-minute session. Instead, therapists "provide individualized care and tools (including social support) to cope with unexpected changes, along with a *daily program of meditation and spiritual connection*, and daily optimistic reminders of the chronicity of their condition and how they're managing it."[1]

Like Wehrenberg, I have met with many clients suffering from depression and anxiety who felt therapy was unable to fully heal their pain. After years of sitting on the "couch," many were still struggling with persistent feelings of worry or sadness. They needed more support than just 45 minutes a week in their psychologist's office. The frustration these clients experienced as they tried various therapies, without feeling lasting results, challenged me to create a comprehensive approach toward depression and anxiety.

Inspired by the work of psychiatrist Viktor Frankl, Chasidic teachings, and the most effective methods available in modern psychology, I developed Torah Psychology, a spiritually-based therapy that encourages clients to find meaning, think positively, and create a spiritual framework that inspires optimism, and helps my clients find purpose in their lives. This book includes client experiences that led to Torah Psychology, along with a summary of traditional therapies, scientific research supporting a spiritual approach, and finally, the principles and tools to apply them.

Let's begin with the far-reaching experiences of my clients whose tenacity to face depression and anxiety inspired this journey to integrate therapy with a spiritual path.

SARAH'S STORY*

When I first met with Sarah, a forty-five-year-old mother of four, she had recently lost both her parents in a car accident. Sarah was struggling with depression and anxiety following this tragic loss. At our first session she described what had happened:

"My parents were coming back to the city at the end of a long weekend upstate. They had planned to join us for dinner. I was busy cooking with two of my daughters when I received the devastating call. I felt my body freeze, and I had severe cramps in my stomach and chest as I listened to the terrible news. At that moment, all time had stopped. I had flashbacks of my childhood, my parents' faces, and felt the tremendous gap this loss would have on my life."

Since that day, Sarah would break into tears and then have moments of deep silence where she seemed unreachable. Her distress was taking a huge toll on the family. Sarah was overwhelmed by what had occurred, and worried she wouldn't be able to overcome her pain and depression.

Sarah had struggled for years trying to overcome the distance she had felt with her parents since she was a teenager. She shared with me what her profound sadness felt like:

---

*All stories in this book are not real cases but composites of many cases. Any resemblance to anyone the reader may know is coincidental.

"I thought my life was going pretty well when G-d threw me a tremendous curveball. My mother was killed just when I felt ready to get closer to her. Yet I could never see her again. This was not how life was supposed to be. I descended into a very low mood filled with doubt about my future and hatred toward myself for not having the relationship I wanted with my mother when she was alive."

Sarah felt guilty that she missed the chance to repair her relationship with her mother before she died. Instead, Sarah felt "a lack of meaning" and was "drowning in sorrow" day after day. While Sarah had tried therapy in the past, she had only experienced partial relief. Now she was looking for something different that would restore her to herself.

MOSHE'S STORY

Moshe was a 32-year-old computer programmer who had struggled with depression and anxiety since he was a teenager. Recently, Moshe had become addicted to the Internet and would look at his phone constantly as we spoke in my office. His addiction was also affecting his family life. When he returned home after a long day of work, he would lay in bed and surf the web, causing his wife and children to feel abandoned by him. Moshe had lost a lot of weight suddenly, and his doctor was concerned about the impact depression was having on his health. He had tried working with therapists in the past, but he was still suffering.

Slumped on the couch in my office, Moshe described what it felt like to be depressed:

"I feel as though I'm living in a dark cloud and there will never be any sunlight. I don't have energy or motivation to feel any happiness. Last week my nephew got married and I couldn't feel anything. I just sat at the wedding staring at people, emotionless. I couldn't smile due to the pain in my stomach. I pretended that I was having a good time to friends and family, but deep down inside I was miserable."

Moshe was overwhelmed by his symptoms of sadness and lethargy, and had lost all hope of feeling better. What complicated his feelings of emotional instability were the various sensations he was having around his body, including aches and pains in his stomach, back and knees. Psychosomatic pain is common in people who suffer from depression, making their lives physically uncomfortable, in addition to their emotional turmoil.

At our second session, Moshe shared traumatic childhood memories he believed were responsible for his long-term depression. Moshe's father used to abuse him and his siblings, hitting them with a belt, and threatening them verbally on a daily basis. He also was abused by two of his teachers, and had significant anger toward his school, and especially toward rabbis. Despite his suffering, Moshe viewed himself as a religious Jew, but had many questions about G-d and the purpose of his life. He had been to other therapists who didn't know how to discuss issues pertaining to G-d, meaning, and religion. Referencing my religious training, Moshe was hoping I could help him feel better.

MIRIAM'S STORY

Miriam was a 28-year-old mother of three young children who suffered from frequent anxiety attacks. Her third child was born prematurely, and spent many months in and out of the hospital. That experience triggered what Miriam described as "postpartum depression." Still reeling from the difficult birth and recovery, Miriam also had to juggle taking care of her two other young children, and helping her mother, who was sick with cancer.

A year before we met, Miriam started having indigestion that worsened over time and was accompanied by dizzy spells and headaches. She had trouble sleeping and would spend many hours on her computer late at night, chatting with friends and watching movies. Before bed, she would obsess about the front door not being locked, and would check it several times each night—to the dismay of her husband and children. Miriam had already been diagnosed with anxiety and was now exhibiting signs of OCD and depression.

Miriam was raised in a family that didn't believe in therapy, and was told that therapists steer people away from their relationship with G-d. Begrudgingly, she began seeing an Orthodox Jewish therapist at a mental health clinic who spent months listening to her problems. Yet, Miriam felt little relief from her symptoms and was looking for a different kind of treatment that could help.

As I continued to work with Sarah, Moshe, and Miriam, I wondered if the missing pieces in their healing process were finding a sense of purpose in life and adopting a positive outlook. In all three cases I suggested that they read a book called "Man's Search for Meaning" and two specific teachings of the Tzemach Tzedek, the third Rebbe of the Chabad dynasty, that would soon change their lives. Their response to finding a higher meaning and focusing on positive thinking, confirmed my belief that living a life of meaning, increasing optimism, and having a spiritual connection are the keys to sustaining the gains made in therapy. Meaning and positive thinking are two inseparable wings that can help a person soar. The third force is spirit, which keeps a person in flight.

FINDING VIKTOR FRANKL (*MAN'S SEARCH FOR MEANING*)

I first encountered Viktor Frankl in the winter of 1989, when I walked into a Jewish bookstore looking for something to read on Shabbos. Heading towards the *parashah* section, I noticed a book about the Holocaust called *Man's Search for Meaning*. Intrigued by its small size and title, I picked up the book, started flipping through the pages, and was hooked immediately. I had read many books about that horrible time period, including the writings of Elie Wiesel and Yaffa Eliach, but Frankl's work was different.

A Jewish survivor of Auschwitz and respected psychiatrist, Frankl developed the third Viennese School of Psychotherapy called Logotherapy (therapy of meaning). In his short but powerful book, Frankl described his experience during the war, as well as his theory that "those who knew that there was a task waiting for them to fulfill were most apt to survive [the concentration camps]."[2]

Frankl credited his work as a psychiatrist for helping him survive:

"As for myself, when I was taken to...Auschwitz, a manuscript of mine ready for publication was confiscated. Certainly, my deep desire to write this manuscript anew helped me to survive the rigors of the camps I was in. For instance, when in a camp in Bavaria I fell ill with typhus fever, I jotted down on little scraps of paper many notes intended to enable me to rewrite the manuscript, should I live to the day of liberation. I am sure that this reconstruction of my lost manuscript in the dark barracks of a Bavarian concentration camp assisted me in overcoming the danger of cardiovascular collapse."[3]

Frankl was not just referring to those interned in the camps or held captive as prisoners of war. He was offering a path forward for *all* people facing challenges. To Frankl, the only way to overcome personal predicament—whether physical or emotional in nature—was to look beyond the limits of self.

After the Holocaust, Frankl spent much of his career trying to persuade his colleagues that modern psychology focused too much on the self, and not enough on the search for meaning. Logotherapy challenged the foundation of theories put forth by the father of modern psychology, Sigmund Freud, and his colleague Alfred Adler, among others.

In Freud's view, the core of human existence was an animalistic impulse that craved pleasure and destruction, called the "id." He attributed depression and anxiety primarily to clients' childhood frustrations and unresolved complexes. Adler took a different approach and believed man's essential desire was attaining power. Frankl disagreed with them both, arguing that a person's most basic need was for a sense of purpose, or what he termed "the will to meaning." If the search for meaning was frustrated, *then* man lowered himself to pursuing pleasure, destruction, or power. [§]

Frankl believed that the greatest challenge to emotional well-being was not low self-esteem or a lack of pleasure, but rather an existential vacuum, or inner emptiness. He perceived that modern psychotherapy would be only partially successful in treating depression if it didn't address its underlying cause, man's frustrated search for meaning.

According to Frankl, three types of values generate meaning:

Creative values: Meaning can develop from a person using his or her skills and talents. For example, a teacher finds meaning through instructing students, a doctor through healing patients, or a mechanic by repairing the engine of a broken car. All three find meaning through their work.

Experiential values: These emerge when a person experiences nature and the wonders of creation, including art and music, or through loving and giving to another person.

[§]According to Chasidic thought there are two souls: the Nefesh Habahamis (the animal soul) and the Nefesh Elokis (the G-dly soul): see the Tanya chapters 1 and 2. Freud's and Adler's comments about pleasure and power reflect the description of the desires of the Nefesh Habahamis (the animal soul). Frankl's focus on meaning seems to refer to the sublime aspects of the Nefesh Habahamis inspired by the desire of the Nefesh Elokis to connect with G-d: See Frankl's "The Unconscious God" where he interprets dreams based on the "religio" or the Godly unconscious.

Attitudinal values: These values surface when a person faces inescapable adversity, yet chooses their attitude toward his suffering. Frankl accessed these values to survive the concentration camps. Others have experienced this while battling serious illness.

ENCOUNTERING THE POWER OF POSITIVITY

The second occurrence that shaped my perspective as a therapist was the heroic, modern-day story of a young yeshiva student named Nachum Sasonkin. In 1994, Sasonkin was shot in the head by a Lebanese terrorist on the Brooklyn Bridge. Gunmen in a passing car opened fire on a van carrying Sasonkin and his friends on their way home from visiting the Lubavitcher Rebbe in the hospital.

After the attack, Sasonkin was still awake as he was transported to the hospital. Within minutes, however, the swelling and bleeding in his brain caused extreme pressure inside his skull. Within an hour, he was rushed into surgery. Dr. Alan Hirschfeld, Sasonkin's neurosurgeon, had to remove part of his skull and brain to keep him alive. The immediate prognosis was devastating. Nachum remained in a coma for three weeks while his family and friends waited, praying he would regain consciousness. Dr. Hirschfeld told a reporter for *The New York Times* that he had "never seen one patient get out of the hospital alive" after such a serious injury. "On a scale of 1 to 10, I would give him a chance of point five," said Dr. Hirschfeld. Though the Sasonkins respected the doctor's' advice, they held on to hope.[4]

Despite the dire prognosis, Nachum's mother was able to look forward and create a positive vision that her son would recover, thrive, and eventually get married. She announced she was "collecting names to invite to her son's wedding," shocking national television audiences with her absolute faith in a good outcome. Onlookers doubted her approach, yet three weeks after the accident, Nachum miraculously woke up. He eventually went on to get married, receive his rabbinic ordination, and build a family.

As I followed the story, I wondered how Mrs. Sasonkin had the power and presence of mind to react with confidence in a good result, against every shred of medical evidence.

TEACHINGS OF THE TZEMACH TZEDEK ("THINK GOOD AND IT WILL BE GOOD.")

Two centuries ago, long before modern psychology promoted positivity, the Tzemach Tzedek utilized the power of having a positive outlook in life. Responding to a distraught father seeking help for his critically ill son, the Tzemach Tzedek advised, *"Tracht gut vet zein gut"* (Think good and it will be good). The Tzemach Tzedek was not offering false hope for healing. He understood that positive thinking can actually influence the outcome of events. In this case, the son recovered fully from his illness at the very moment his father began thinking positively.

The *Tzemach Tzedek* explained that "thinking good" involves developing a deep sense of *Bitachon* (trust) in G-d. And yet, complete faith in a positive outcome does not deny the importance of taking responsibility for your actions. He was not suggesting that you should avoid dealing with difficult situations and challenging your desires. Taking personal responsibility for your actions, working to uncover possible motivations, and finding solutions are essential steps to overcoming feelings of emotional distress. However, "thinking good" reminds you to "Cast your burden upon G-d" (*Tehillim* 55:23); to turn your attention toward Him as the source of your comfort. According to the *Tzemach Tzedek*, when you deepen your trust and rely on G-d alone for assistance, G-d responds in kind, bestowing "visible and manifest good upon you." [5]

I have found that a spiritual outlook guided by religious beliefs can have a powerful effect on emotional well-being. In fact, the search for meaning and positive thinking are two of the most powerful tools to assist us in dealing with depression and anxiety. The third tool is creating a daily spiritual program to strengthen faith and trust in a Higher Power. And yet I wondered how many of us—therapists and clients—had approached depression or anxiety with the perspective of ongoing treatment.

HOW TO RECOGNIZE DEPRESSION AND ANXIETY

Individuals like Sarah, Moshe, and Miriam are not alone. Almost 15 million American adults experience depression, and nearly 40 million have various symptoms of anxiety. [6] Both of these illnesses can interfere with daily life and functioning. In severe cases, depression or anxiety may limit a person's ability to experience joy or pleasure, and make it hard to work, raise a family, and lead a productive life.

Depression in adults is sometimes experienced as sadness, but it is possible that a person suffering from depression or anxiety has other symptoms that include:

Depression
- Feelings of hopelessness, pessimism, worthlessness, or guilt
- Loss of interest in things that used to be important
- Lack of energy
- Difficulty sleeping
- Lack of appetite or weight changes (without dieting)
- Difficulty concentrating or reading
- Irritability
- Physical pain such as muscle, head, or stomach aches
- Thoughts of suicide

Anxiety
- Restlessness or feeling wound-up or on edge
- Being easily fatigued
- Difficulty concentrating or having their minds go blank
- Irritability
- Muscle tension
- Difficulty controlling worry
- Sleep problems (difficulty falling or staying asleep or restless, unsatisfying sleep)[7]

There are many factors that may affect the onset of depression or anxiety. Common triggers include family history, physiology or traumatic events such as the loss of a relationship or loved one, a car accident, and sexual molestation. Both illnesses have more severe forms including "Major Depression" or "Panic Disorder." Some people may experience Seasonally Affective Disorder (SAD) during the winter, or Postpartum Depression after giving birth. Others suffer with social anxiety or phobias, and avoid people, places, and things. Obsessive Compulsive Disorder (OCD) is a form of anxiety that causes people to have intrusive and repetitive thoughts, and practice ritualistic behaviors like constant hand washing or checking stove tops or locks on doors.

TREATMENT STRATEGIES

Psychologists have been searching for a cure for anxiety and depression for the past 100 years. Their efforts have resulted in various therapeutic approaches including: Psychoanalysis (Sigmund Freud), Cognitive Behavioral Therapy (Aaron Beck), and *Eye Movement Desensitization and Reprocessing* (Francine Shapiro), to name just a few. All three approaches have influenced the practice of psychotherapy and have helped many individuals achieve *some* success in overcoming depression and anxiety.

Psychoanalysis

According to Sigmund Freud's psychoanalytic theory of personality, the mind has three components: the id, ego, and superego. Freud described how the conflict among these three parts can cause anxiety or depression during adulthood. Freud believed that these conflicts were mostly unconscious, revealing themselves in the choices people make. When left unresolved, these conflicts turn into neurosis. For example, if a person was rejected by his father as a child and years later his boss fires him, his job loss could lead to depression.

Psychoanalysis is a lengthy process that requires a person to attend therapy sessions several times per week. During these sessions the therapist listens carefully to the client's remarks, as the client uses "free association" and says whatever comes to mind. The therapist looks for connections by sifting through the client's unconscious material in order to make the themes conscious. Dreams are also explored as a means to uncovering unconscious desires.

In Freud's view, depression is caused by the perceived or actual loss of a parent during childhood. To resolve depression, the client needs to mourn this real or perceived "loss." Anxiety results from the unconscious fear of losing control of the id's desire (i.e., pleasure). Freud's main point was that many people experience emotional suffering caused by their conflicts during childhood. He therefore believed that therapy must focus on a person's past, in order to change their present condition.

Cognitive Behavioral Therapy

Aaron Beck took a different position on the causes for depression or anxiety, creating a new approach he called Cognitive Behavior Therapy (CBT). CBT is built on the concept that a person has different levels of thoughts, including automatic thoughts, intermediate thoughts, and self-beliefs. When these thoughts are distorted, they cause negative emotions like sadness or excessive worry, as the following diagram illustrates.

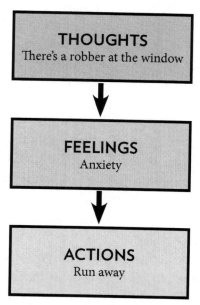

In CBT, a person heals by exploring his thoughts while the therapist works to modify negative and rigid thinking patterns. The goal is to form a more realistic view of oneself by using "coping statements" to reduce feelings of anger or disappointment.

For over 30 years, CBT has been the standard in treating depression and anxiety. It is one of the most utilized and successful types of therapy in the world today. CBT focuses on exploring past and current issues, yet it does not necessarily move a person toward finding meaning, nor does it orient individuals towards fulfilling their future goals or spiritual ambitions. (A more detailed discussion of anxiety and CBT can be found in chapters 2 and 4).

Eye Movement Desensitization and Reprocessing

Renowned psychologist Dr. Francine Shapiro created EMDR to treat Post-traumatic Stress Disorder (PTSD) nearly 30 years ago. While taking a long walk, Shapiro began thinking about traumas she had experienced in the past. Shapiro was able to reduce her emotional response to her memories almost immediately by moving her eyes and back and forth. Dr. Shapiro believed that using the eye-movements during exposure to her traumatic memories lessened her post traumatic stress, reoriented her thought patterns, and transformed her negative self-beliefs into positive cognitions.

EMDR was quickly recognized as an effective therapy for treating people with PTSD (Post Traumatic Stress Disorder). Since then, it has been used to help victims of terrorism, war, sexual abuse, life-threatening accidents and illnesses, and to treat depression and anxiety.

In EMDR, a person revisits the past in order to have a more functional present. This involves exploring initial traumas in detail together with a therapist trained in this technique. As the client recalls the details of the trauma, the therapist guides him to explore his emotions and beliefs about himself.

For example, someone who had been molested during childhood is exposed to his memories of the event(s). He also delves into his beliefs about himself, which may persist for many years. Common reactions include feeling responsible that he somehow "caused" the trauma, or carrying a sense of powerlessness that he is currently unsafe. The goal is to change thought patterns like powerlessness into self-empowerment and positive self-esteem.

According to EMDR, it is important to navigate through the history of a person's big "T"s and little "t"s (traumas). The goal is to gain access to repressed experiences, feelings, and memories. Repression of memories often plays a protective role, shielding a person from facing painful experiences head-on. The conscious mind represses or pushes away pain in order to cope better. On the surface level it seems that the traumatic memory has disappeared. However, painful memories eventually push their way to the surface. When a person doesn't want to face these feelings, they can reemerge as anxiety or depression.

THE LIMITATIONS OF THERAPY

Working with Sarah, Miriam, and Moshe, I began therapy by exploring their past histories, utilizing psychodynamic principles (maybe it's your parents' fault?), CBT, and EMDR. In Sarah's case, it was clear that the big trauma (big "T" or "Touchstone Memory") that was causing her depression was the loss of her parents. Facing their death was not an easy process. It takes tremendous courage to open up old wounds. However, by following the EMDR protocol over a two-month period, EMDR was successful in reducing the severity of some of the trauma Sarah experienced—but not all of it.

Sarah's other trauma was the emotional distance she felt from her mother that began when she was a teenager. She believed (like many teenagers) that her mother didn't respect or understand her. Sarah chose to study education, whereas her mother wanted her to go to nursing school. Her mother was not happy with Sarah's choice of friends. These issues were a major source of contention between the two of them for thirty years.

Utilizing EMDR, Sarah was able to address the conflict with her mom, which helped her understand the nature of parent/teenager interactions, and reduced the feelings of guilt and anger she had carried for so many years. However, despite our progress, Sarah was still in a depression. At times she would spend most of the day sleeping or trying to distract herself on the Internet until late at night. Though we had tried many therapeutic approaches, Sarah could not overcome the loss of her mother, describing it as a "pain that would never go away."

In Miriam's case, we aimed to reduce her anxiety and OCD by utilizing CBT and exposure therapy. Exposure therapy gradually exposes an anxious person to their fears. For example, if a person worried that gas was leaking from their stove, exposure therapy would increase the amount of time they were supposed to wait between checking the stove for gas leaks. Or, if they consistently avoided walking by the neighbor's house because the neighbor had a dog, treatment would involve having them walk past the house several times a day to learn how to cope with their fears.

The truth is that the more a person avoids their fears the worse they get. However, exposure to fears allows a person to face and overcome them. The mind eventually habituates to any fear or stimulation, causing less of a reaction over time. It is similar to someone who avoids jumping into a cold pool of water. Instead, they step in one foot at a time and stay there for a few moments. Gradually their body habituates to the new environment and they slowly submerge deeper into the water.

In Miriam's case, I asked her to control her compulsive stove-checking habit by only checking for leaking gas once per night. Practicing relaxation skills, such as calm breathing and guided meditation, helped her reduce her compulsions. Although she experienced significant relief after a few sessions, she still felt a pervasive sense of emptiness that therapy did not resolve.

During Moshe's sessions, we explored the multiple forms of abuse he experienced using EMDR. One of the most frightening episodes occurred when his father asked him to help physically abuse his siblings. He was forced to choose the "weapon" with which his father would abuse his siblings. This memory haunted Moshe for years. He would have frequent flashbacks of his sibling's pain, and of his guilt for not being able to save them.

After several EMDR sessions, however, we were able to reduce the intensity of his posttraumatic feelings. Moshe gradually learned how to manage his emotions and focus on loving his own children, despite the ghosts of his past. Although he had been taking an SSRI (antidepressant) for depression, Moshe continued to struggle. He longed for a more comprehensive approach that would allow him to function at a higher level.

I wished I had an easy answer, a proven method to guide Moshe, Miriam, and Sarah toward lasting recovery. I knew a comprehensive approach would not only address their early childhood traumas or cognitive distortions from the past, but also orient them toward the future by finding more meaning in their lives.

This shift however, needed to be towards the future and into the world of spirituality as the following diagram illustrates:

On the left side of the diagram we see that the focus of tradition-al therapies has been on the past (i.e. drives—Freud, cognitions—CBT, and trauma—EMDR). However, if you have already been in therapy and have not experienced comprehensive relief, you will need to move to-ward the right side of the diagram and shift your focus to the future. This is where a person enters into the world of what Frankl calls "Noos" (the dimension of meaning) or what Torah Psychology defines as spirituality.

Unfortunately, modern psychotherapy has for many years avoided focusing on meaning and spirituality. To the detriment of their clients, most therapists are not comfortable entering into these dimensions with their clients, as secular schools of therapy have historically avoided these topics. As a licensed therapist I also still had professional reservations about introducing spirituality in psychotherapy.

Chapter 1

IS THERE ROOM FOR SPIRITUALITY IN THERAPY?

SHOULD G-D BE ALLOWED INTO THE THERAPIST'S OFFICE?

While this may sound ridiculous, psychology has kept G-d and religion separate from the therapeutic process for over 100 years. In graduate school, we were taught to avoid the "G" word in therapy, and counseled never to discuss religion with our clients. We were told to keep a strong boundary between church and state, and to avoid mixing science with religion or spirituality, which were presented as "irrational" or "superstitious."

In fact, in 1981, the National Academy of Sciences passed a resolution stating that "religion and science are separate and mutually exclusive realms of human thought whose presentation in the same context leads to misunderstanding of both scientific theory and religious belief." [8] It's no accident that psychology is devoid of spirituality. These scientists wanted to keep G-d in the waiting room.

Please don't misunderstand me. It is important to maintain a level of professionalism that avoids personal issues such as religion and spirituality. I also firmly believe that the academic training and professional standards inherent in the licensed practice of psychology are crucial to providing clients with successful therapy. However, there are many clients who view spirituality as an integral part of their lives and wish to discuss their religious beliefs when confronting difficult situations such as death, loss, or hardship. Unfortunately, many psychologists aren't equipped to accommodate their needs.

The wedge modern psychology placed between G-d and man is perhaps a continuum of the Western world's drive toward secularism and rationalism. For thousands of years, man accepted the soul as part of the human condition. The soul gave man purpose and formed his identity, giving him the strength to rise above challenging circumstances and bravely weather the conditions he faced.

FREUD'S REJECTION OF THE SOUL

The fathers of modern psychology disagreed. Freud, for example, regarded G-d, and the soul, as an illusion man "created" from his infantile need for a powerful father figure. Religion, Freud claimed, was necessary to help restrain violent impulses in the development of early civilization. Worse, Freud asserted that religious thinking and training contributed to a weakness of intellect. He argued, "In the long run nothing can withstand reason and experience, and the contradiction which religion offers to both is all too palpable." Freud predicted that "science will go beyond religion, and reason will replace faith in G-d."[9]

Due to the overwhelming popular acceptance of these secular theories, many people seeking relief from depression or anxiety in therapy were only "allowed" to look inward to work through their "misperceptions" of reality or distorted cognitions. Modern secularism took away the emotional and spiritual orientation toward a higher purpose that had guided humanity for thousands of years. Unfortunately, Orthodox Jews and millions of other individuals who believe in G-d were actually discouraged, as part of their therapy, from turning to their faith for inspiration. Instead they were told by therapists that their beliefs were irrational and that they lacked scientific validity. It is no wonder that many Orthodox Jews have remained skeptical of modern psychology.

Yet, despite modern psychology's insistence that G-d be kept out of therapeutic treatment, research shows that many people continue to turn toward spirituality to overcome feelings of depression, anxiety, trauma, and addiction. A Pew research study found that over 89 percent of Americans believe in G-d or a higher power, and look to religion and G-d for guidance, stability, or for gaining a sense of meaning in their lives.[10]

SPIRITUALITY AND THE TWELVE STEPS

Although faith is not sufficiently discussed in the practice of psychology, it is a major component of the most successful self-help movements in the world. Alcoholics Anonymous (AA), Overeaters Anonymous, Sexaholics Anonymous, Al-Anon for the families of addicts, and the like have helped millions of people overcome addictions or emotional pain by utilizing the "Twelve Steps."

Created originally to treat alcoholism and other forms of addiction, Twelve-Step programs offer hope to people who have lost control of their lives. Following the steps encourages people to turn to G-d to overcome their addiction, cope with a family member's addiction, or to deal with feelings of anxiety or depression.

The first three steps are based on the following premises: (1) a person has lost control and is no longer able to pull himself out of his addiction, (2) he needs to "go above" and ask G-d to restore him to sanity, and (3) turning over one's will to the care of G-d brings serenity and healing. The second and third steps are about accessing a Higher Power capable of helping a person overcome their predicament by reaching beyond their inner world.

Twelve-Step programs address one of the greatest problems facing addicts, the lack of meaning in their lives, which Viktor Frankl calls the "existential vacuum." Addictive behaviors involving alcohol, drugs, sex, Internet, and food, among others, are an attempt to numb these feelings of emptiness. It seems as though addictive behaviors have seeped into almost every area of life. And yet, the quest to find a cure for alcoholism may guide us in finding the answers for depression and anxiety as well.

In the 1930s, Bob Smith and Bill Wilson, who were themselves alcoholics, began a revolution to cure their addiction and add meaning to people's lives. The result of their efforts was the creation of Alcoholics Anonymous (AA), with the stated mission "to stay sober, and help others achieve sobriety." Eventually AA's founders wrote a guidebook to recovery from addiction, known as the "Big Book," listing the famous "Twelve Steps" that have helped millions of people recover and build meaningful lives.

Here are the original Twelve Steps of AA. Over the years, these have been adapted by Twelve-Step groups to address various other addictions and behaviors:

1. We admitted we were powerless over alcohol—that our lives had become unmanageable.
2. Came to believe that a Power greater than ourselves could restore us to sanity.
3. Made a decision to turn our will and our lives over to the care of G-d as we understood Him.
4. Made a searching and fearless moral inventory of ourselves.
5. Admitted to G-d, to ourselves, and to another human being the exact nature of our wrongs.
6. Were entirely ready to have G-d remove all these defects of character.
7. Humbly asked Him to remove our shortcomings.
8. Made a list of all persons we had harmed, and became willing to make amends to them all.
9. Made direct amends to such people wherever possible, except when to do so would injure them or others.
10. Continued to take personal inventory and when we were wrong promptly admitted it.
11. Sought through prayer and meditation to improve our conscious contact with G-d as we understood Him, praying only for knowledge of His will for us and the power to carry that out.
12. Having had a spiritual awakening as the result of these steps, we tried to carry this message to alcoholics and to practice these principles in all our affairs.[11]

The Twelve Steps begin with a person admitting that he is powerless in the face of his addiction. Then, he is asked to deepen his relationship with G-d, and to make amends to other people. Finally, the person is asked to mentor others in recovering from alcoholism.

CARL JUNG AND THE ROOTS OF ADDICTION

Correspondence in 1961 between AA founder Bill Wilson, and Carl Jung, one of the world's leading psychologists, offers a surprising perspective from the medical establishment on the roots of addiction. Jung wrote that alcoholism results from a deep and unfulfilled desire for spirituality. He referenced a Latin phrase about addiction that states, "*Spiritus contra Spiritum*," meaning "Higher Power opposes alcoholism." *Spirit* is the Latin root for both wine and spirituality, implying that wine is a lower-level misguided attempt to achieve a profound sense of spirituality. To support this point, Jung quotes the Psalms, *Tehillim* 42:1 "As a hart cries longingly for rivulets of water, so does my soul cry longingly to You, O G-d." Here, water is interchanged with wine, alluding to a human craving which is, in actuality, a cry for G-d.[12]

Jung's remarkable letter continues, "I am strongly convinced that the evil (alcohol) principle prevailing in this world, leads the unrecognized spiritual need into perdition, if it is not counteracted either by a real religious insight or by the protective wall of human community. And ordinary man, not protected by an action from above and isolated in society cannot resist…. You see, alcohol in Latin is "*spiritus*" and you use the same word for the highest religious experience as well as for the most depraving poison." Jung was telling the leaders of AA that the only way out of addiction was by replacing it with spirituality and a higher calling for G-d.[13] Jung's understanding of alcoholism is clearly reflected in the Twelve Steps, as they both guide a person to develop a spiritual relationship with G-d.

Noah and PTSD

The Torah provides insight into how addictions are formed and how people can recover. The *Midrash Tanchuma* tells the story of Noah, his posttraumatic stress, and the development of the first recorded addiction in history:

"When Noah set out to plant the vine, Satan encountered him and asked upon what errand he was bent. 'I am going to plant the vine,' said Noah. 'I will gladly assist you in this good work,' said Satan. When the offer of help was accepted, the Satan brought a sheep and slaughtered it on the plant, then a lion, then a pig, and finally a monkey. He thus explained these symbols to Noah. When a man tastes the first few drops of wine he will be as harmless as a sheep; when he tastes a little more he will become possessed of the courage of a lion and think himself as strong; should he further indulge in the liquid produced by your plant he will become as objectionable as a pig; and by yet further indulgence in it, he will become like a monkey."[14]

According to this *Midrash,* lurking behind alcohol is a devil (Satan) who entices a person by first appearing to be helpful, but then leading him to the point of addiction. The Satan offers to help Noah in his desire for wine. When Noah acquiesces, Satan offers him a series of animals whose blood can be used to help grow Noah's vineyard. Although the offer is seemingly "free," the alcohol begins to change Noah's personality. At first the wine seems harmless. Then the drug is powerful enough to make Noah uninhibited, providing temporary elation. Finally, Noah loses control and becomes mocked like a monkey.

We need to appreciate what Noah had experienced previously. He had just witnessed the destruction of the entire world. He and his family were the only survivors of this significantly traumatic period in history. After the flood, Noah was left without friends, cousins, or material resources. Now he had to face a new world alone, with just his nuclear family intact. Noah was experiencing posttraumatic stress, along with a profound sense of loneliness. In order to cope, he turned toward alcohol to numb his feelings. He reasoned, "I can have one drink and then I'll stop. I'm still in control." Then Noah has another drink, and starts to feel powerful. Eventually he becomes inebriated and loses all control. Noah not only damages himself, but is hurt by his son, who is then cursed for the rest of history.

In truth, addiction is a misguided attempt for people—who may have been hurt, traumatized, or simply feel depressed—to seek relief from their pain. However, alcohol doesn't end the pain. Rather, alcohol and drugs trap a person, as their addiction takes on a life of its own. The addict loses self-control, and begins to believe that he doesn't have a choice whether or not to indulge in his drug of choice. He feels he has lost the "space" between his thoughts, feelings, and actions, becoming a slave to his addiction.

Feeling "powerless" in the face of addiction, an addict needs something greater than himself to pull him out of his predicament. Frankl describes this struggle by saying that you can't reach behind your back and lift yourself up. Rather, you need something beyond yourself to recover and go higher. For the majority of my clients, whether they are facing addiction or have anxiety or depression, G-d can be the higher power, providing guidance, inspiration and a sense of healing.

It is important to note that Frankl also believed that neuroses (depression and anxiety) are sustained by a person paying excessive attention to himself (which may paradoxically be reinforced by therapies that focus a person on their past). If you are searching for relief from anxiety or depression, you may find that actualizing a deep and spiritual longing, augments what you have already gained in therapy. You can be "pulled" upward beyond your emotional limitations by focusing less on yourself, and more on transcending yourself.

Chasidic thought teaches that the power to go beyond yourself exists within. In Kuntres HaHitpa'alut (Tract on Ecstasy), Rabbi Dovber of Lubavitch (the "Mitteler Rebbe"), the second Rebbe of Chabad, describes five spiritual states (based upon the five levels of your soul) of transcendence that a person can experience. Accessing these five states depends on your ability to lose yourself and think more about G-d. Rabbi Dovber explains that thinking deeply about the existence of G-d and focusing on how He is the source of creation and divine guidance, allows a person to experience transcendence. By losing yourself—attaining a state of flow in the state of contemplation—you can move away from your materialistic self toward your G-dly self, connecting with G-d. The more you "forget" yourself the greater chance "hitpa'alut" or "ecstasy" (happiness in psychological terms) will ensue.

SPIRITUALLY-INTEGRATED TREATMENT

Belief in G-d has not only been one of the keys to overcoming addiction, it has an equally effective impact on treating mental health disorders. Groundbreaking research by Harvard professor Dr. David Rosmarin shows the connection between increasing trust in G-d and reducing anxiety. Rosmarin's study, entitled "Spiritually-Integrated Treatment," found that treating anxiety with a faith-based intervention for 30 minutes a day over a two-week period, was more effective than traditional forms of therapy like Progressive Muscle Relaxation (PMR). Based on *Duties of the Heart* by Rabbi Bachya Ibn Pakuda, the intervention includes the following exercises:

- Introduction about the purpose of the program (to increase trust in G-d)
- Inspiring anecdotes about belief
- Reading four passages from Torah sources about belief
- Picturing a person you trust and imagining that he/she was sent by G-d to help you
- Thinking about a precious item and trying to imagine that G-d sent it to you
- Thinking about a stressful time in the past that turned out better than expected, and then contemplating G-d's role in the event
- Thinking about G-d's role while engaging in physical activity (standing up, lifting, etc.)
- Praying for help to increase trust in G-d[15]

The study required participants to read inspiring stories highlighting trust in G-d and how stressors may be blessings in disguise. Participants also read teachings of *Chazal* (Rabbinical stories) about trust and belief. Additionally, they used guided imagery to envision someone they trusted being sent as a messenger to provide help, as well as to generate appreciation for something important in their life. Finally, the participants spent time thinking about how things had turned out better than expected during stressful times in their life. They learned to attribute positive outcomes to G-d's benevolence, and prayed to increase their trust in G–d, so that things would turn out well for them in the future.

SIT participants showed significantly reduced levels of stress, worry, and symptoms of depression from following the prescribed regimen. They also reported "greater belief in treatment credibility, greater expectancies from treatment and greater treatment satisfaction than PMR participants." The SIT group also improved in their ability to tolerate uncertainty, which leads to an overall reduction in anxiety, compared to the Wait List Control Group [those who did not receive any therapy].[16]

MINDFUL-BASED STRESS MANAGEMENT (MBSM)

Mindful-Based Stress Management (MBSM) is another spiritually-based program aimed at reducing stress and worry. Developed by Rabbi Adam Stein, a clinical instructor at the Stony Brook University School of Medicine, MBSM is a series of 8 workshops based on guided meditations that teach participants ways of "'Living in the Moment' devoid of stress, worry and anxiety." Stein's meditative exercises, which take 15 minutes per day, are based on the concept that G-d recreates the world continuously, every single moment. By focusing on how G-d creates and sustains the world at every moment, participants are able to assuage feelings of anxiety or stress.

In a recent assessment of the MBSM Program, Rabbi Stein asked 44 college students who participated in the workshops to take an online anxiety test. The test consisted of 42 questions that would rate their stress and anxiety levels from 1 to 100. Participants took the anxiety test before MBSM, and after completing the course. Stein then compared the initial scores to the same participants' test scores upon concluding the program. Care was taken to only collect data from participants whose stressful lifestyle remained constant, and did not change from the beginning of the course till the end. From that control group, 17 students subjectively remarked that the MBSM approach "worked very well" in reducing their "stress, worry, and anxiety." Recorded anxiety test scores for these 17 participants showed a 21 to 81 percent decrease in anxiety.

Additional feedback from participants described MBSM as "nothing less than life changing." Another student said the program, "enabled me to achieve a full presence of being and look at everything from a completely different perspective." And, unlike other non-Jewish "mindfulness" programs based on Buddhism, one participant noted that "Most approaches to mindfulness encourage you to embrace the moment. [The MBSM] approach focuses on how the moment embraces you."[17]

Additional studies have shown similar evidence that religious participation and beliefs lead to better mental health outcomes, including "fewer symptoms of distress and depression".[18] Researchers found individuals with strong religious convictions often used positive coping behaviors to assist with stress reduction and emotion regulation, leading them to concede that "spirituality may assist in lowering depression levels." Not surprisingly, those who regularly attended religious prayer services showed "50% less risk for depression as opposed to those who did not."[19]

Attending religious services has a proven positive emotional impact on depression and overall mental health for the following groups:

- Adolescent girls
- Pregnant women
- Mothers with young children
- Elderly patients
- Nurses
- Hospice workers
- Parents of children with disabilities
- Those at risk for suicide
- People grieving from the loss of a loved one
- Family members of patients with dementia and Alzheimer's disease [20]

THE CONNECTION BETWEEN PRAYER AND MENTAL HEALTH

Researcher Walter Muelder has documented ten positive psychological benefits of prayer, including: awareness of needs and realities; confession and harmonious adjustment; trust and relaxation; perspective and clarification; decision and dedication; renewal of emotional energy; social responsiveness; joy, gratitude, and relaxation; loyalty, perseverance, and integration; and personality." He found that prayer helps people find inner peace and become more self-aware, resulting in "improved mood and a state of peace and calm." [21] These studies show that being conscious of G-d's presence can influence all aspects of a person's life.

What emerges from the research is that Torah concepts such as belief and trust in G-d, prayer, and a positive outlook are highly effective when used in the context of therapy. In fact, the benefits of psychology can be *enhanced* by adding a spiritual dimension to therapy that addresses religious yearnings as well.

The Lubavitcher Rebbe and Viktor Frankl

Perhaps this is the reason why religious leaders such as the Lubavitcher Rebbe spoke highly of Viktor Frankl's work, as it focused on goals and values that were more compatible with Torah concepts. Answering someone who wrote to him about mental illness, the Rebbe advises a spiritual, yet practical approach:

"…I would like to take this opportunity to add another point albeit this is her field, that the medical condition of . ..... proves (if proof is need ed in this area) the great power of faith—especially when applied and expressed in practical action, community work, observance of *mitzvot*, etc.—to fortify a person's emotional tranquility…minimizing and sometimes even eliminating inner conflicts, as well as 'complaints' one may have to his surroundings, etc."

"This is in spite of the philosophy that faith and religion demand from a person the 'acceptance of the yoke', to restrain and suppress natural instincts and drives, and is, therefore, undesirable for any person, particularly in the case of a person who requires treatment for emotional anxiety."[22]

The Rebbe was responding to a prevailing theory in psychology that religion—which demands the discipline to restrain and suppress natural instincts—would somehow act in opposition to a person's treatment in therapy. According to the Rebbe, the opposite is true: a Torah perspective and *mitzvah* observance only enhance a person's ability to heal their emotional disturbances.

The Rebbe continues the letter, recommending Frankl:

"I particularly took interest in the writing of Dr. Frankl (from Vienna) in this matter. To my surprise, however, his approach has apparently not been appropriately disseminated and appreciated. Although one can find numerous reasons as to why his ideas are not accepted so much, including the fact that such treatment is related to the personal lifestyle exemplified by the treating doctor, nevertheless the question [as to why it is not appreciated] still remains."[23]

Aware that modern psychotherapy did not sufficiently address his followers' spiritual needs, the Rebbe was also concerned that therapy would steer religious Jews in the wrong direction, away from their faith. Perhaps the Rebbe highlighted Frankl's work, and encouraged its dissemination, because it focused on finding meaning beyond the limits of self-reflection.

Reading the Rebbe's correspondence on mental health strengthened my resolve to find a way to integrate the best practices therapy could offer within a spiritual framework. My goal was to allow my clients to discuss their desire for meaning, and learn effective skills to cope with depression, anxiety, or addiction. Torah Psychology emerged from the Rebbe's inspiration, extensive scientific research, and my experience with clients.

TAKEAWAYS

- Some of the most successful self-help groups in the world are based on spirituality.
- Scientific evidence shows that prayer and meditation increase healing and emotional well-being.
- Viktor Frankl's logotherapy can act at a bridge between psychotherapy and religion.

Chapter Two

INTRODUCING TORAH PSYCHOLOGY INTO MY PRACTICE

The need to provide my clients with a comprehensive approach to mental health led me to design a spiritually-based therapy I called Torah Psychology. My aim was to relieve depression or anxiety by moving a client toward finding more meaning in their life, and deepening their relationship with G-d. Torah Psychology transforms negative thinking patterns using powerful spiritual concepts to encourage clients to think positively, and find greater meaning. It does not reject other forms of therapy. Rather, it integrates the best psychological practices in a spiritual context.

THE SIX STEPS OF TORAH PSYCHOLOGY

Torah Psychology consists of six steps to improve emotional well-being:

- Creating Space
- Going Above
- Thinking Good
- Designing Your Future
- Doing Good
- Being Connected

The first three steps—Creating Space, Going Above and Thinking Good—form the initial stages of therapy. The next three—Designing Your Future, Doing Good, and Being Connected—are part of the therapy maintenance plan discussed in later chapters.

Creating Space—The mind rules over the heart
(Moach shalit al halev)

"Creating Space" is based on the Chasidic principle of "*Moach shalit al halev*," or "The mind rules over the heart" (Chapter 16, *Tanya*). This seminal concept implies that you have the unique capacity to restrain your emotions. For example, you are annoyed at a colleague for being rude, yet remain calm by giving him the benefit of the doubt. Or, when you are suddenly cut off by an aggressive driver, but refuse to react, and instead you switch lanes quietly to avoid greater conflict. "Creating Space" helps slow down your thoughts and choose your response by utilizing the power of will and imagination.

Going Above - Everything that G-d does is for the good
(Kol mah de-avid Rachmana l'tav avid)

"Going Above" involves stepping back and looking at life from a broader perspective. This includes seeing a situation from another person's viewpoint, and gaining greater objectivity. For example, a husband is asked to spend more time with his wife's parents, and despite his discomfort with the idea, empathizes with her and tries to accommodate her needs. He goes "above" the situation by seeing another point of view. Or, someone is treated rudely by a coworker but doesn't respond. She later finds out that her colleague's parent was just diagnosed with a serious illness and was overwhelmed with grief. "Going Above" allows us to step back from a difficult situation that is beyond our control.

Thinking Good—Think good and it will be good
(Tracht gut vet zein gut)

"Thinking good" helps us achieve a cognitive shift to view life optimistically. When you think positively, you view your cup as half-full. You constantly look for good points in other people and yourself. You are open to the idea that goodness exists in the world because of G-d's desire to bestow His kindness to all of His creation.

These three fundamental concepts form the foundation of Torah Psychology. Let's now explore Torah Psychology in depth, examining each principle and its practical application, beginning with "Creating Space."

Creating Space

Your thoughts are racing and your heart is beating too fast. You're feeling irritable and nothing seems to calm you down. It feels like you're running on a treadmill and you can't get off. You feel like you're living in a dark cloud and there is no way out.

These are some of the feelings depression or anxiety can cause on an ongoing basis. There is no "space" to slowly analyze your thoughts. They keep coming at you like a fast moving train, and there is no escape. For example, if you are depressed, and have an unfriendly encounter, your mind may magnify the problem leading you to feel friendless. You are overwhelmed as your thoughts and feelings are fused together and actually become one.

Now try something different. Allow your thoughts to emerge, but this time, see if you can slow them down by watching them, gaining control over them one by one. Stop fighting them. Accept your thoughts as if they are simply a series of neurons in your brain flickering on and off. Create space between you, your thoughts, your feelings and your actions. Realize that right now you are placing too much emphasis on your thoughts, and that your mind has hundreds of other possible thoughts you could concentrate on instead. After a few seconds, your thoughts begin to slow down. You are starting to become the master over your thinking.

Let Your Mind Rule Your Heart

One of the central principles of Torah Psychology is "*Moach shalit al halev*" (the mind rules over the heart) a Chasidic concept that describes the power of the mind over one's emotions. Following this precept enables you to utilize the power of your mind to override the pull of your emotions. You can then exercise control over your thoughts and make decisions about how you would like to respond.

There are many examples throughout Jewish history where great individuals used this power to overcome tremendous distress. The Modzitzer Rebbe, for example, avoided taking anesthesia during surgery by singing a *Niggun*. Rabbi Moshe Meisels, a Chasidic spy against the French army, was able to stay calm and maintain a steady pulse when Napoleon himself placed his hands upon Rabbi Meisels' chest to see which side he was on.

"Success in Time"

One of the most instructive examples of "*Moach shalit al halev*" is the story of Rabbi Yosef Yitzchak Schneersohn, the sixth Lubavitcher Rebbe. He coined the term "success in time" to describe how he was able to focus on the needs of his disciples, despite facing violence at the hands of Russian officials.

Rabbi Yosef Yitzchak Schneersohn was about to travel to Moscow for a meeting with one of his supporters who was arriving from abroad. The danger was that the Rebbe was under close scrutiny from the Soviet secret police, and attending this meeting was virtually playing into their hands. Shortly before the Rebbe was scheduled to leave his apartment, his son-in-law and future heir to the Chabad dynasty, Rabbi Menachem Mendel Schneerson, entered the Rebbe's room.

Finding the Rebbe alone, Rabbi Menachem Mendel Schneerson was surprised that his father-in-law did not seem "the least bit agitated about the task ahead." He saw his father-in-law sitting "totally at peace as if it was an ordinary afternoon." The future Rebbe wondered to himself: Here was a man who was asked to carry out a mission that would put his own life and the future of the Jewish community at tremendous risk. Despite this danger, his outward composure projected a calm and collected manner. Knowing of the specific doctrine of "*Moach shalit al halev*" (the mind rules over the heart), Rabbi Menachem Mendel turned to his father-in-law in bewilderment, and asked, "but to such an extreme?" He wanted to know how his father-in-law the Rebbe had achieved such a great degree of self-mastery.

Rabbi Yosef Yitzchak explained that he learned "success in time" from his grandfather Rabbi Shmuel of Lubavitch, the fourth Chabad Rebbe. Essentially "success in time" is the ability to be fully immersed in the here and now by focusing sharply on the task at hand to the exclusion of other concerns. He linked this concept to the famous Rashba, Rabbi Shlomo ben Aderet, who gave three Torah classes a day and answered complex questions in Jewish law – yet still managed to take a leisurely stroll every day. The secret of the Rashba was "success in time" and the ability to hyper focus on whatever he was doing, even if the current activity was relaxation."[24]

Although these great individuals were living examples of self-mastery, every single one of us has the power to exercise our willpower to some degree. When facing intense emotion, if we pause and decide to not react, we have tapped into the power of "*Moach shalit al halev.*"

Frankl described this power from a psychological perspective when he stated, "Between stimulus and response there is a space. In that space is our power to choose our response. In our response lies our growth and our freedom." Following on this idea, Steven Covey, the author of *The Seven Habits of Highly Effective People* explains, "Within the freedom to choose are those endowments that make us uniquely human."[25] The main point is that all of us have the ability to slow down and choose how we respond. When we exercise this mental control, we are able to transcend and transform our thoughts.

Steven Covey uses a diagram to describe this phenomenon, which I modified.[26]

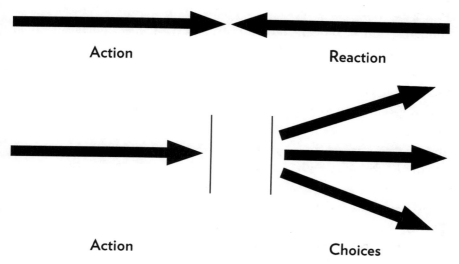

Action   Reaction

Action   Choices

The first diagram shows a typical reaction to a stimulus i.e., someone pushes you, or you have an anxiety-producing thought. In this case, stimulus (the push or the thought) is followed by an emotional reaction (pushing back or feeling anxiety). In the top diagram, you are reacting automatically to someone or something that bothers you.

The second diagram introduces space between the stimulus and the response. According to Frankl, that space gives us the power to choose how we react. Detaching and watching ourselves think is the first step in this direction.

There are various methods to create more space. Here are six introductory techniques that provide relief from depression or anxiety: Contemplating Your Thoughts, Videoing Your Thoughts, Depersonalization, the G-dly Self, Thinking Traps, and Judging Others Favorably.

EXERCISES

—*Contemplating Your Thoughts*

You can begin to create "space" by engaging in a process known as "*Hitbonenut*" or contemplation. Instead of fighting your negative thoughts, first try to reflect on *how* you are thinking, and where your thoughts are coming from. By doing this, you can slow down your thoughts, and *then* decide how to respond. *Hitbonenut* creates a small "space" that gives you the opportunity to distance yourself from your negative emotions and feelings.

Hitbonenut comes from the Hebrew root word *Binah*, understanding. *Binah* is one of the ten *Sefirot* in *Kabbalah*, and represents the mind's ability to reflect deeply on an idea. Let's take a look at how the *Kabbalah* views the human mind, so we can understand the power of *Binah*. To begin with, *Kabbalah* describes 10 *Sefirot*, G-dly emanations, that act as a blueprint for the way G-d creates and sustains life. The *Sefirot* also describe how the mind and body work, as the following diagrams illustrate.

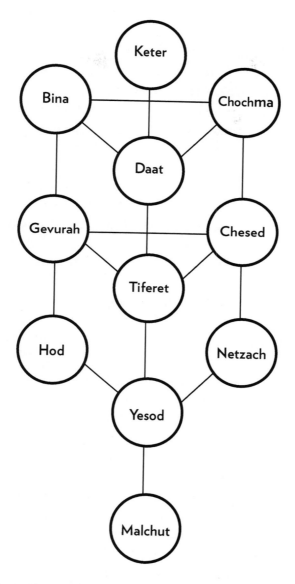

Notice how the *Sefirot* mimic a human form, with energy flowing from the mind downwards into feelings and actions. We will discuss here the three *Sefirot* that parallel human consciousness are *Chochmah* (Wisdom), *Binah* (Understanding), and *Daas* (Knowledge). *Chochma* is the first level of conscious thought. At the level of Chochmah, the mind is able to sense an undefined idea. *Chochmah* is often described as a spark or point of insight. In *Bina*, however, the mind examines the point, as all of its details come into focus. In other words, the original spark (*Chochma*) is developed and amplified in depth and breadth (*Binah*).

Think of an artist who looks at his canvas and envisions his new work of art (*Chochma*). At first, he does not have a plan for all the details of his painting. Then, as he begins his artwork, he sees how to fill in all the details (*Bina*). He first uses *Chochma* for inspiration, and then he uses *Bina* to create his painting. Finally, *Daas* is the ability to concentrate and to gain knowledge about things outside of oneself.

Practicing *Hitbonenut* creates a "space" or "distance" from anxiety, since it is only possible to concentrate on one thing at a time. At the moment of contemplation, you are no longer overwhelmed by your thoughts, as you become absorbed by something more important.

Psychologists have only recently identified the power of this contemplative process, which they term *metacognition*. Metacognition is a "deeper level of thinking that includes your ability to think about your thinking; how you understand, adapt, change, control, and use your thought processes."[27] By engaging in *Hitbonenut* about how the mind works, you learn how to detach from your habitual stream of consciousness. You obtain an objective perspective on how you are processing your thoughts and experiences. In other words, you achieve a "deeper level of thinking".

Let's take a look at how to do this practically. I often tell my clients that when they feel anxious, they first need to stop, take a deep breath, and imagine "pushing" a slow-motion-instant-replay button in their mind to review the thoughts that led to feelings of anxiety.

For example, one day you feel your heart racing. You're panicking about flying for an upcoming business trip overseas. Instead of fighting your thoughts ("Stop being scared, the flight will be okay!"), actively examine the flow of your thoughts and describe them to yourself. You can say, "I can see my mind conjuring up pictures of the plane crashing and people screaming." Then say, "I see how those thoughts are affecting my emotions and causing me unwanted anxiety." The goal is to describe your thoughts, allowing you to "watch" them from a more detached perspective.

Here's another example. Imagine that you made a mistake at work and felt overwhelmed with thoughts of shame and embarrassment. You might automatically say to yourself, "I'm such a failure and I hate my life!" Instead, reflect on your thought process. Describe your thoughts by saying, "I see how my mind thinks that one mistake somehow defines my entire personality. I notice how quickly my thoughts turn into emotions, and I start flooding with negative feelings".

Exercise

Developing the skill of *Hitbonenut* (contemplation) takes time and practice. Many people find it unusual at first, since it's not a common way of using your mind. However, as I have seen with my clients, this ability develops gradually with time. To start with, commit to taking five minutes a day to experience *Hitbonenut*.

Choose an object you see or feel, and describe it in all its details. Or, focus your mind on a painting or picture, and describe all of its colors and nuances. Looking at a picture of a forest you might say, "In the picture I see trees. They are about forty feet tall. They have dark green leaves, and their branches spread outward in all directions. I can see the rays of the sun beaming over the treetops and spreading out through the forest. The trees have different thicknesses. Some of their branches start higher up on the trunk, and some lower. Some trees are bearing fruits, while others are empty etc." The longer you spend noticing minute details, the longer your mind will be deeply engaged in the process. As you distract your mind, you will become disconnected from your original feelings. As you practice calmly describing a picture or a scene every day for a few minutes, notice if you gain more control over your thoughts.

Next, try describing your own thoughts. Start by closing your eyes and watching a random thought emerge in your mind. Now, simply describe your thought process in detail, e.g., "I was insulted in school today. This is causing me to feel sad and unwanted." Then, imagine that the thought remains at an intellectual level, disconnected from your emotions, e.g. "These are just thoughts about being criticized."

Now, allow a different thought to emerge in your mind, describe it to yourself, and notice if you can envision it as being distant from your emotions. Practice this once a day for a week to see if you can slow down your thoughts and "Create Space."

—Videoing Your Thoughts

Another way to "Create Space," is to project an image of yourself dealing with an unpleasant thought onto a screen. Now, watch this video of yourself from a detached perspective, and identify the thoughts you are feeling. You may say, "I'm thinking a critical thought about myself," or "That's a judgmental thought that's causing anxiety."

For example, let's say your boss criticizes you at work, and you return home feeling angry or depressed. However, if you play back the scene from a detached perspective, similar to watching a video, you may be able to identify your thoughts and feelings without reacting to them. While detaching and watching this projection of your thoughts, you become an impartial spectator, allowing you to create more "space".

Exercise

Find a quiet place where you can sit calmly and practice this exercise for five minutes. Imagine that something that bothers you is happening to a projection of yourself on a screen. Notice your thoughts and feelings as a spectator. Identify them and imagine not reacting to those thoughts. Instead maintain a sense of distance by choosing not to react on an emotional level.

—Depersonalization

The next exercise helps depersonalize a difficult situation by imagining it happening to someone else who is able to react differently. Watch the difficult scene like a movie about this "other" person from a broader perspective. Notice how, despite his agitation, the imagined person is able to pick himself up, and isn't overwhelmed by his boss's criticism. To the contrary, he doesn't react by feeling depressed or anxious because he doesn't believe that he is defective or worthless. Rather, he is less reactive and does not get overwhelmed by his thoughts.

The next step is to further de-personalize the situation. Imagine that the "other" person hears that his boss just received a medical diagnosis and was feeling scared that morning. He feels more empathy and reacts with less emotion. By doing so, he creates more "space".

Exercise:

Sitting quietly, imagine a painful emotional experience you have had as if it were happening to someone else who responds differently. Describe the person's flow of thoughts and how he is able to respond without feeling agitated. Imagine him finding empathy for the person who insulted him, and replacing his anger with compassion.

—The G-dly Self

Think about your "G-dly" self to become aware that you are not your thoughts, feelings, or actions. Rather, you have a soul that is beyond these three dimensions. The soul is given to you by G-d and is pure without blemish. In fact, it is untainted by any memories or experiences that you have had. It is not affected by your parents, upbringing, or any traumas you may have suffered. It remains untainted despite your mistakes or transgressions, as we read in the morning prayers "Lord, the soul that you have placed inside of me is pure. You created it, You formed it, You blew it into me. You protect it inside me..." (*Siddur*, morning prayers).

You can now view whatever happens that bothers you as affecting only your external self. It has no influence on your G-dly self. You realize that at any given moment, the G-dly soul has an endless and unbreakable connection to its Source. The idea is that you are not the same as your thoughts, but someone much greater. Instead of reacting, you can detach from the moment and keep your eyes on the bigger picture, viewing people's insensitivities as brief nuisances that will quickly pass.

Exercise:

Sitting calmly, close your eyes and imagine that inside you is a precious diamond that just needs to be polished. Become aware that any dark spots are merely external blemishes that cover over your brilliance. Gently polish away any blemishes (mistakes you have made) noticing that you are a beautiful person who shines from the inside out. Picture your diamond lighting up the space around you, and sharing the light with people in your life.

Exercise

This is particularly good for someone experiencing low self-esteem and deeper feelings of sadness or depression.

Sit in a relaxing position and take two calming breaths. Sense your body becoming totally relaxed. Relax deeper and deeper. Watch your thoughts and notice if there are any negative feelings emerging. Now, dig deeper than those negative thoughts. Go lower and lower until you find a point of goodness within you. Imagine that point of goodness is a light. Begin to magnify that point and make it bigger and bigger until the light is radiating throughout your entire mind and body.

Now, imagine that above you there is an even greater light, shining into you and connecting to your light within. Your own light draws you toward the greater light. Slowly move closer and closer as you are enveloped by the light radiating into every part of your being - your thoughts, feelings and bodily sensations. You are now experiencing pure goodness and attachment with G-d. As you move even closer, notice the light becoming even brighter. As you approach the light, lose yourself and become even more absorbed in it. You are part of infinite goodness. This is the real you, totally good, and illuminated by your G-dly self.

—*Thinking Traps*

Once a person begins to "Create Space," they can identify and rectify their "thinking traps," or what psychologists call "cognitive distortions." According to Aaron Beck, the founder of Cognitive Behavioral Therapy, thinking traps are "dysfunctional thought patterns that cause negative emotional reactions".[28]

Thinking traps can also be viewed as "rules" that cause a person to feel anxious or depressed. For example, a common thinking trap is "Black and White Thinking," which often affects people who have depression. "Black and White" thinking works like this: someone expects an "A" on their math test, but receives a "B," and concludes, "I'm an absolute failure in math. I will never succeed!" Another example is a young mother whose child is having a temper tantrum and believes that she is a failure despite all of her other positive qualities as a parent. These distortions cause undue emotional distress and need to be challenged.

Other thinking traps include:

Catastrophizing

The person assumes the worst possible outcome, no matter how unrealistic it is.

Example: Getting an average evaluation at work and thinking "I'm going to be fired".

Magnifying or Minimizing

Grossly exaggerating a small problem or minimizing an achievement.

Example: The boss says "You did a good job" but the employee discounts it as just a little bit of luck.

Mind Reading

You assume someone doesn't like you without any knowledge of that fact.

Example: The teacher wasn't very friendly with you today so you assume he doesn't like you.

Mental Filter

You focus only on negative aspects of the situation and not on the positive.

Example: You only get second place in the competition and you believe you're a failure, instead of focusing on your achievement.

Jumping to Conclusions

You assume the worst conclusions in a given situation.

Example: Your best friend doesn't call you back for one hour, and you assume she is no longer interested in your friendship.

Shoulds, Musts, Nevers

You walk around feeling that you or other people "should" be a certain way.

Example: I should never make a mistake when I speak in public. I never give a good presentation at work.

Exercise:

Choose an issue which is making you anxious, such as an upcoming test, public appearance etc. Write down some of the possible thinking traps you're using. Perhaps you can discover if your mind is prone to using "black-and-white" thinking, or if you focus only on the bad. If so, try to catch yourself using these thinking traps in the future, and work on changing your thinking patterns (more about this in upcoming chapters).

—Judging People Kindly

People tend to judge others quickly, often without evidence. This may be a function of the "fight or flight" mechanism that protects a person from danger. The unconscious mind believes that if a person is critical first, they will be spared being criticized later on. In other words, the best defense is a good offense. This may be true in the world of sports or combat, but it is not helpful in the world of human relationships.

Judgment sometimes gets conveyed in subtle body language, while other times it's perceived by the tone of a person's words. Being critical and judging others is both painful to the person being judged and to the person judging. Judging others also creates bad feelings, since people tend to feel negative emotions when someone else judges them.

Being judgmental is especially counterproductive for those who suffer from social anxiety. Paradoxically, when someone is judgmental, they also tend to be self-critical. Although a person may believe that other people don't like him, in actuality, it is often the person himself who doesn't like others. That's why if someone wants to feel more accepted, he's best off trying to accept others first.

The Torah shows us the importance of reducing judgmental tendencies when it instructs us to judge other people favorably, saying, "Judge your fellow man justly" (Lev. 19:15). The *Sefer HaChinuch* explains that this means that you should "judge your fellow man favorably and interpret his actions and words only to the good" (Sefer HaChinuch 235). This tells us that one should not only avoid being critical, but actively look for the good in others.

This idea is reflected in one of the most important commandments in the Torah, "To love your neighbor as yourself." Just as you do not want to be judged by others, you should not judge them. The Torah states: "Do not favor the poor or show deference to the rich; judge your neighbor fairly...You shall not hate your kinsman in your heart. Reprove your neighbor, but incur no guilt against your kinsfolk. Love your neighbor as yourself: I am the L-ord" (*Vayikra*, 19:18).

The Torah's emphasis on loving others shows us how important it is to catch one's tendency to be judgmental, and to change this habit. Instead, try giving others the benefit of the doubt. Those who judge others favorably often experience a significant reduction in negative and depressing feelings, leading to more emotional freedom. Reducing judgmental tendencies also frees up emotional energy and builds greater camaraderie between people, bringing more happiness and joy into your life.

Exercise:

Think of someone who has hurt you in the past. Imagine for a moment that you forgive them in your heart. Then, try to notice the feelings of relief that may come up, as you feel less angry and vindictive than before. If this works, consider calling up the person or meeting with them to forgive them for hurting you. Pay attention to how you feel afterwards.

PUTTING IT ALL TOGETHER

Let's see how these various techniques to "create space" helped clients like Miriam, Sarah, and Moshe reduce their symptoms of depression or anxiety.

Miriam benefitted from learning how to watch her thoughts in her struggle with OCD (Obsessive Compulsive Disorder). Miriam was a classic hand-washer. She would wash her hands three to four times an hour to "protect" her from fears of a "disaster" happening to her or to her children. While treating Miriam, I asked her to stop or significantly reduce washing her hands, and instead, to address her fears in therapy.

With practice, Miriam learned how to control her thoughts of impending disaster, and not react to them. She also mastered allowing her negative thoughts to emerge, calming her body down by changing her breathing patterns, and letting her thoughts dissolve into the air.

I explained to her that just like the conductor of an orchestra, each of us has many different "instruments" (thoughts) in our minds. We can arrange the sounds (thoughts) together by increasing the volume and speed of our instruments (thoughts). In the orchestra, if the drums are beating too loudly, they drown out the violins. If the horns are blasting with too much intensity, the audience cannot hear the cellos. I asked Miriam to look at herself as the conductor of her thoughts, and to try to synthesize them together. It was up to her to orchestrate the speed and intensity of her thoughts and blend them together. She could accomplish this by separating her thoughts from her emotions, allowing other neutral and positive cognitions to come through.

Over several sessions, Miriam practiced watching her thoughts by imagining that they were happening to another person who reacted calmly to them. I then asked her to think about her G-dly self, so she would see how her obsessive thoughts were only distractions that didn't represent her true self. As we practiced these steps, Miriam's situation began to improve. Eventually she was able to "create space" by reacting less to her negative thoughts.

In Sarah's case, I helped her identify and correct her thinking traps. She reported that she often fell prey to "magnifying and minimizing," "mental filter," and "should" statements. At times, she focused exclusively on remembering the conflicts with her mother when she was a teenager. She would "filter" out any of the positive experiences she shared with her mother while growing up.

To increase her recollection of positive experiences, I asked Sarah to bring in family pictures showing the quality time she spent together with her mother as a child, taking trips to parks and zoos and going on long walks together. There were many occasions when Sarah and her mother laughed together and experienced bonding and attachment. These memories helped refocus Sarah on the good times, and not just the bad ones.

Being somewhat of a perfectionist, Sarah discovered that she operated with many "should" statements like, "I *must* be perfect and can never make mistakes," "I *should* be a better mother," "I *should* have been even closer to my mother when I had the chance to be," and "Life *never* turns out the way I expect it to."

Sarah and I created coping statements that helped her feel better. A "coping statement" is a short motivational script that can neutralize intense anxiety. It is usually one to two paragraphs long, and is simply a good reminder that can reduce fears. Creating and keeping a file of coping statements handy is particularly useful in confronting one's thoughts before they become overwhelming. Sarah's coping statements included: "I *prefer* to be the best mother possible, but I know most parents make some mistakes and that's okay." Or, "*Sometimes* life doesn't turn out the way I expect it to, but often it does."

When Sarah confronted her thinking traps, she was able to watch her thoughts, analyze them, and then shift toward a more realistic view of herself and her relationship with her mother. This enabled her to create more "space," and lessened her feelings of worthlessness and helplessness.

I also asked Sarah to be aware of her tendency to judge others and herself negatively. Some of the conflicts with her mother were based on her tendency to judge her unfavorably. Although her mother had already passed away, adopting a more favorable view of others – and herself - would help improve Sarah's mood. Even retroactively, when Sarah judged her mother more favorably, she felt more compassion towards her, and had more positive feelings about their relationship.

Moshe's therapy plan focused on developing different skills, though he also needed help learning how to watch his thoughts and disconnect them from his emotions. Over several sessions, we practiced using guided visualization to call up and watch his thoughts flow without criticism. Between sessions, I asked Moshe to:

- Spend five minutes per day simply watching his thoughts and noticing them without reaction.
- Review any daily negative interpersonal interactions as an "impartial spectator"
- Watch his negative thoughts by projecting them onto a screen and viewing them objectively.
- Imagine someone else experiencing a similar situation but reacting more positively.

- Call friends and family members he appreciates and who make him feel more optimistic every day.
- Read stories of outstanding individuals and religious leaders who overcame difficult situations.

After a few weeks of practicing these steps and reviewing them together in therapy, Moshe reported feeling greater control over his emotions, and his life. He felt less overwhelmed and believed he was moving in the right direction, since he already noticed some improvement.

Also, after learning to watch his thoughts and separate them from his feelings, Moshe chose to practice forgiveness. He started by forgiving one of his supervisors at work, who was critical of him. After doing so, he noticed a slight change in the intensity of the energy the supervisor directed towards him.

A week or so later, Moshe asked for a meeting to discuss with his supervisor what had occurred. Moshe shared his feelings about the situation, and his supervisor actually apologized. Moshe also said he was sorry for the misunderstanding, and was appreciative that he had a chance to talk openly with him. For Moshe, taking a small step to forgive people in his present life opened up the possibility of overcoming his negative feelings toward people who had hurt him in the past.

It is important to note that the "creating space" exercises are not an end in themselves. Rather, they are means to a higher end: to transcend the limits of self and choose a pathway different from depression or anxiety. Once a person creates space they can then move to the next stage of Torah Psychology, "Going Above".

TAKEAWAYS

- We need to "Create Space" between our thoughts, feelings, and actions.
- When Viktor Frankl says "Between stimulus and response there is a space," this means that we need to develop our ability to not react negatively to everything that happens to us.
- By watching our thoughts and feelings, we can slow them down to the point where they become less powerful.

- Correcting thinking traps helps reduce emotional reactions to distorted thought patterns.
- After "creating space," we need to "Go Above" to view our situation from a higher perspective.

Chapter Three

GOING ABOVE

Overcoming depression often necessitates going above one's natural inclinations to find new emotional resources and discover new possibilities. Take David, for example. David was a 32 year-old father of four who had suffered from depression since he was a teenager. When David and I first met, he had already been in therapy for several years, and had tried various anti-depressants, which had a limited effect on his low mood. He seemed to have lost hope in life, and in his own abilities to overcome his depression.

David's history pointed to some of the reasons why he was suffering for so long. He was raised in a dysfunctional family, where his father, the son of Hungarian Holocaust survivors, suffered from depression. David's father was also highly abusive, hitting and kicking David, and harshly punishing his children for small errors like spilling milk and not scoring 100 percent on their tests. He grew up fearful of angering his father, who could snap at any moment.

As an adult, David was doing the best he could, working long hours to provide for his family while trying to be an affectionate and attentive husband. David, however, had a very low self-image and had trouble attending synagogue services and maintaining his friendships. He admitted to me that he was grappling with many issues pertaining to his faith. He wanted to lead a more spiritual life. Yet his inability to trust other people clouded his perception of all relationships, including his relationship with G-d.

EXPLORING YOUR SPIRITUAL ATTITUDES

Aware that David had already tried the standard therapeutic treatments, I suggested he consider a new approach that would help him "go above" his persistent symptoms of depression. We began by exploring his spiritual attitudes towards faith and trust in G-d, using the following questions:

- What role does your relationship with G-d play in your life?
- Are you satisfied with your level of trust in G-d?
- What were you taught about how G-d relates to the world?
- Which religious practices do you observe e.g. prayer, study, acts of kindness?
- Do you have anyone to confide in about your religious feelings and attitudes?
- Do you experience G-d in a positive or negative light? What did you learn growing up that affected your view?
- Did a trauma affect your belief in G-d?
- Do you see a role for faith and trust in G-d in your current predicament?

The last question about G-d's role in David's life sparked an engaging conversation about faith. David revealed that he was unsure of his belief in G-d. He had never understood why his grandparents were allowed to suffer during the Holocaust. It is a well-known fact that children (and grandchildren) of survivors have their own unique challenges. They grew up with parents who were highly traumatized during the war. Some survivors were separated from their families, while others witnessed parents, siblings, or children killed in front of their own eyes.

After the war, they had to uproot their lives again, immigrating to foreign countries without support from friends, family, or community. Despite their traumas, many married and began building their own families in the United States. Unfortunately, few received proper emotional or financial support. Even fewer had access to mental health services that would have made their lives easier.

There are generally two types of survivors: those who speak about the horrors of the war, and those who refuse to talk about it, insisting that no one has the right to ask questions. The combination of survivors' intense emotional experiences and physical hardships often leads to severe posttraumatic stress disorder.

In David's case, his grandfather was emotionally closed and refused to share his experiences during the war. Suffering from PTSD, he would rage about his financial problems or complain that his children "didn't live up to his expectations." David's father struggled with depression and anger management issues that grew from his grandfather's erratic and violent style of parenting.

Like many people who were raised in religious homes and had difficult childhoods, David's perception of G-d was damaged by how he was treated by his parents and teachers. Overall, a child's initial under-standing of G-d comes from his parents and authority figures. Religious children with a loving father and mother, who protected and nurtured them, have a greater chance of envisioning a benevolent higher power who acts the same.

However, if the child grows up in an abusive home or school where they saw a distortion of power and experienced harsh forms of control that denied their basic needs, they may have developed a cynical view of G-d as well. Worse, in a situation where someone experienced abuse, G-d and religion may also be perceived as harsh and controlling. Unfor-tunately, as adults, they find it difficult to turn towards a higher power, their spouse, friends - or even a therapist - for help.

Exploring your current perception of G-d is a therapeutic way of helping repair the damage from early childhood. In David's case, I asked him to re-examine his perception of G-d from a more detached, adult perspective. I challenged him to think of people in his life currently who he is able to trust or love. Who has been kind to him at work or in his community? Are there any special people in his life who supported or encouraged him when he felt down? If someone like David can see the possibility of love and goodness in the world, they may also be able to accept the existence of a power who confers that goodness.

Also, a person who has experienced long-term emotional pain often needs someone or something *higher* to lift them out of their suffering. In Torah Psychology, this "lifting up" is accomplished by seeing the world from a viewpoint beyond oneself; from a G-dly perspective, as this diagram describes:

ZOOMING OUT

Perceiving life from "above" is similar to a video camera zooming out and viewing the scene from a broader perspective. For example, picture a videotaping of where you are standing at the moment. Next, the video zooms out, showing you a view from above your head, slightly above the first image. In the next frame, the camera zooms out even further, hovers above your city, country, the earth, and finally displays a view from outer space.

Psychologically speaking, when you are "stuck," or emotionally reactive, you have zoomed in, became frozen in the present moment. You're unable to see the situation from a higher point of view. However, when you pull back, you can begin to understand your predicament from a slightly different angle. As you zoom out even further, you may even discover some hidden good in what you have experienced.

The next stage of "Going above" is accepting that there is a higher power that guides you, and "speaks" to you even during life's predicaments. This higher power observes your life from the broadest perspective. "Going Above," means recognizing a Divine hand in your life that is guiding you with care and benevolence. This optimistic outlook is based on the idea that G-d is the ultimate good, and wants to share His goodness with others.

In the 1700s, Rabbi Moshe Chaim Luzzatto, known as the Ramchal, was one of the most prominent rabbis to discuss the importance of gaining a higher perspective. In *Derech HaShem* (1:2:1), the Ramchal explains that G-d desires to do good to His creation by giving of His own goodness. G-d's purpose in creation is to "bestow of His good to another." The Ramchal writes: "He alone is the ultimate good and He wishes to bestow His good for Himself to another since He is the absolute good."

According to the Ramchal, everything that G-d does is for our good, and His goodness permeates the universe at all times. Studying the Ramchal's descriptions of how G-d relates to the world can create a paradigm shift in dealing with depression. There is nothing more positive than the idea that everything is ultimately good, especially if that goodness is pursuing you, and only need to perceive its presence.

As King David said, "only good and kindness pursues me all the days of my life" (*Psalms*, 23). Utilizing this verse as a powerful meditation is more effective than simply changing a distorted cognition about yourself. Faith in G-d's goodness provides an all-encompassing awareness that the Creator is constantly sharing His goodness and intimately caring for each human being.

Viktor Frankl: Finding Meaning in Suffering

If you have suffered from trauma, it is important to note that "Going Above" is just one aspect of coming to terms with what has happened in your life. You also need to find a way to examine the possible reasons behind your suffering.

During an interview, Viktor Frankl explained the relationship between meaning and suffering as D=S-M, where D is for despair, S is for suffering and M is for meaning. This equation implies that suffering minus meaning equals despair. However, finding meaning (M) in suffering can change a person's perception of himself and his life. He is able to view his hardships as serving a greater purpose.[§]

[§]Frankl's approach to finding meaning in suffering reflects the Talmud's instruction that "Just as one should bless G-d for the good, so he should bless Him for the bad" (Berachot 60b). This is not a revealed good visible to our eyes but originates from a Hidden World (Tanya, 26). This concept is considered to be the ultimate path to relieving depression and anxiety.

But who can answer the question of why bad things happen to good people? A therapist doesn't have any greater knowledge of the existential reason his client had to suffer than the client himself has. Specifically, a psychologist can't tell a person "why" he is suffering. He can, however, facilitate a therapeutic discussion by asking the client to consider the following questions:

- Have you ever seen any good come out of a seemingly hopeless situation?
- Have there been times in your life when you have been instructed to do something you didn't want to do, but in the end found out that it was actually good for you?
- Did experiencing a difficult time in your life ever make you stronger?
- Using your imagination, could you write a story about how a person may experience something initially as painful, but in the end it saved their life?
- Is there any possible good that emerged from your own trauma?

David and I spent many sessions pondering these questions. During one discussion, he recalled visiting Israel as a student. On his way to the Kotel, he missed his bus and had to take a taxi. That very same bus was in a terror attack 20 minutes later. He remembered feeling like he was saved from disaster.

Reflecting back on that tragedy, he was able to see the possibility of goodness hidden in life's circumstances. Still, David was not sure what good came out of the Holocaust. He did believe, however, that his own personal suffering made him more sensitive to other people's pain, and that his ability to empathize with others was one of his greatest skills in life.

Other clients have shared how trauma actually served as a wakeup call in their life. At his first session, one of my clients shared his harrowing story:

"I was a college student living on a campus known for its party scene. I decided that I wanted to take advantage of all the pleasures I could. I started drinking and trying crazy things that I never knew were possible. After one year I became addicted to opioids. My life was spiraling out of control. There was no way out.

One day, I decided to rent a sports car and go on a daring drive in the mountains. On the way up I was in a terrible car accident, and almost broke my back. Although the initial pain was agonizing, and my recovery difficult and arduous, that accident saved my life. At the hospital I met a fantastic psychiatrist who suggested I join a 12-Step program. Joining the group gave me a greater sense of meaning, and I found a new calling for helping other people overcome their addictions. If I didn't have the accident, I'm sure I would've died from an overdose."

Another client of mine grew up with an uncle who was in a sporting accident and lost his leg. The mishap left his uncle an invalid, struggling both emotionally and physically for the rest of his life. In reaction to the pain he experienced watching his uncle suffer, my client decided to go to medical school. He went on to become a world famous foot surgeon, inventing a post-surgical prosthesis for amputees. Overcoming trauma can transform a person's life and the lives of many other people.

One of the stories I shared with David was about a well-known outreach rabbi who created a network of successful programs to help young religious women. At a public lecture about addiction and recovery, he revealed how he was abused by two teachers as a young child. He had lived with this secret for many years, developed a gambling addiction, and eventually saw his life spiraling out of control.

One day he decided to take back control, swearing to himself that he would never let any of his friends be hurt the way he had been. He created a new organization to help others develop healthy lifestyles. At the lecture, he proclaimed that if he was given the chance to relive his life, he would never give up his trauma, since his response to it shaped his calling in life.

Here are some other examples of people who were able to "go above" their situation and turn their tragedy into a triumph.

A man whose father was a paranoid schizophrenic and was almost killed in a car accident.	He became a psychiatrist helping children overcome trauma and other difficult childhood issues.
Rabbi Kalonymus Kalman Shapira, the Piaseczno Rebbe, who was orphaned after the death of his father at age 3.	He dedicated his life to helping young children in Warsaw and wrote numerous books on education.
A prime minister whose brother was killed in an anti-terror operation.	He founded an institute studying how to combat international terrorism.

A war hero who was badly wounded in battle.	He founded an international organization to help people with disabilities.
A young woman who was diagnosed with terminal cancer.	She survived and went onto become a leading expert in healthy lifestyles
A man born with muscular dystrophy.	He became a manufacturer of wheelchair accessible vehicles.
An upcoming sportsman who broke his neck in a diving incident and became paralyzed.	He went on to complete a PhD in psychology to help injured individuals find meaning in their lives.

These individuals were able to transform their disabilities and challenges by dramatically changing the lives of others. They discovered a unique opportunity to answer a higher calling that may not have arisen had they not encountered their initial trauma.

INTEGRATING MEANING INTO THERAPY

If you are finding it difficult to find meaning in your own painful experiences, I suggest you begin by reading the key writings of Viktor Frankl, who suffered in three concentration camps. And, this is exactly the approach I took with Sarah, Moshe, and Miriam.

With Sarah, I started the process by reading passages aloud from *Man's Search for Meaning* to give Sarah hope. Losing her parents had made Sarah feel she had lost control over her life. She had counted on her parents' love, turning to them for guidance and reassurance. Now she felt alone. Facing depression, she believed she had lost the ability to feel anything but pain. Reading through Frankl's work, we found a quote that deeply affected Sarah's perception of her own emotional freedom:

> *"Forces beyond your control can take away everything you possess except one thing, your freedom to choose how you will respond to the situation."*[29]

Sarah found that Frankl's belief in the freedom of choice, *despite* one's condition, encouraged her to move forward. She was able to articulate the possibility that one day she could make a choice to feel less depressed, even if her feelings at the time seemed overwhelming.

Another powerful Frankl quote that made a strong impression on Sarah was the following:

> "Don't aim at success. The more you aim at it and make it a target, the more you are going to miss it. For success, like happiness, cannot be pursued; it must ensue, and it only does so as the unintended side effect of one's personal dedication to a cause greater than oneself or as the by-product of one's surrender to a person other than oneself. Happiness must happen, and the same holds for success: you have to let it happen by not caring about it. I want you to listen to what your conscience commands you to do and go on to carry it out to the best of your knowledge. Then you will live to see that in the long-run—in the long-run, I say!—success will follow you precisely because you had forgotten to think about it."[30]

Sarah had spent the last few months *trying* to be happier. However, the more she tried to feel better, the worse her depression seemed to get. Based on Frankl's insight, Sarah decided to stop pursuing happiness, and instead, work on finding meaning. This was a major revelation, since Sarah had started therapy with the goal of ending her depression. She now decided to stop trying to be happy, and focus on finding positive ways to honor her parents' memory, inspired by the following reading:

> "It did not really matter what we expected from life, but rather what life expected from us. We needed to stop asking about the meaning of life, and instead to think of ourselves as those who were being questioned by life—daily and hourly. Our answer must consist, not in talk and meditation, but in right action and in right conduct. Life ultimately means taking the responsibility to find the right answer to its problems and to fulfill the tasks which it constantly sets for each individual."[31]

From our work with Frankl's principles, Sarah decided to shift her attention away from her problems by fulfilling a greater cause. Her parents had supported an organization for children with cancer. She decided to volunteer for the same organization, and raise money for a fund in her parent's honor. Each week, Sarah shared her journal with me detailing her progress and the steps she was taking to build the organization.

For the first time, I started seeing a glimmer of hope in Sarah's eyes. Discussing Frankl's writings resulted in some very powerful sessions. Together we were able to create a therapeutic "space" using Logotherapy that allowed Sarah to experience more meaning in her life. We had found a pathway to healing - one that most schools of psychology would not necessarily encourage traveling on.

I also introduced Frankl into my sessions with Moshe. We focused on what Frankl called "experiential" values, which focus on the possibility of finding meaning in the wonders of nature.

Frankl writes:

> *"Let us ask a mountain-climber who has beheld the alpine sunset and is so moved by the splendor of nature that he feels cold shudders running down his spine – let us ask him whether after such an experience his life can ever again seem wholly meaningless."*[32]

After reading this passage together, I suggested Moshe try an experience that would help him move past his pain. He wrote a list of activities he used to enjoy. One of his greatest childhood pleasures was bicycling, and for several years he had wanted to buy a bike. I encouraged him to do so, as well as to join a local biking group of religious young men that organized outward-bound experiences where he lived.

After several weeks, Moshe started biking, enjoying the beauty of nature while building friendships with fellow bicyclists. He slowly began to discover a new energy for life, which created a small opening for the next stage of therapy: to increase his positive thoughts. I also suggested that Moshe increase his acts of love and kindness toward his wife, who had been very supportive of him, despite his depression.

With Miriam, instead of trying to relieve her symptoms of anxiety, we tried Frankl's "Paradoxical Intention" exercise. The following passage describes how it works:

> A young doctor had major hydrophobia (fear of sweating uncontrollably). One day, meeting his chief on the street, as he extended his hand in greeting, he noticed that he was perspiring more than usual. The next time he was in a similar situation he expected to perspire again, and this anticipatory anxiety precipitated excessive sweating. It was a vicious circle . . . We advised our patient, in the event that his anticipatory anxiety should recur, to resolve deliberately to show the people whom he confronted at the time just how much he could really sweat. A week later he returned to report that whenever he met anyone who triggered his anxiety, he said to himself, "I only sweated out a little before, but now I'm going to pour out at least ten liters!" What was the result of this paradoxical resolution? After suffering from his phobia for four years, he was quickly able, after only one session, to free himself of it for good. [33]

Miriam had a constant fear of having dizzy spells and collapsing in public. Instead of trying to challenge her cognitive distortions, I asked her to attempt using Frankl's "Paradoxical Intention." We agreed that if she was in public and feared passing out, she would actually try to faint as hard as possible. At first she found the idea to be overwhelming. However, within several sessions, Miriam's fear of collapsing had disappeared.

DISCOVERING THERAPY IN TORAH

The Torah also provides numerous ways of "going above" to find more meaning. In fact, many phrases throughout the Torah can be used as mantras to help deal with feelings of depression or anxiety, and to go "above" them. For example, if you find yourself in an immediate state of distress, a mantra acts as emotional first aid to help break your intense reaction to your emotions. Powerful Torah-based mantras that help a person view the world from a higher perspective include:

- *Ribono shel Olam* (Master of the universe)
- *Ein od milvado* (There is no one besides Him)
- *Shema Yisrael Hashem Elokeinu Hashem Echad*
- Shaviti Hashem Lenegdi Tamid (I have placed G-d in front of me, all times Psalms 16:8).

If you feel a sense of despair and helplessness, saying the words *Ribono shel Olam* (Master of the universe) over and over again can shift your thoughts and improve your mood. You can also repeat the phrase *Ein od milvado* (There is no one besides Him) until your mind enters into a different state of consciousness. These phrases can be used therapeutically to arouse thoughts of G-d surrounding and protecting you at all times.

I encourage you to make a note of phrases and prayers from the Torah that you find soothing, adding them to the list of mantras you repeat in times of distress. I also recommend studying Rabbi Bachya Ibn Paqudas's powerful book, *Duties of the Heart, The Gate of Trust.* Daily study of *Duties of the Heart* provides a spiritually-focused strategy to shift your psychological orientation toward trust and faith in G-d. This shift creates an overall sense of calmness and enhances feelings of attachment and security, reducing symptoms of anxiety. A comprehensive daily study program based on *Duties of the Heart, The Gate of Trust,* can be found in the second section of this book.

TEN LEVELS OF EMOTIONAL SECURITY

Most importantly, Torah-based mantras and a daily study program of *Duties of the Heart, The Gate of Trust,* can help you envision G-d as your "secure base" and "safe haven." This is highlighted at the conclusion of *Duties of the Heart, The Gate of Trust,* where Rabbi Bachya enumerates ten reassuring beliefs that a person who deepens his faith will experience: "*Mivtach* (trust), *Mishan* (support), *Tikvah* (hope), *Machse* (protection), *Tochelet* (waiting), *Chikui* (expecting), *Semichah* (reliance), *Sever* (resting), *Misad* (confidence), and *Chesel* (assurance)".

David joined a support group that studies *Duties of the Heart, the Gate of Trust* every day as part of his treatment plan. He found that the exercises and mantras reduced his depressive thoughts. Though David had stopped praying a few years ago, he was surprised to find that the meditations made him more open to attending synagogue services, which provided additional social interaction and reduced his feelings of loneliness. I also suggested that he increase his positive associations about G-d by using the following meditation, which awakens a sense of being loved and cared for.

EXERCISES

—Feeling the World Love You

The *Kabbalah* provides one of the most important guided meditations on how to "go above," by acknowledging G-d's continuous role in creating and sustaining the world. The *Kabbalah* attempts to explain the paradox of how G-d could know everything about His creation, but at the same time give those He created the power of free will. To make sense of this conundrum, *Kabbalah* uses a metaphor called *Tzimtzum* (contractions/constrictions) to explain how the world was created:

The *Zohar* teaches us that before the world existed, there was only G-d. G-d decided to form the world in several progressive steps. The first step was to make a space so that the world could exist. This "vacated space" created a potential "place" for the world. Then, G-d allowed His light inside this vacated space, but didn't want to refill the space entirely. G-d progressively then concealed His light within four separate worlds: *Atzilus, Briah, Yetzirah*, and *Assiyah*.

The physical world we live in is called *Assiyah* (the world of action). In *Assiyah*, G-d's light is concealed almost to the point where it cannot be perceived. That is why the physical world often seems devoid of G-d's infinite light and presence. *Kabbalah* explains that G-dly light is present in *Assiyah*, it merely exists in a state of concealment, as the following diagram describes:

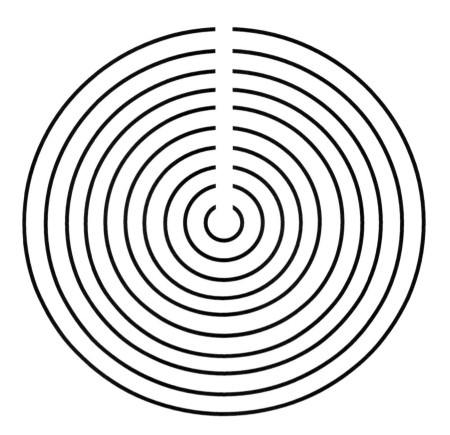

According to *Kabbalistic* understanding, everything in the world is indeed G-dly, existing in a state of hiddenness. This includes things that may seem "bad" to us. By contemplating this teaching, we come to realize, that in truth, nothing is truly bad. Negativity is merely concealed goodness.

The *Kabbalah* takes this idea even further, asserting that G-d created this world as the ultimate act of love. Another way of saying this is that the universe is a "creation of love." Although we may not always perceive this love, we can believe that G-d's guidance is "loving" us every moment.

The following meditation is especially helpful in identifying G-d's love.

Look around at the walls in the room where you are sitting.
Understand that those walls are there to protect you from the
wind and from any disturbance outside of your home.

Look up at the sky and notice the clouds that bring rain to nurture the earth, and the sun that gives us light and warmth. Imagine that if the sun ceases to shine its rays for just a few moments, the earth will cease to exist. All of this is sustained for you by G-d at every moment.

Consider how the piping in your home brings life-sustaining hydration; that water was created for you to live and to enjoy. Also consider the tens of thousands of people who are involved in maintaining the quality and delivery of water to your home. All of this is sustained for you by G-d at every moment.

Notice yourself breathing in and out, in and out. Become aware of the wondrous power of your lungs breathing in oxygen and breathing out carbon dioxide. Look at your hand and notice the complexity of its shape, muscles, bones, and its dexterity. All of this is sustained for you by G–d at every moment.

Feel the chair behind your back holding you as you sit comfortably. Notice the floor under your feet that is maintaining your balance and keeping you securely grounded. All of this is sustained for you by G-d at every moment.

Consider that every part of creation and every aspect of the universe is created for you by G–d. Contemplate how the universe loves you and is giving you life at every moment. Now, increase your awareness of all the love that is directed toward you from G-d, available for you at all moments.

—*Feeling Pursued by Goodness: Tehillim 23*

Words and phrases in the Torah serve as powerful meditations when they are read slowly while concentrating on the meaning of the words. Psalm 23 has helped many people seeking calmness and serenity. Here is a thoughtful meditation on each line that describes how G-d is our Shepherd guiding us through difficult times.

1.   A Psalm by David. The L-rd is my shepherd, I shall lack nothing.

> *I am guided and protected at all times by G–d, who cares*
> *for me as a shepherd cares for his flock. Due to His love and*
> *benevolence, I should never worry that I will be left alone and*
> *lack something that I need.*

2.   He lays me down in green pastures; He leads me beside still waters.

> *My relationship with G–d allows me to experience calmness*
> *and relaxation. At times, I will be able to sleep calmly, as*
> *if I am taking a nap on the grass in a park on a beautiful*
> *spring day. Others times, I will sense a feeling of tranquility,*
> *like someone sitting by the lake and enjoying the calmness of*
> *nature.*

3.   He revives my soul; He directs me in paths of righteousness for the sake of His Name.

> *Despite the difficulties life may bring, each day I wake up*
> *feeling renewed with optimism to face and overcome any*
> *obstacles. G-d wants me to succeed and opens up opportunities*
> *for me to make good choices, enabling me to follow my*
> *conscience by doing what's right and meaningful.*

4.   Though I walk in the valley of the shadow of death, I will fear no evil, for You are with me; Your rod and Your staff-they will comfort me.

> *Even if I face adversity, I can turn towards my Shepherd*
> *who will hold me and ensure that He is with me at all times.*
> *Although I may face emotional "enemies," I'm still "anointed*
> *with oil," meaning that I'm granted protection from Above.*

5.   You will prepare a table for me before my enemies; You have anointed my head with oil; my cup is full.

Although at times my thoughts may be painful, You have opened up other possibilities that life may improve for me. You have given me unlimited opportunities to experience spirituality and positivity in the world.

6.   Only goodness and kindness shall follow me all the days of my life, and I shall dwell in the House of the L-rd for many long years.

There is ample goodness in the world, and goodness is pursuing me at all times. I just need to open my eyes to become aware that abundance and goodness are surrounding me every moment. I am a child in G-d's "home," protected and cared for by my Father in heaven.

In addition to this meditation there are many examples of how various passages in the Torah can be used therapeutically. Some of the most important ideas appear in the following lines in *Tanach*:

*   I trust in your kindness, I rejoice in your salvation. (Tehillim 13)
*   "You shelter me, You preserve me from distress, with songs of deliverance to envelop me." (Tehillim 32:7)
*   G-d is my strength and my shield, my heart trusted in Him and I was helped. (Tehillim 31)
*   G-d is with me, I shall not fear, what can man do to me? (Tehillim 118)
*   Hear O Israel, the Lord our G-d, the Lord is one. (Devarim 6:4)

David benefitted by incorporating some of these phrases in his daily meditations. Gradually, he was able to improve his ability to both go "above" and stay "above" when confronted by feelings of sadness or loneliness. He now had practical tools to view life from a broader perspective, having learned key skills that enabled him to see the world from "above." He was ready for the next step, to focus on thinking good thoughts.

TAKEAWAYS

- "Going Above" helps a person broaden their perspective on life.
- Strengthening one's relationship with G-d has been shown therapeutically to be helpful in alleviating depression.
- Studying *Duties of the Heart, The Gate of Trust* and various portions of the Torah can play an important role in therapy.

Chapter Four

THINKING GOOD

The *Tzemach Tzedek* captured the power of positive thinking which can be used to overcome depression and anxiety. When he said, "Think good and it will be good," he stretched beyond viewing the proverbial cup as being "half full" instead of "half empty." He was providing a profound strategy for changing your life. More than just adopting a positive attitude, The *Tzemach Tzedek* proposed actually filling the cup with positive thoughts. Filling the cup with positivity has the power to reduce depression and anxiety, and, as science is now discovering, create lasting neurological changes.

There are two categories of "thinking good" that may change the way you think about life: categories A and B. Category A is about distracting your thoughts and focusing on positivity. Category B instructs you to consciously determine a positive outcome through your profound trust in G-d.

CATEGORY A: THE LETTER OF THE TZEMACH TZEDEK

How does "thinking good" work? How can you utilize the power of positive thinking?

In one of his letters, the Tzemach Tzedek elaborated on a remarkable psychological and spiritual approach to treating anxiety or depression. He detailed how to distract one's thoughts and focus primarily on the positive:

The Letter of the Tzemach Tzedek:

"In response to the question concerning the matter of fear in your heart, even though it is "nothing" in nature, I will not withhold writing what is in my heart. A person should request from G-d to experience happiness of his soul, as mentioned in the saying, 'Make the soul of your servant happy' (*Tehillim* 86:4) and also 'to remove his feelings of sadness and helplessness' (*Siddur*). He should also avoid causing himself distress since a person has the ability to avoid arousing negative feelings. Proof for this approach can be found in the commandment 'to not fear going to war,' as it is written, 'When you go out to war against your enemies, and you see horse and chariot, a people more numerous than you, *you shall not be afraid of them*, for the Lord, your God is with you Who brought you up out of the land of Egypt' (*Devarim*, 20:1). What happens if, despite this commandment (to not be scared), a person still feels fear in his heart from the battle? There must be a way to accomplish this since all *mitzvos* are only given to us [man], who has the free will to accomplish or not to accomplish them as is mentioned in the second chapter of the Eight Chapters of the Rambam.

"The explanation is as follows: a person has three garments [of his soul] - thought, speech and action. And, a person is able to think, speak, and act according to the power of his mind. Even if his heart is afraid, he is able to remove his thought, speech and actions [from his fears] and most importantly, not to think and speak about them, but rather do the opposite, as is written in the *Tanya* chapter 14. In this way we are commanded to 'not be afraid of them.' This implies that we shouldn't *think* about fear at all....

"Immediately as he stops thinking about them, his fear will become nullified. At this point his fears will be similar to one who is sleeping who doesn't have any feelings at that moment. After several days [the fear] will be totally be gone and [these foreign thoughts] will not be considered.

"The reason for this [ability] is that through *removing* your thoughts, fear will also disappear. This is according to how the mind works. Emotions emerge from *Daas* (Knowledge - the third *Sephira*) which is known as the 'key' to the other six *Sefirot* [The focus of the mind influences the emotions]. Through removing [negative] thoughts, they will automatically be forgotten without further emotional reaction.

Greater than even this is the statement that 'a person is not forced [into lust]'. Even if he is confronting a [powerful desire] he is not forced to do so. For if he hadn't placed his thoughts on it, it wouldn't have been aroused (even though he is Chayav Skilah as is mentioned in the Rambam, in the first chapter of Isurei Biyah). It is also inferred in the Talmud that a person can choose to be afraid or not be afraid (Talmud Brachot 60a).

"The key to forgetting your thoughts is to absorb your mind in other matters - especially matters of this world that arouse happiness. Also, [learning] Torah makes a person happy, and studying Torah daily at organized times especially with others (including the revealed Torah and the inner dimensions of the Torah [Chasidut]) can be very helpful.

"Additionally, a person should not think of depressing matters. Rather, he should always strive to be happy as if his heart is happy, even if he doesn't feel this at the moment, since in the end, he will feel happy. This is due to the fact that through repetitive behaviors a person comes to feel it in their heart, as the Rambam says 'a person should do it once, twice, and three times until it becomes habit" (Hilchot Deot, 1). See the Rambam's "Eight Chapters" and the Pardes" (Rabbi Moshe Cordovero), The Gates of Colors, Chapter 1. (A translation of this meditation can be found later in this book)

"The main principle is that a person shouldn't focus on matters that bother him and make him scared. Rather, he should do the opposite [by focusing on the positive], and by doing so, G-d pours upon him happiness from above. I heard this from my father [The Saintly Shneur Zalman of Liadi], that the Maggid of Mezeritch commented on the line 'The appearance of man is from Above.' This means that according to the emotion a person shows 'below,' this will be shown to him from 'Above.' This is why he held me back from singing a melancholy melody until after the evening prayer was completed and he waited until I finished my prayers and afterwards explained to me [this idea] in the name of the Maggid.

"A person should therefore teach himself to avoid depressing thoughts and to distract his mind from his fears even when he has a reason to fear something, and especially when there is nothing to fear at all, whether it pertains to his health or his finances. Also, a 'strand of lovingkindness was drawn upon him' [G-d was gracious to him] the previous summer, and it is known from our Rabbis that 'When a good

thing is given to a person, it isn't quickly taken away from him'
(Baba Kama 80:b). These [the fears mentioned above] are simply ways by
which a person's negative inclinations fool him. And thusly, they [the
disturbing thoughts] must be thrown away, as it says, 'and you shall
not wander after your hearts and after your eyes after which you are
going astray' (Numbers 15:39) in regards to distracting your mind from
thinking about transgressing'...as is written in the Rambam, second chapter
of Hilchot Avodat Kochavim, halacha 3..." [34]

The Tzemach Tzedek's approach instructs those who are dealing
with depression or anxiety to use "distraction" as a means of focusing
on more positive and important matters in one's life. Distraction-based
activities such as counting backwards, noticing other bodily sensations,
doing math or watching a video, are some of the most powerful tools
that have been proven to provide immediately relief. A person also
needs to focus on good thoughts by thinking positively and
contemplating spiritual concepts. There is a second category of
positive thinking (category B) which can be accomplished by deepening
one's relationship with G-d.

CATEGORY B: THE DISCOURSE OF THE LUBAVITCHER REBBE

In a remarkable discourse delivered by Rabbi Menachem Mendel
Schneerson, the Lubavitcher Rebbe, discussed the power that the
Tzemach Tzedek ascribed to thinking positively in the case of an actual
medical emergency. As mentioned in the introduction to this book,
Rabbi Yosef Yitzchak Schneerson, the previous Rebbe, told the story of
the Tzemach Tzedek that when a father came to him seeking help for his
deathly ill son, the Tzemach Tzedek responded, "Think good and it will
be good". According to the story, when the father began to "think good",
his son miraculously recovered.

In the discourse the Rebbe explained that positive thoughts actually
cause positive outcomes and that this is accomplished through developing
complete trust in G-d. He maintains that this level of trust is distinct
from a general faith in G-d (believing in His existence and providence).
Trust implies that a person will "'rely and depend on G-d *alone* to the
extent that he casts his lot entirely upon Him, as it is written: 'Cast your

burden upon G-d,' (Tehillim, 55:23) i.e., the person has no other dependency in the world except upon G-d".[35]

In quoting Duties of the Heart, the Rebbe explained that the level of trust needed to affect a positive outcome should resemble that "'of a prisoner in a dungeon in his master's domain.' The prisoner puts his trust only in his master, for "he is given over to his hand. No other person can cause him harm or help him (Duties of the Heart, the Gate of Trust)." "This itself" explained the Rebbe, "is the foundation for a person's trust that G-d will bestow apparent and manifest good upon him, *even* if he is not worthy of this kindness."[36]

The Rebbe is speaking about a *total* relationship and trust in G-d which can manifest spontaneous changes in the physical world. It is completely opposite to the way by which a person experiencing anxiety believes he is helplessness and has lost all control. In this case, a person gives up *all* fears and turns *solely* towards G-d for relief. This itself "causes a corresponding approach toward him in the spiritual realms. G-d protects him and showers mercy upon him even when, were one to make a reckoning, he would not be worthy, and He enables him to appreciate manifest and apparent good."[37]

For those who are open to this approach, I ask them to work toward "casting" their fears to G-d and to trust that He has the power to affect change in their lives. Many of my clients have reported to me that this was the defining moment in their battle against depression and anxiety.

THE PSYCHOLOGY OF POSITIVE THINKING

To understand how to utilize the psychological power of positive thinking, we first need to explore how the human mind experiences anxiety. We all know what it feels like to be scared, or avoid situations that make us uncomfortable. It is normal to feel an "extra" heartbeat before taking a test, or to get butterflies before making a presentation at work. However, if a person's heart races too frequently, and they constantly break out in a sweat when they're in public, these are signs that they may be suffering from an anxiety disorder.

Like depression, anxiety can take on different forms. Some people who suffer from anxiety often exist in a state of high alertness, fearing that something bad might happen at any moment. Others have fears and phobias of people, places, and things. Independent of which type of anxiety a person suffers from, there is one common denominator: they are experiencing fear too frequently, and their persistent states of anxiety have made their life unmanageable.

Take Rachel, age 37, who came to my office looking for help for Generalized Anxiety Disorder. Over the past five years, Rachel had seen several psychologists who treated her for anxiety symptoms including heart palpitations, dizzy spells, and nausea. She was also given Klonopin (a tranquilizer used to treat seizures) to take for periodic panic attacks. At our first session she shared her story:

> *"The last five years of my life have been a nightmare. My anxiety begins the minute I wake up. I immediately start worrying that something bad is going to happen, and often feel that I could have a heart attack at any moment. I keep on checking my chest and arms for any sign something is wrong. I can't stop worrying that something bad might happen."*

Rachel's symptoms were so severe that she had trouble caring for her children, and had to reduce her work hours in order to cope with her anxiety. Yet now she was feeling that her anxiety was getting worse, with no end in sight.

Rachel's story is similar to the hundreds of individuals I have treated for anxiety. Many have fears of leaving their home and find it hard to go to the bank or the doctor's office. The persistent physiological symptoms of anxiety can also be overwhelming. Someone with anxiety may experience muscle tension, headaches, and stomach pain that lasts hours or days. Worrying about an impending disaster, they may constantly scan their environment and bodies to make sure that something bad won't happen to them or their loved ones.

When a person presents with what seems like a pretty clear cut case of anxiety, I usually begin by explaining to them the science and psychology of anxiety, addressing these frequently asked questions:

Where does anxiety come from? Is it real? How does it start? Can I get rid of it without medication?

WHAT IS ANXIETY?

Who hasn't felt nervous before taking an exam, presenting in front of their peers, or waiting of the results of a medical test? Anxiety is a part of our lives; it just depends how big a part it plays and to what degree feelings of anxiety overwhelm us. Fear is a normal human response to danger. Anxiety is an ongoing condition where your senses are overwhelmed by a perceived threat, even when no real danger is present.

Let me give you an example of fear: One day you are walking outside your home on the street when suddenly, without any warning, a dog leaps towards your arm and tries to bite you. Without thinking, your body springs into action and does one of three things: it fights the dog, runs away or freezes. This is what psychologists call the "fight or flight" mechanism. When a person is in danger, his body is able to take rapid and evasive action to fight off impending danger or even death.

The fight or flight response is no simple maneuver. It is a powerful mechanism that happens at the speed of electricity. Fight or flight is so powerful that it takes effect even before the logical brain, or frontal cortex, can process what is occurring. Just think about it, a person doesn't slow down and say, "Hey, there's a dog going to bite me. Hmm, I think it's time to move out of the way, or raise my right arm up and smack it in the head." Instead, a process takes place where another part of the brain, known as the limbic system, rapidly recognizes danger, and swings into action. Only after the immediate impulse reaction, can a person begin to process what is happening and make a coherent decision.

The Amygdala is a little organ in the brain where the rapid evaluation of danger takes place. When the Amygdala senses danger it sends out a signal to another part of the brain that releases adrenaline, the most powerful hormone in the body. Adrenaline rushes through the entire nervous system, stimulating the sympathetic nervous system. In battle, adrenaline makes everything in your body go into overload: your heart starts beating faster, blood pressure goes up, your pupils may dilate, and you may begin to breathe rapidly. Muscles receive a rapid burst of energy to punch, jump, lift or run away from danger.

It is important to note that adrenaline does not harm the body. Those who suffer from anxiety may worry that the extra heartbeats or hyperventilation are signaling a heart attack. But the extra adrenaline cannot kill you! It may feel like you are going to stop breathing, but adrenaline can only make you feel uncomfortable—nothing more.

When a person is anxious they experience almost exactly the same sensations as the person warding off a vicious dog. During an anxiety attack the body goes into overdrive, the same way it does when fighting off danger. The difference, however, is that now THERE'S NO DOG. Anxiety causes the body to react "as if" there is a present deadly danger without a current and verifiable threat.

If "there's no dog," why does the adrenaline flow with equal vigor? The answer lies in how the brain, the most powerful organ in your body, works. Our imaginative faculties have the same ability to trigger the overwhelming torrent of chemicals as a physical threat. The body will respond as if the danger is real.

To experience a slight adrenaline rush, imagine driving on a highway in a January blizzard in a small car that's swaying back and forth due to violent winds and blinding snow. Suddenly, a Mack truck is tailgating your car. You desperately try changing lanes but you feel your car skidding. Then, in front of you, a car spins out of control. You slam on the breaks, sensing you are about to collide.

Extending this guided visualization for a few more seconds may cause you to start sweating and feel anxious. Your heart may pump a little faster and you may feel a tightening of your breath. This is because your brain can imagine various scenarios that start the flow of adrenaline in your body. Just like your brain can increase the flow of adrenaline, it can also reduce it.

The Robber by the Window

Dr. Aureen Wagner Pinto illuminates the connection between thoughts and their power to cause anxiety. Imagine yourself lying in bed, cuddled up in your blanket about to fall asleep. Suddenly you hear a scratching noise at the window. For a second you imagine the worst case scenario and believe it's a robber trying to break in. How do you feel? I'm sure you answered "anxious" or at least "on guard". Now, imagine that it's just leaves rustling by your window. How do you feel now? In the first case you will sense the danger and you may begin to panic, heart racing as you prepare to protect yourself or fight the impending danger. In the second case, you'll probably roll over and go to sleep.[38]

Our thoughts have tremendous power. A person can literally sit in a room alone and create a masterpiece of music, a new paradigm in physics, or conjure up thoughts of danger or personal disaster. He has the ability to envision himself flying on an airplane and the engine failing. Or, he can picture himself sitting calmly by a stream, watching lily pads gently float by and disappear into the horizon.

"What Ifs" and "What People Think" (WPTs)

According to Dr. Howard Liebgold, author of *Freedom from Fear*, there are two kinds of thoughts that generate fear: "What Ifs?" and "What People Think" (WPTs).[39] "What If" fears are a train of thoughts that drag you into a state of anxiety. For example, while driving over a bridge you picture it collapsing. Or, after checking the lock on your door several times, you ask yourself, "Did I really lock the car door? If I didn't, then someone may pass by, open the door and steal the car."

"What If" fears transform common situations into a state of full blown panic. Some people may feel some tightness in their chest and pain in their left arm, and begin to think that they are having a heart attack. Yet, the more you worry about the symptoms, the more anxious you become. Then you begin to think, "What if I'm really having a heart attack?" As the "What If" fears intensify, your heart races and you begin to hyperventilate.

The other kind of fear Dr. Liebgold describes is "What People Think," or WPTs. WPTs occur when you imagine what others are thinking about you, or how you are perceived. For example, you walk into a crowd of people. Out of the corner of your eye, you see someone whispering something to his friend. You think, "They're probably talking about how poor I look, and how ugly my clothes are." Or, you are about to give a speech in front of your peers at work, and you think, "I'm going to make a fool out of myself when I open my mouth!" WPTs cause you to see yourself in the worst possible social position, either becoming an outcast or a scorned failure.

One thing is for sure: "What If" fears and WPTs take a tremendous amount of creativity and imagination. It would take a Hollywood screenwriter to conjure up some of the disastrous scenarios that people with anxiety live with on a daily basis.

A child who suffered from OCD once told me that he imagined he would be kidnapped by a terrorist, tortured, and burned to death on the stake by the Inquisition. Another woman told me of her fear that if she walks across the street, she will certainly be hit by a car, so she avoids crossing streets without bringing a friend or family member along. She had imagined a creative chain of events that would lead to her being hit: a dog breaks free from his leash and runs in the road, a car swerves and hits another car, that car spins out of control and crashes into her.

Treating Anxiety

Cognitive Behavioral Therapy has been the gold standard when it comes to treating anxiety for over 40 years. The goal of CBT is helping people understand the nature of their thoughts, and changing their cognitions and perceptions about life. More recently, however, a new generation of therapists is looking to improve the results of CBT by increasing the ratio of positive thoughts to anxious ones.

A person experiencing prolonged anxiety is likely consumed by negative thoughts about people, situations, and, especially, their safety. The trick is to learn how to increase positive thoughts, while limiting the impact of negative ones.

The Positivity Ratio

One of the leading proponents of increasing positivity is psychologist Dr. Barbara Fredrickson. She maintains that the best way to reduce anxiety is by arousing positive emotions like love, joy, and gratitude. Fredrickson believes that a positivity/negativity ratio of 3:1 must be maintained to experience the benefits of positive thinking.[40] This means that if you have three positive thoughts for every negative one, you are on the right track. If, however, you have three negative thoughts to every positive one, then you are probably on the road to depression or anxiety.

Fredrickson developed a method to increase positive thinking using "Positivity Portfolios" to develop a person's capacity for happiness.[41] The portfolios contain photographs and mementos of the people, places, and things that generate a heartfelt feeling of positivity. The ten portfolios Fredrickson suggests are: joy, gratitude, serenity, interest, hope, pride, amusement, inspiration, awe, and love.

The system works like this: Let's say that in the "joy" portfolio you collect pictures, or write down notes about all the joyful moments in your life, like the birth of a child, birthday party, graduation day, wedding, etc. In the "gratitude" portfolio, you make a list of all the people you feel grateful for. You read through your portfolios a few times a day to increase overall positivity, especially at times when negative thoughts occur. The portfolio helps you shift toward positive thoughts in order to awaken feelings of happiness.

Fredrickson's positivity-enhancing exercises are the key in helping clients like Rachel overcome their generalized anxiety. In Rachel's case, we first measured her "Positivity Ratio" and found out that she had a 4:1 negative ratio, meaning four negative thoughts for every positive one. While picking up her daughter after school, she would think to herself "I love my daughter." This would be followed by "I can never do anything right," "I might be too sick one day to care for my daughter," "I can't do anything to stop my anxiety" and "I'm going to be suffering for the rest of my life". She discovered that her negative ratio was consistent throughout the day, especially when she would put her children to sleep or eat dinner with her husband.

Rachel lived in a world filled with negative thoughts that were eating away at her ability to experience positive feelings and an overall sense of optimism. Over the past five years, she had lost her spontaneity, and now felt totally isolated in confronting her perception of helplessness. Sharing the benefits of positivity, I asked Rachel to commit to a daily program of positive thinking that could change her thought ratios and reduce her anxiety.

Over a three-week period Rachel's Positivity Portfolio focused on the times she felt gratitude toward her friends and some of her teachers at school. She wrote down a collection of memories including her seventh grade English teacher who gave her special attention and encouragement. Despite struggling with her grades, she felt gratitude towards being made to feel special and that someone believed in her. She also put in her portfolio the love she experienced in her grandparent's home. She would visit them every weekend and would be greeted with hugs, kisses and chocolate chip cookies! These memories aroused positive emotions and the more she focused on them—opposed to her anxiety-inducing thoughts—the happier she felt.

The Science of Positive Thinking

The power of positive thinking is one of the most talked about and researched topics in the world of psychology today. There have been hundreds of well-known books and articles published on the ideas of positivity and positive thinking. Most of these studies point to the fact that positive thinking leads to healthier emotional outcomes.

One study conducted at the Maytiv Center for Research and Practice in Positive Psychology, in Jerusalem, followed sixty-six children, ages 5 to 12 facing life-threatening illnesses, as they participated in Make-A-Wish Israel. Half the group wasn't certain their wish would be fulfilled, while the others knew their wish would come true within six months.

Both groups were asked to complete a questionnaire rating their levels of optimism and overall emotional wellbeing. It turned out that the children who had their wishes fulfilled had higher levels of optimism, lower levels of depression and anxiety, and improved health-related quality of life. These findings show the important role that hope and optimism play in increasing the overall well-being of people who suffer from illness.[42]

The opposite is also true. Spending considerable time focusing on negative or catastrophic thoughts leads to excessive worry and depression. The key is to increase the level of happiness by filling your mind with positive thoughts.

Research from the Mayo Clinic

Researchers at the Mayo Clinic also found a connection between positive thinking and physical well-being. Interestingly, their research clarified that positive thinking doesn't mean ignoring life's realities, but approaching life in a more positive and productive way. Someone with a healthy attitude anticipates that good things will happen, not the worst.

According to the Mayo Clinic study positive thinking may provide benefits to overall well-being, such as:

- Increased lifespan
- Lower rates of depression
- Greater resistance to the common cold
- Better psychological and physical well-being
- Reduce risk of death from cardiovascular disease
- Better coping skills during hardships and times of stress.
- Researchers also found that for every point that increased optimism, risk of early death decreased by 19 percent.[43]

I have seen first-hand the powerful impact of positive thinking. One client who suffered from bipolar disorder told me that when she was struggling with her worst episodes of depression, she read positive stories about other people overcoming difficulties in their lives, and staying optimistic despite their conditions. When reading the newspaper, she skipped to the comic section first. She also tried to avoid hearing about any stories about violence or tragedy. Another client, who had lost a child, started printing positive sayings from the Internet on magnets and giving them out to her friends. Despite her own tragedy, she felt uplifted by making other people happy and watching the impact it had on their lives.

Changing Brain Chemistry

Positive thinking actually changes a person's brain structure. Dr. Susumu Tonegawa and his colleagues at the Center for Neural Circuits Genetics at the Massachusetts Institute of Technology studied how positive experiences change how the brain works in mice. In their lab, mice overcame chronic stress by reactivating neurons that had been used during positive experiences (like being with a mate) to prevent depressive behaviors.

Dr. Tonegawa's research showed that the hippocampus, a structure of the brain that changes in response to stress and depression, also responded to positive thoughts. Stress reduced the creation of new neurons in the brain, making it vulnerable to depression. However, reactivation of neurons that had been active during a positive experience restored neuron development in the hippocampus and reversed the effects of depression. In other words, the process of activating positive thoughts is enough to restructure the brain to reduce anxiety or depression.[44]

Positive thinking also changes a person's brain chemistry by elevating serotonin levels, which play a vital role in the development of depression and anxiety. A study in the *Journal of Psychiatry and Neuroscience* engaged actors who were able to maintain intense memories of either positive or negative experiences. The actors underwent brain scans when they were focused on happy thoughts and memories. The scans showed that their brains increased the production of serotonin, which reduces depression and anxiety. However, when the actors focused on negative memories, serotonin levels in the brain decreased, showing the connection between thoughts and brain chemistry.[45]

THE SEVEN STEPS AND EXERCISES TO POSITIVE THINKING

For many people thinking "good" is not something that comes automatically. To "think good" a person often needs to view life from a different perspective. One way to achieve this is to practice the following seven steps daily:

1. Increase the use of positive words.
2. View life from a broader perspective.
3. Practice positive affirmations.
4. Read books about positivity.
5. Think Joyfully.
6. Offer Gratitude.
7. Forgive yourself and others.

These seven steps form a comprehensive strategy to increase positivity. Clients begin by adopting positive speech, and progress towards using positive affirmations. By step 7, clients are able to forgive others, setting them free from bearing grudges or feeling jealous. However, the process doesn't have to occur in this exact order, and you can choose what is most needed in your life.

—1.   Increase the Use of Positive Words

The words you use to describe people, places, and things shape the way you think about them. Speech is a powerful tool that can create negative associations, or elevate one's attitudes toward life. For example, you can choose to negatively describe another person or to find the goodness in them, by judging their behavior from a place of kindness and empathy.

Try to notice the words you use every day. If they are negative in nature, then introduce more positive words like:

Abundant, Agreeable, Appreciation, Astounding, Beautiful, Calm, Caring, Complete, Connected, Enjoyable, Friendly, Gratitude, Happy, Harmonious, Good, Grateful, Innovative, Joyful, Marvelous, Optimistic, Perfect, Peaceful, Positive, Remarkable, Resilient, Resourceful, Responsible, Safe, Sparkling, Thankful, Together, Valuable, Wholesome, Wonderful, and Youthful.

These words are known to trigger positive associations and create more optimism. When describing yourself, try inserting words like "resilient" and "calm." While describing other people, use words that point out their best qualities like "friendly" or "youthful."

When a 28-year old mother reported to me that her son was "bratty" and "*chutzpadik*," I suggested that she substitute terms like "struggling" or "overwhelmed" to describe his shortcomings more accurately. Whenever she started to use negative adjectives to describe her son, I advised her to replace them with more positive attributes such as "youthful", "vibrant" and "energetic." At the next session, she reported that using positive words helped her to feel better about her son, and he began to behave differently, reflecting her new attitude.

I often share the advice of a prominent community organizer who asks parents dealing with "rebellious" teens not to label them "at risk." Rather, he suggests calling them "kids in pain" or KIPS. These are just some examples of how language can transform our attitudes and affect relationships in our lives.

Exercise:

Try to become aware of the words you use on a daily basis. Are they predominantly negative or positive in nature? If you find yourself in the negative zone, try increasing the number of positive words, and notice a difference in your life and relationships.

Make a list of the positive characteristics of people you work or live with. During the next few days use those words when speaking about them or speaking with them. Notice if your words affect a change in attitude between the two of you.

—2.   *View Life from a Broader Perspective*

"Thinking good" can help broaden your perspective on life, especially when confronting challenges. The *Talmud* tells about the trials and tribulations of Rabbi Akiva who declared, "*Kol mah de'avid Rachmana letav avid*," or "Everything that G-d does is for the good." Though Rabbi Akiva was subjected to extreme cruelty and torture at the hands of his Roman persecutors, he was able to maintain his positive attitude toward life.

Despite his personal pain, Rabbi Akiva taught us a pivotal concept: When facing difficulties, a person needs to call upon their faith in G-d, trusting that everything He does for us is good. Rabbi Akiva's legacy can inspire us to shine a light of positivity on life's challenges.

It is interesting to note that the name Rabbi Akiva uses for G-d is *Rachmana,* or "The merciful One." When we speak of G-d in this way, we understand that He acts with mercy and compassion toward us. The Merciful One is always looking out for us and guiding us even if we don't perceive His Providence. Rabbi Akiva's powerful phrase, "*Kol mah deavid rachmana ltav avid*," "Everything that G-d does is for the good," reassures us of G-d's care, and offers a powerful way to access positivity at any moment.

Rabbi Nahum Ish Gamzu took the concept of "thinking good" to an even greater level. Dealing with challenges, he said, "*Gam zu letovah*," meaning, "This too is good." In other words, things that happen to us that may seem negative, are essentially good. Rabbi Nahum Ish Gamzu understood that behind every blemish is beauty, waiting to be revealed. This is the ultimate expression of Divine providence and "thinking good."

Exercise:

- Make a list of instances in your life which at first seem to be negative, but turned out to be positive.
- Have there been any times in your life when struggling through a difficult time has strengthened your identity and enhanced your resourcefulness?

—3.   *Practice Positive Affirmations*

Positive affirmations help a person change their core self-beliefs and recognize their positive value. In Torah Psychology, we understand that each person has inherent value, since they were created by G-d and given a soul which uniquely defines who they are. This concept is rooted in the Torah's description of man's creation, as it says, "G-d breathed into man a breath of life" (*Bereishis 2:7*). *Kabbalah* describes this "breath of life" as G-d blowing a part of Himself into man, imbuing him with a G-dly dimension known as the soul. The presence of a G-dly soul ensures that a person is totally good, devoid of any defects, since his soul is a reflection of infinite goodness, and a mirror image of the Divine. This soul is the true self, which is greater than a person's external manifestations of negative thoughts, feelings and behaviors.

Here are some helpful affirmations that can increase positive thinking.

Affirmations about oneself

- I am unique.
- I am the child of my Parent in Heaven who longs after me and loves me

like His most precious treasure.

- I am a good person who deserves to be loved.
- I am a person who deserves to be treated with kindness and affection.
- I totally accept and embrace myself as I am.
- I am happy just to be alive breathing and experiencing all the wonders of life.
- My soul within me makes me capable, talented and loved by others.
- I love who I am because G-d loves me and sustains me every day.
- I love who I am and I do not need to justify my existence to others.
- My soul is like a precious diamond that can shine light outwards to others. Fulfilling a commandment or doing an act of kindness draws me closer to G-d.
- My very existence gives pleasure to the One above, like a child who gives his parent's pleasure just by being born.
- Although I may make mistakes, they are simply external blemishes which cover up my ultimate goodness that's inherent within me.
- I am a channel of positivity in this world.
- My body is healthy and able to heal from any illness or pain.

Affirmations about others

In order to "Think Good" about other people, it is helpful to focus on their G-dly dimensions. Unfortunately, it is human nature to view other people negatively, especially when one feels rejected. For example, one day you attend a gathering to hear the words of a well-known speaker. At the end of the lecture, participants gather around the speaker to ask him questions. You wait until the crowd thins out, and walk towards the speaker gesturing that you would like to ask him a question.

As you're about to approach him, he continues talking to someone else, and then abruptly exits the room. It is natural to feel slighted by the speaker, and even to imagine that he has rejected you and doesn't value you enough to spend time speaking with you. It is also human nature to label the other person, claiming that he is egotistical, snobbish, or simply a mean individual who disregards other people's feelings. However, it is also reasonable to assume that the speaker was merely tired after his lecture, or he may have had to rush to another event.

The Torah gives us positive direction in our relationships by asking us to avoid judging others unfairly. In the second chapter of *Ethics of the Fathers*, Hillel warns, "Do not judge your fellow until you have reached his place." This dictum cautions us against jumping to conclusions about other people, unless we have experienced the exact same situation in our own lives. Until we "stand in their place," we shouldn't judge others' intentions or their actions.

Instead of focusing on negativity, we should aim to ascribe positive qualities/motives to people on an ongoing basis. Giving others the benefit of the doubt and finding the good in them frees us from constantly feeling disappointed by other people. When we attribute goodness to others, we also experience a reflection of goodness towards ourselves.

Here are some key affirmations to help view other people more positively:

- I accept that all people are created by G-d and they deserve to be loved as I do.
- G-d, not other people, takes care of all of my needs and no one can take away something which G-d does not want me to have.
- "Love your neighbor as you love yourself." This is the great principle of the Torah.
- The only impediment that separates me from another person is our bodies, and not our souls, which are one.
- I can share my goodness with others by treating them kindly and thinking good thoughts about them.
- I have abundant love and desire to share goodness and love with other people.
- Because I have an infinite soul, I have the ability to love others with infinite love and kindness.
- I can judge other people favorably, and give them the opportunity to improve their ways.
- Sometimes people may not appear good in my eyes because they are suffering in their own way.
- With patience and kindness my relationships with other people (even difficult people) can work.
- I can learn something new from everyone I meet.

- G-d is guiding me through other people's interactions with me; He is giving me direction through everyone I meet.

Affirmations about life

These positive affirmations are based on the Torah view of the nature of life. Repeating them enhances positive thoughts to better handle the ups and downs of life.

- Every moment and place is the right moment and place for me to be.
- I fully trust in G-d. He will give me everything I need in its proper time.
- Life has meaning in all circumstances and at all times.
- Everything that G-d does is for the good.
- This too is for good.
- Everything is working together for me right now, guiding me to the right destination.
- I accept G-d's plan for me. He will show me step-by-step what I need to do.
- G-d gave me the power to overcome all potential roadblocks in my life.

Exercise

Create a list of positive affirmations that would improve your situation. Read these affirmations to yourself twice a day for the next week. Try to notice if you feel a difference in your overall emotional wellbeing.

—4.   Read Books about Positivity

It is important to spend time each day reading about positive behaviors, and people who acted positively to improve the world. Instead of following the news, try to find stories about those who have sacrificed for others, or have changed people's lives. Choose books that inspire you to live with positivity. There are also numerous online resources, blogs and WhatsApp groups about optimism and positive thinking you can read daily, or subscribe to their email lists to receive updates.

As you encounter negative cognitions during the day, pick up your book to distract your thoughts. After a while, you will become used to reading about positivity and see how it influences your unconscious mind to produce happier thinking. The more you read about positivity, the more you will be drawn to it in all parts of your life.

Some great works of inspiration I suggest to my clients include:

- Stories about the Lubavitcher Rebbe's personal interactions with people
- The writings of Viktor Frankl
- Books on happiness by Rabbi Zelig Pliskin
- Stories of Rebbeim and Tzadikim
- Books by Rabbi Dr. Avraham Twerski
- The writings of Rabbi Eliyahu Dessler
- A Tzaddik in Our Time: The Life of Rabbi Aryeh Levine
- Jewish heroes throughout history
- Stories about random acts of kindness

Exercise:

Go to the library or Jewish bookstore and choose one book on positivity. Read it daily for 15 minutes.

—5. *Think Joyfully: Ramak's Meditation on Colors*

Thinking about joy can help you to feel more joy. In fact, it is possible to change negative thought patterns by concentrating on the nature of joy and associating situations that bring more joy into one's life. I recommend creating a list of positive images and connecting them with happy and optimistic thoughts. For example, while repeating the word "joy," imagine picking up and kissing a newborn child, watching children laugh, or seeing an elderly person smile as they play with a puppy. When saying the word "goodness," imagine a volunteer helping someone who is handicapped, feeding someone who is hungry, or protecting someone who is innocent.

If any negative thoughts arise during this exercise, do not fight them. Gently return to repeating the positive words and images until the negative thoughts subside.

Some joyful words and concepts to consider:

- Joy
- Goodness
- Love
- Happiness
- Abundance
- Kindness
- Laughter
- Freedom
- Harmony
- Peacefulness
- Add your own words and associations

When I teach this meditation, clients are often surprised when they begin to smile and even laugh as they evoke positive thoughts and associations. By spending time making these positive connections, you can increase feelings of positivity and joy in your life.

Exercise:

Meditation on Colors

The *Tzemach Tzedek* remarked on the importance of a meditation by Rabbi Moshe Cordovero, the Ramak, to boost happiness .In *Pardes Rimonim,* Gate Nine "Gates of Colors," the Ramak explains that there are physical qualities in the world that reflect spiritual realities. Thinking about these concepts can bring you to a happier state of mind. For example, the color white reflects *Chesed* (lovingkindness), whereas red represents *Gevurah* (sternness). The Ramak suggests wearing white clothing to awaken feelings of happiness and lovingkindness. For help falling asleep, the Ramak recommends thinking of water, which also reflects *Chesed* (lovingkindness).

Here is another Kabbalistic meditation for when you feel stressed, or simply want to elevate your emotional state, that focuses on the connection between *Sefirot* and the following colors:

Keter (Invisible)
Wisdom (All colors)
Knowledge (Yellow)
Kindness (White)
Judgment (Red)
Beauty (Violet)
Victory (Light pink)
Glory (Dark pink)
Foundation (Orange)
Kingship (Blue, Purple)

The Meditation

"*You are entering an enchanted garden. As you walk in, you notice how the flowers around you smell, and how they feel. In front of you is a small pond, a pool of water. On the surface, you see the color green. As the green enfolds, you feel it and sense its true nature. Green helps things grow into abundance through envy, which motivates all life. Sense the different shades of green. Feel the beauty of light green and the purpose of darker shades.*

As you look further into the pool you see the color blue. Blue is like the sky over all things, filled with truth. Sky blue is the color of beginning. Blue is the color of G-d's presence, the Shechinah.

Shift your assemblage point into the color purple. Purple is mysticism and royalty. Visualize blue and white garments laid upon your body, with a crown upon your head. Before you is your castle, and within is your greatest treasure room. Proceed towards the room. When you reach the door, notice that you have a key in your hand that will open the lock. Inside there are stacks of gold coins and other monetary treasures. Seek out the greatest treasure in the room. It might be a large ancient book upon a pedestal. Feel free to open the book to a particular page. Imagine what you see on the page. It might be a single letter, like the letter caph. *In the* Book of Creation, caph *signifies life. From here we learn that the greatest treasure in the world is just to be alive.*

Visualize the color yellow and become one with it. Feel yellow all around you. Yellow may represent the intellect and illumination of ideas.

Yellow overwhelms all personal deceptions. It may dissolve the delusions of one's own identity and hence, there may be dissonance while remaining in its healing glow.

Shift into the color orange. Orange is sensuous and relaxing, succulent like an orange. Orange nourishes the emotions and calms the nerves, and is regenerating for the body and soul.

Now move out of the colors and back into your enchanted garden. Step out of the garden and back to the present, feeling renewed. Take the gifts of the colors and their lessons with you. Open your eyes."[46]

—6. *Offer Gratitude*

Appreciating others who have been kind to you is another important way to increase positivity. Gratitude helps a person recognize all the goodness they already have.

One of my clients shared with me that when she wakes up in the morning, the first thing she does is write down all the things she appreciates. She starts her day by focusing on all the good in her life. She thanks G-d for the health and welfare of her children and spouse, and is grateful that she's been given an opportunity to re-experience life in a new way.

Here are lists of some of the people and things you may appreciate:

People and religious ideas

- A friend
- Your neighbor
- G-d
- A teacher who helped you
- Your parents
- Your grandparents
- A worker at a store
- A customer service agent
- Your superintendent
- A religious leader who inspired you
- Your doctor
- Your dentist

- The bus driver
- Your children
- Your spouse
- Your boss
- Your clients

Material Objects
- Your home
- Your bed
- Your electricity and water
- Your car
- Your pet
- Clean streets
- Trees
- Community parks
- Nature
- Your bicycle
- Your job
- Your furniture
- Your kitchen
- Your artwork
- Your money and investments

Exercise:

Make your own gratitude list of all the special gifts in your life. Include all prized possessions, as well as the simple things in your life that you take for granted. Read your list daily and notice the difference in your positivity levels. If necessary, read the list twice a day.

—7.   *Forgive Yourself and Others:* Ramak's Tomer Devorah

Perhaps the greatest form of "Thinking Good" is learning to forgive others for what they may have said or done to us. Acting with mercy and compassion toward others gives us the opportunity to transcend ourselves.

In addition to the color meditations, and many other important *Kabbalistic* works, the Ramak wrote a treatise called *Tomer Devorah* which outlines the way G-d forgives His creations despite their behavior towards Him. The Ramak asks us to emulate G-d's ways by forgiving others who may have hurt or wronged us as well.

The Ramak's treatise is based upon a stanza from the Prophet Micah who describes G-d's thirteen attributes of Mercy emanating from the *Kabbalistic Sephira* of *Keter* (Crown). The Ramak explains that since man is created in the image of G-d, man can actualize this potential by imitating G-d's ways in this world. Reflecting on these attributes offers a comprehensive psychological approach toward letting go of one's anger and disappointment in others—two of the most common sources of ongoing emotional distress.

The Thirteen Attributes of Mercy are:

מיכה פרק ז (יח) מי אל כמוך |נשא עון ועבר על פשע |לשארית נחלתו |לא החזיק לעד אפו |כי חפץ
חסד הוא: (יט) ישוב ירחמנו| יכבש עונתינו |ותשליך במצלות ים כל חטאותם:(כ) תתן אמת ליעקב |חסד
לאברהם |אשר נשבעת לאבתינו |מימי קדם:

MIDDAH 1: To accept being Insulted מי אל כמוך

Just as G-d gives us the power to sin against Him, we too must be patient without overreacting to offense

MIDDAH 2: נשא עון Nurture even those who hurt us.

Just like G-d continues to nurture the very people who sin against Him, so should we be patient when we are insulted. We should not to refuse to do good to those who do wrong to us.

MIDDAH 3: עבר על פשע Forgive the Sinner

Even though people sin against G-d, He still continues to take care of them with kindness. Just like G-d forgives our sins and washes them away, we too should pardon those who sin against us, and forget their wrongful deeds.

MIDDAH 4:לשארית נחלת Wish others the best

When we are hurt, G-d also "feels" our hurt and shares our pain. We too should look out for the honor of our neighbors, and treat them like family by desiring their well-being.

MIDDAH 5: לא החזיק לעד אפו Letting go of anger

Just as G-d does not allow His anger to persist, we too should not harbor anger towards people who may have hurt us.

MIDDAH 6: **כי חפץ חסד הוא** Desire good for you neighbor

Just like G-d rejoices in our success and goodness, so too should we delight in our neighbors' goodness, even when we are insulted by them.

MIDDAH 7: ישוב ירחמנו Show even greater kindness to those who have hurt us and repented their ways.

Just like G-d accepts those who repent and considers them to be greater than those who are righteous, so too should we embrace those who have hurt us and repented for what they did to us.

MIDDAH 8: יכבש עונתינו Nullify your neighbor's negative points, not his good ones.

G-d does not extinguish our good points due to the negative traits that we exhibit. So too, we should not forget the good points those who wronged us may have.

MIDDAH 9: ותשליך במצלות ים כל חטאותם Forgive and cast away a person's sins.

G-d allows us to suffer, yet He still has mercy on us. We should also view those who may have hurt us with compassion.

MIDDAH 10: תתן אמת ליעקב Be truthful, even to those who hurt us.

Just as G-d judges the world in truthfulness, so too should we behave truthfully to our neighbors without perverting justice.

MIDDAH 11: חסד לאברהם Show kindness to others.

Just as G-d bestows great kindness to His children, so too should we be patient and show compassion to our neighbors and friends.

MIDDAH 12: אשר נשבעת לאבתינו Be good to others since we all share the same Father.

Just as G-d loves all Jews as the sons of Abraham, so too should we forgive those who sin against us because we share the same Father.

MIDDAH 13: מימי קדם Be good to those who have hurt us, since there was a time when they were good.

Just as G-d remembers that there was a time before the sin, we should remember that those who hurt us also displayed many good points before we were hurt by them.

Ultimately, through forgiveness, a person can take control of his life, freeing himself from feelings of revenge and anger. When a person emulates G-d's mercy toward others, he moves from being the victim to the one who rises above emotional limitation. He transcends all boundaries, exemplifying higher virtues such as temperance and benevolence.

MEDICAL BENEFITS OF FORGIVENESS

When a person holds on to resentment, he is ultimately the one that will suffer the most, not the perpetrator. Holding on to anger can lead to various physiological symptoms including heart disease and hypertension. Studies have found that when you forgive someone, you actually lower your risk of heart attack, reduce cholesterol levels and blood pressure, and can even influence your levels of anxiety and depression.

Dr. Karen Swartz, Director of the Mood Disorders Adult Consultation Clinic at The Johns Hopkins Hospital, asserts there is an "enormous physical burden to being [emotionally] hurt." In Swartz' experience, chronic anger ignites a "fight-or-flight mode, which results in numerous changes in heart rate, blood pressure and immune response." The ongoing emotional distress can "increase the risk of depression, heart disease and diabetes, among other conditions. Forgiveness, however, calms stress levels, leading to improved health."[47]

Forgiveness releases a person from their self-imposed negativity, and frees up their energy to actualize important values, like building healthy relationships. It also gives a person more strength to do good for others.

Affirmations of forgiveness

- I forgive anyone who may have hurt me in my life.
- Nothing can harm me if it is not willed so by G-d.
- I forgive myself and realize that I'm not perfect.
- I did the best I could, given the circumstances.
- I forgive my parents for any pain they may have caused me.
- The past cannot change, but my attitude can.
- I wish others only goodness and happiness.

Exercise:

Study the thirteen *Middos* daily, repeating them until you experience feelings of mercy toward those who have hurt you. Many of my clients have reported significant emotional benefits from doing this exercise within a few days. In fact, some found that learning how to forgive was more beneficial than many years of talk therapy.

Make a list of people who have hurt or bothered you. Although this may be difficult, contact them and forgive them for what they did. Notice afterwards if you feel relieved and happier than before.

TAKEAWAYS

- Positive thinking correlates with a reduction in depression and anxiety.
- Positive thinking transforms neurological patterns and elevates serotonin levels in the brain (The key neurotransmitter that affects depression and anxiety).
- Increasing positive thinking and gratitude are the keys to emotional well-being.
- Forgiving other people has both psychological and physiological benefits.

Chapter Five

CARRYING IT FORWARD

In a NASA rocket launch, the first three stages of takeoff are fiery and dramatic. The big boosters produce the enormous energy to blast off and fight the powerful forces of gravity. Once the rocket is in orbit, it doesn't need as much power to continue moving forward. It is the smaller payload modules on top that journey forward into space, leaving the large, dramatic launchers behind.

In the same way, overcoming the "gravity" of depression or anxiety takes enormous courage. The power of the first three steps of Torah Psychology: "Creating Space," "Going Above," and "Thinking Good," takes a person out of their comfort zone, into a new way of thinking. Three additional steps help you maintain the gains of feeling better: "Designing your future," "Doing Good," and "Connecting with Others."

DESIGNING YOUR FUTURE

Many people who suffer from depression or anxiety for a prolonged period of time can't remember what life was like without their symptoms, and find it hard to envision freedom from emotional distress.

Torah Psychology asks you to construct a new emotional reality, different from the one you live in presently. Imagine a resilient future empowering you to be the architect of your destiny, moving beyond where you are at the current moment.

Speaking at a lecture, Frankl used the analogy of airplane navigation to express the importance of defining an idealistic future.

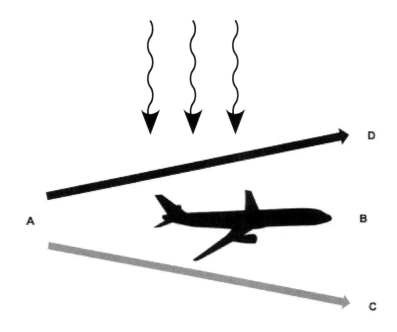

An airplane is flying from the West to the East, from point A to point B. There's a crosswind blowing from the North to the South, so if the pilot aims directly at Point B, he will drift South of his destination to point C. Instead, he must aim North of his destination to point D so that the crosswind will bring him where he intends to go. Quoting the famous German writer Johann Wolfgang von Goethe, Frankl explains that the same is true of man: "If we take man as he is, we make him worse, but if we take man as he should be, we make him capable of becoming what he can be."[48]Frankl maintains that a person needs to have a higher vision of what he *can* become, to turn into the architect of his future.

An architect needs to have a vision of what a new building will look like before he can begin designing its details. He needs to ask several questions that might include: Will it be an office building or a home? What size will it be? How many people will it be able to hold comfortably?

In the same way, the process of designing one's future begins by asking the following questions:

- What would my life be like without depression or anxiety?
- What changes will take place when my life is better?
- What would I be doing differently when all of the problems have been resolved?
- What would I like to become in the future?

Once you are able to envision the future, you can begin to fill in the "architectural" details.

SOLUTION-FOCUSED THERAPY

The need for designing a positive future and thinking positively led to the creation of a revolutionary approach in helping people overcome depression and anxiety called Solution-Focused Therapy. Similar to Logotherapy, Solution Focused Therapy looks into the future to undo the rigid patterns or solutions that were tried in the past, but have failed.

Solution-Focused Therapy maintains that there are two types of language: "problem" talk and "solution" talk.[49] By engaging in negative talk, we enhance the negative aspects of our life experience. However, concentrating on the positive makes it our reality.

One of the most powerful techniques in Solution-Focused Therapy is the "Exception Question." The "Exception Question" asks the client to recall times when they didn't experience the problem. For example, "What were you doing differently at those times when you weren't feeling depressed," and in what ways can you make it possible for more of those exceptions to occur?"[50] Questions like these shift the focus to solutions.

Another powerful technique called the "Miracle Question" invites a person to look beyond the problem and imagine what life would be like without it.[51] A "Miracle Question" would be, "Imagine a miracle happened one night while you were sleeping, and your problem was solved. How would you know things had changed? What would you do differently?" The "Miracle Question" introduces a person to a new world of possibilities, as he contemplates life without emotional illness.

The purpose of Solution Focused Therapy is to help the client maintain an optimistic view of himself. For example, the therapist might ask, "Between this session and the next, please observe what good things happen in your life that you would like to continue to happen in the future."[52]A person is encouraged to engage in these positive activities as often as possible.

The therapist cautions the client to "Go slowly, and don't expect rapid changes," reducing the likelihood the client will return to a self-fulfilling prophecy of failure.[53] The overall goal is to increase the person's strengths, and shift his focus away from the negative.

I also suggest that my clients develop relationships with people who believe in them, and instill them with feelings of optimism about their future. Try to be aware of "frenemies," or people who make you feel bad about yourself. Choose to be around people who are able to see the positive in others. You want to spend time around people who bring out the best in you and see what you *can* become, not what you lack.

NARRATIVE THERAPY: REWRITING YOUR STORY

Another way to boost positive gains in therapy is to tell a new "story" about yourself.[54] A story is a personal narrative that summarizes how a person views himself. Some people live with a personal story that they have a "depressing life" or face a "daily battle against addiction." Sarah's initial narrative was a "tragic life of loss and pain." Miriam's narrative was a "life of anxiety and excessive worry," while Moshe's was "a depressed father who couldn't cope." Narrative Therapy helped them to begin viewing themselves in a positive light.

In Narrative Therapy, the therapist explores the "stories" people tell about themselves, since these stories are the way a person understands their life experiences. A person can hold onto a self-defeating story, or change that story to a more successful one. In Narrative Therapy, a person's story doesn't just reflect the person's life, it actually shapes it.

One of the key techniques of Narrative Therapy is to "externalize" the problem. To accomplish this, narrative therapists encourage the client to think of himself as struggling *against* the problem.[55] Similar to Solution-Focused Therapy, Narrative Therapy seeks to understand the problem's impact on the individual.

Therapy begins by asking the client to tell his story and then, with guidance, carefully externalize the problem. For example, instead of saying "Tell me about the depression you're experiencing," a narrative therapist would ask, "How does depression affect you? What does depression tell you?"[56] The main point of Narrative therapy is to show that the problem is not the client; rather, the problem is trying to control the client. Instead of saying that the client has a problem, the client is told that the problem has them. These problems are then described as powers or "voices" working against the client, rather than internal issues that need to be fixed.

The next step in Narrative Therapy is to give control back to the client by exploring "Who is in charge, the person or the problem?" Here, the goal is to understand how the problem began to control the person, instead of how much control they can exert over it. By asking "relative influence questions," it becomes obvious that the problem is disturbing the person and not the other way around. For example, narrative therapists pose questions like, "When did that problem not exert influence over you? When did you have the power to overcome the tremendous pull of your depression to go out and have fun with your friend?"[57]

Overall, the goal of Narrative Therapy is to help you re-author your own story, and tell a new one that highlights your ability to overcome anxiety, depression or trauma. In creating a new narrative, the therapist orients you toward the future, where you can envision rising to face your challenges in a successful way.

Joseph's Remarkable Narrative

I often share the story about Joseph and his brothers to illustrate the idea of changing a narrative. In *Bereishis* (Genesis), we learn that Joseph was Jacob's favorite son, and received a multicolored coat to symbolize his special relationship with his father. However, Joseph's brothers saw him differently.

Feeling that Joseph was a threat to their survival, Joseph's brothers devised a plan to kill him. Abandoned in the infamous pit, Joseph was eventually sold into slavery and purchased by an Egyptian assistant to Pharaoh. In Egypt, Joseph was falsely accused of attempting adultery and was sent to prison. During his imprisonment, a remarkable change of events transpired as Joseph was elevated to be the viceroy of Egypt, eventually saving the entire world from starvation.

One could just imagine Joseph's feeling toward his brothers, and how he might have originally viewed his own narrative: "Jewish child, hated by his brothers, tragically abandoned by his family, suffers in prison." Most of us would have experienced a significant case of posttraumatic stress under similar circumstances. Yet Joseph didn't see himself as a victim. Despite his pain, seeing his brothers kneel before him, he says:

"'Please come closer to me,' and they drew closer. And he said, 'I am your brother Joseph, whom you sold into Egypt. But now do not be sad, and let it not trouble you that you sold me here, for it was to preserve life that G-d sent me before you.'" (*Bereishis* 45).

In a remarkable act of bravery, Joseph pushed aside his trauma, changed the narrative of his life, and recognized that his suffering had meaning. He understood that everything he went through had a purpose, guided by G-d, even though it was only revealed later in his life. Joseph connected to a higher purpose as he turned his turmoil into a human triumph.

I have seen many people successfully change their own narrative. Even the subtlest shifts can improve one's vision of himself. Combining a Solution-Focused approach and Narrative Therapy, I helped clients like Sarah, Miriam, and Moshe to become the authors of their own success stories.

For example, Sarah was able to describe her life without depression. To achieve this, I had her create her own guided visualization about what life would look like when she wasn't depressed. She described how she would spend her time, who she would speak with, and what she could accomplish when she wasn't feeling down. She wrote a new narrative where she was "a successful mother who had turned a personal tragedy into a triumph."

Miriam learned to articulate what it would mean to lead a life without anxiety. She described what her day would look like, from the moment she woke up, until the moment she went to sleep. In the morning she would feel energetic in taking care of her children, and during the day she would enjoy full-time employment. At night, she would have energy and patience to interact positively with her husband, as they put the children to sleep and retired for the evening. Her new story was "despite the anxiety, I'm providing a loving home for my children."

Moshe began to envision his life without addiction and depression. He described what it would be like to not feel out of control, enslaved to the Internet. He described enjoying his family when he would play with his kids, eat dinner with them, or put them to sleep. During family time, he would be present, focused, and feel connected. His new story was, "father working hard to provide for his family's physical and emotional needs."

—Affirmations to Re-envision Yourself

To help you re-envision yourself, I have included some positive affirmations that have helped my clients grow:

Relationships

I envision myself:

- Attracting new friends and building close relationships.
- Spending quality time with people I love and enjoying our relationship.
- Improving my marriage and increasing my attachment with my spouse.
- Connecting with a parent with whom I have been distant in the past.
- Marrying someone who loves and appreciates me for who I am.
- Being cared for by my family and friends.
- Building a positive relationship with my child or children.
- Responding empathetically to a difficult relative or spouse.

Finances

I envision myself:

- Earning more money
- Being successful at work
- Getting a good job

- Succeeding academically
- Being happy in my job
- Having enough money to pay for education, clothing, family trips
- Receiving the promotion I've been waiting for

Health
I envision myself:

- Feeling better
- Being healthy
- Healing from discomfort or illness
- Exercising and improving my feelings of wellness
- Eating well and not losing control
- Accomplishing an exercise goal: climbing a mountain, biking a long distance, running a marathon, walking a long distance
- Living longer
- Appreciating my body as it is

Education
I envision myself:

- Passing the test
- Getting good grades
- Working hard and succeeding
- Exceeding my expectations of myself
- Gaining knowledge
- Getting into the program of my choice
- Completing study objectives
- Finishing complete tractates or books

Parenting
I envision myself:

- Dealing kindly with my children
- Not over-reacting to their misbehaving
- Being patient and diligent

- Not being afraid to discipline when necessary
- Keeping calm during difficult situations
- Actively listening to my children's emotions
- Seeing my children maintain my values
- Not yelling at them when I'm upset
- Never hitting them or hurting them inadvertently
- Being loved and respected by them
- Feeling appreciated for all my hard work

For Depression, Anxiety

I envision myself:

- Feeling happier
- Being less depressed or anxious
- Enjoying life
- Being less overwhelmed
- Viewing life optimistically
- Enjoying family and friends
- Thinking good thoughts
- Appreciating other people
- Valuing myself
- Feeling more energy and creativity
- Not worrying about the future
- Connecting with G-d and religion

I envision myself:

- Having a closer relationship with G-d
- Understanding His ways in the world
- Feeling protected by Him
- Receiving guidance from Him
- Opening my heart to Him
- Praying with sincerity
- Witnessing His wonders
- Appreciating His creation

Exercise:

Write down a new image of who or what you want to become. Then spend a few minutes each day writing positive affirmations about how you will carry out this vision successfully, i.e. "I envision myself succeeding in…" or "I see my plan being carried out and feeling happy that I accomplished my tasks."

Doing Good

Giving transforms feeling of helplessness into empowerment, limitation into abundance. The act may be as simple as holding the door for someone, giving somebody a lift, preparing a meal for a postpartum mother, lending money, or simply saying good morning to people, and smiling. Acts of random kindness create a domino effect: the person who receives the good often turns around and does good to others. Giving to others enhances progress made in therapy, and helps maintain a positive outlook.

Recently researchers have discovered the link between doing good and feeling better. One study, conducted by Dr. Suzanne Richards and her colleagues at the University of Exeter Medical School in England, found a connection between volunteering and health. The study found that "volunteering is associated with lower depression, increased well-being, and a 22 percent reduction in the risk of dying."[58]Other studies showed, "Americans who describe themselves as 'very happy' volunteer an average of 5.8 hours per month. Those who are "unhappy"? Just 0.6 hours."[59]

Medical Benefits of Giving

In the book *The Paradox of Generosity*, sociologists Christian Smith and Hilary Davidson studied the habits and lifestyles of 40 families to see if there is a correlation between doing good and feeling good. They found that "Americans who donate more than 10 percent of their incomes (41 percent say they rarely or never experience depression versus 32 percent for everyone else.) And, giving away money isn't the only way to reap the psychological rewards of generosity: Americans who are very giving in relationships—being emotionally available and hospitable—are much more likely to be in excellent health (48 percent) than those who are not (31 percent)." The authors also observe that doing good creates neurochemical changes, "giving people more pleasure chemistry in their brain… [and] a sense of reward for having done something good."[60]   I asked Sarah, Miriam, and Moshe to choose one act of giving to complete at least once a week. They could choose something as simple as giving more charity, or helping a family in need.

EXAMPLES OF RANDOM ACTS OF KINDNESS

Exercise:

Choose one act of random kindness to do this week.

- Giving *Tzedaka* (charity)
- Raising money to send a child to sleep away camp
- Volunteering with a child who has special needs
- Setting singles up to get married
- Giving bags of food to those in need
- Finding a job for someone out of work
- Driving people to medical appointments or to the hospital
- Raising money to help someone defray the costs of a wedding
- Creating a *gmach* (lending center) for clothing, toys, items for babies, used furniture, food, and distributing these items to needy families
- Visiting someone who is sick or in the hospital
- Visiting the elderly
- Becoming a big brother or big sister
- Helping out at a food pantry
- Inviting guests for a meal
- Tipping someone generously
- Lending your expertise
- Complimenting someone
- Holding the door for someone

- Listening empathetically to another person's problems
- Each day, plan or be involved in acts of kindness.

Being Connected

One of the greatest causes of anxiety or depression is loneliness. In fact, feelings of emotional isolation from friends and family are one of the most common conditions of depression or anxiety. Many people describe their loneliness as even more painful than their depression. Loneliness, however, is not only associated with mental health issues. It is also an unfortunate reality of modern life that people are dealing with more than ever before.

In a recent study, scientists at Duke University "observed a sharp decline in social connectedness over the past 20 years." According to their findings, "25% of Americans have no meaningful social support at all—not a single person they can confide in. And, over half of all Americans report having no close confidants or friends outside their immediate family." The study goes on to say that "the situation is much worse today than it was when similar data were gathered in 1985. (At that time, only 10% of Americans were completely alone)."[61]

A few generations ago, people had more connection with close family members. Family size was larger and people lived closer to home, and visited their families more frequently. Today, family connectivity has changed dramatically. Many people choose to attend college or find employment in remote locations, far away from their family members. Also, many jobs can be accomplished via Internet, allowing people to work in isolation from each other.

Affiliation and participation in religious and community institutions are at an all-time low. For years, the synagogue or the community center provided opportunities to volunteer, build engaging friendships, or even meet your spouse. Unfortunately, these forms of social engagement have been replaced by social media, which has become the primary means of communication between people. Modern technologies such as the iPad and cellphones have replaced meaningful opportunities for satisfying human interaction.

In his book, *Choice Theory*, William Glasser notes that lack of friendship is often a decisive factor in depression. Glasser writes, "good friends are our most reliable source of long-term happiness."[62] I once heard him share the following analogy at a lecture:

A person who suffers from depression had a terrible day. He was late to work in the morning, since he missed his bus. His boss was mean to him at work, and it was raining, and a car drove by and splashed his pants with water. He's in a terrible rut that he can't shake off easily. Just when he's feeling at his lowest point, he gets a call from his best friend, whom he hasn't seen in years. They strike up a conversation about the "good old days." They both share a laugh together as they reminisce over positive childhood memories about their friendship. Within a few moments, his mood has changed, and he feels like a different person. Suddenly his depression subsides and he is no longer feeling as sad as he just felt a few minutes ago. What happened? The answer is that friendship is a powerful emotional experience that can transform even the lowest of spirits. A good friend makes you feel loved, accepted, and connected. Being in their presence, your feelings can be transformed almost immediately, as you are lifted up from your emotional isolation.

Friendship is in fact a spiritual experience that heightens a sense of oneness with other human beings. When friends "become connected," intense self-reflection is replaced by transcendence. Perhaps this is why loving one's neighbor is the *ad maxim* of religious behavior. As Rabbi Akiva said, "Love your neighbor as yourself," (*Leviticus*, 19) This is the most important rule in the Torah" (Jerusalem Talmud, Nedarim 30 B).

As part of an emotional maintenance plan, I suggest actively trying to build relationships with friends, *despite* feeling down. This means scheduling time to go out with friends, to relax and have a good time.

Exercise:

Connect with one friend or participate in one communal activity this week. Reach out to someone in your life—a friend, family member, or neighbor—and nurture that relationship.

Some ideas for connecting include:

- Call a friend and make a date
- Schedule quality time with a spouse or family member

- Reach out to relatives with whom you may have lost touch and reconnect
- Attend a weekly or daily lecture in a synagogue
- Invite guests for Shabbos or accept an invitation by others
- Attend a lunch with a group of friends
- Join an organization
- Talk to your colleagues at work
- Offer to help a friend with a task

Chapter 6

ONGOING SUPPORT

Designing Your Future, Doing Good, and *Being Connected* are only a part of a comprehensive approach to mental health that includes positive thinking and practicing daily meditation based on Torah concepts. Using these strategies along with tools from *Creating Space* and *Going Above*, and *Thinking Good*, form an ongoing support system to supplement the progress made in therapy.

Daily Study of Duties of the Heart, "The Gate of Trust" —*Chovot Halevavot, "Shaar Habitachon"*

In addition to the steps outlined in this book, studying the book *Duties of the Heart*, the section called, "The Gate of Trust," has been used by people for over 1000 years to cope with depression or anxiety. As we have seen throughout the book, the results are impressive.

Letter from the Lubavitcher Rebbe on Studying Duties of the Heart, Gate Four, "The Gate of Trust"

The Lubavitcher Rebbe promoted the importance of studying *Duties of the Heart*, "The Gate of Trust," on a daily or weekly basis in a letter to an individual struggling with depression:

By the Grace of G-d
15 Menachem Av, 5711 [1951]
Brooklyn

Greetings and Blessings!

Just now I dispatched a telegram to you: "Am most surprised
at your low spirits. You should follow the directives of two
medical specialists, and muster strength in your trust in G-d,
Who will no doubt restore your former health. With blessings
for a speedy recovery. [My signature.]

People study, and study — but when it comes to practical
application, where's the trust?

You should study, three or four times over, "Shaar HaBitachon (The Gate of Trust)" in Chovos HaLevavos (Duties of
the Heart). It goes without saying that I do not mean that you
should study it all at once, but in the course of a few weeks.

With blessings for a speedy recovery, and awaiting good news
of your physical and spiritual health."[63]

I have seen firsthand that the Rebbe's instruction have helped many
people I have worked with over the last few years. Clients like David,
Sarah, and Miriam have committed to daily study of *Duties of the Heart*,
"The Gate of Trust," and joined support groups that focus on increasing
their sense of faith and reliance on G-d. The following portion of this
book includes a new English translation of *Duties of the Heart*, the Gate
of Trust, presented for the first time as daily readings that take only a few
minutes to complete. The translation includes extensive commentaries
to enhance your faith and trust in G-d, while overcoming depression,
anxiety or addiction.

Online Support Groups at *www.ItWillBeGood.com*

Online and phone-based support groups, along with recorded guided meditations, are available on the resource page at www.ItWill-BeGood.com.

TAKEAWAYS

- Explore and focus on the "exceptions" to the times when you don't feel anxiety or depression and then repeat those successful behaviors.
- Remember that problems can be externalized as outside forces affecting a person; and not that the person *has* the "problem".
- Doing good for others and building friendships can increase a person's feelings of attachment and well-being.
- Find ways of giving and connecting to other people daily.
- Study *Duties of the Heart,* "The Gate of Trust" every day

SECTION II

Section II

A DAILY GUIDE TO GATE FOUR OF *CHOVOS HALEVAVOS / DUTIES OF THE HEART*

by Rabeinu Bachya ibn Paquda, zt'l

Contents II

Translator's Foreword

The following is a translation of the fourth gate of one of the earliest of the classic *mussar* works, *Chovos HaLevavos* by Rabeinu Bachya. The book has inspired many great men to walk in its ways and review it throughout their lives. The fourth gate deals with what Rabeinu Bachya regards as "the most necessary of all things for the service of G-d."

I have found that the gate must be read in its entirety to understand it properly. In this second revision, I added select commentaries and also checked/compared every sentence against the brilliant translation by Rabbi Moses Hyamson, O.B.M., the former chief Rabbi and head Dayan of England between 1911 and 1913. The translator studied in various yeshivas under great Torah scholars such as Rabbi Dov Shwartzman,*zt"l* (~2 years); Rabbi Nachman Bulman,*zt"l;*and Rabbi Nissan Kaplan (~5 years). He also completed a degree in physics at the University of Massachusetts, Amherst and was a research associate in nuclear physics for some time before heading off to yeshiva.

—Yosef Sebag, Jerusalem, Tamuz 5775/ June 2015

ABBREVIATIONS USED IN THIS TRANSLATION:

MH - Manoach HeLevavos commentary by Rabbi Manoach Hendel (1540–1611)

TL - Tov HaLevanon commentary by Rabbi Yisrael Halevi (1700–1777)

PL - Pas Lechem commentary by Rabbi Chaim Avraham Hacohen (1740–1815)

ML - Marpe Lenefesh commentary by Rabbi Refael Mendel (1825–1895)

LT - Lev Tov commentary by Rabbi Pinchas Lieberman (1929–2005)

MC - Matanas Chelko* commentary by Rabbi M Solomon (with permission)

* MC commentary available from Israel Bookshop Publications

"Shaar Habitachon—The Gate of Trust"
Gate #4 of *Chovos HaLevavos—Duties of the Heart*
by Rabeinu Bachya Ibn Paquda, zt"l

(Please note: the following daily portions are for "simple" years. For leap years in Adar II, repeat each day for two days)

TISHREI 1

Introduction

The author says: Since our previous treatise dealt with the duty to assume the service of G-d, I deemed proper to follow it with what is more necessary than all other things for one who serves G-d—placing one's trust in Him for all matters, the reason being the great benefits this yields both in religious and in secular matters.

The benefits in religious matters: Among them, peace of mind, and trusting in G-d as a servant must trust in his master, because if one does not place his trust in G-d, he will place his trust in something else, and whoever trusts in something other than G-d, the Al-mighty will remove His providence from such a person, and leave him in the hands of the one he trusted...

TISHREI 2

[This person] will be as it was written: "For My people have committed two evils; they have forsaken Me, the spring of living waters, to dig for themselves cisterns, broken cisterns that do not hold water" (Yirmiyahu 2:13), "They exchanged their Glory for the likeness of an ox eating grass" (Tehillim 106:20),"Blessed is the man who trusts in the L-ord; the L-ord shall be his refuge" (Yirmiyahu 17:7), "Praiseworthy is the man who made the L-ord his trust, and did not turn to the haughty and those who turn to falsehood." (Tehillim 40:5), "Cursed is the man who trusts in man, who makes flesh his strength and whose heart turns away from the L-ord" (Yirmiyahu 17:5).

TISHREI 3

(*Matanas Chelko*: "If one does not place his trust in G-d, he will place his trust in something else...they have forsaken Me" - this is a great fundamental principle, namely, that every person trusts his life in something or someone. One who claims he does not trust in anything [unless he is 100 percent sure] is fooling himself. Since this is the way of the world. A man who purchases a loaf of bread from the baker trusts that no poison was placed there. If he takes his automobile to the mechanic for repair and afterwards drives it on the highway, he trusts that it was repaired properly. Likewise for trusting his life with the doctors and other similar matters. Hence, one who trusts in these things cannot say "I cannot trust in G-d until I fully understand everything and fully see everything". This is false! For behold, he trusts his life on many things and many human beings without fully knowing all that happened.

TISHREI 4

(*Matanas Chelko*: If he places his trust in his wisdom and tactics, physical strength and industriousness - he will toil for nothing, his strength will weaken, and his tactics will fall short of accomplishing his desire, as written "He traps the wise with their own cunning" (Iyov 5:13) (that their tactics result in bad instead of good - *TL*), and "I returned and saw under the sun, that the race does not belong to the swift, nor the war to the mighty; neither do the wise have bread, [nor do the understanding have wealth, nor the knowledgeable, favor for time and chance happens to them all]" (Koheles 9:11), and "Young lions suffer want and are hungry, but those who seek the L-ord lack no good" (Tehillim 34:11).

TISHREI 5

Matanas Chelko: "Whoever trusts in something other than G-d...the Almighty will leave him" - i.e. that he places his trust (peace of mind) on the country or on the alarm system in his home, or the like of the various cause and effect calculations. There are grounds for a claim against him for he does trust on things, just not on the Master of the world. His punishment is that G-d leaves him to "nature" and to the framework to which he placed his trust. Therefore, he is ruled over by that system of nature, with its many statistics of causes and effects. Hence, he who thinks his own strength and ingenuity earned for him all of his success, and he relies on this, G-d will leave him under that system of causes and effects. Through this, certainly he will eventually stumble and be lost. [because: "the race is not to the swift, nor the battle to the strong...."]

TISHREI 6

If he relies on his wealth, it will be removed from him and left to someone else as written "He lies down rich, but there shall be nothing to gather; he opens his eyes, and his wealth is not" (Iyov 27:19), "Do not weary yourself to grow rich; cease from your own understanding." (Mishlei 23:4), "Should you blink your eyes at it, it is not here; for it will make wings for itself, like the eagle, and it will fly toward the heavens." (Mishlei 23:5), "so it is he who gathers riches but not by right; he shall leave them in the midst of his days, and at his end he stands dishonored" (Yirmiyahu 17:11) (since if he placed all of his trust on his riches, certainly, he will not be clean from various forms of theft and dishonesty - PL)

TISHREI 7

Or, he will be prevented from its benefit as the wise man said "the Al-mighty will not give him the ability to eat from it" (Koheles 6:2), and it will be by him like a deposit that he guards from damages until it reaches someone worthy of it, as written "[For to a man who is good in His sight, He has given wisdom and knowledge and joy,] but to the sinner He has given an occupation to gather and to accumulate, to give to him who is good in G-d's sight; this too is vanity and frustration." (Koheles 2:26), and "he will prepare, but a righteous man will wear them; and the pure shall divide the silver" (Iyov 27:17). And it is possible that the money will be the cause of his destruction (in this world) and ultimate downfall (in the afterlife) as written "There is a grievous evil that I saw under the sun; riches kept by their owner for his harm." (Koheles 5:12).

TISHREI 8

(*Matanas Chelko*: A person thinks that if he attains great wealth, he will be free of worries. The truth is that it is not so. For example, a very wealthy man may be in constant worry and fear that his children will be kidnapped for ransom. Hence, his wealth has become the cause of his worry. For due to it, he is in fear of bad people. If he attains great wealth, he will see that he cannot trust in it and worries about potential mishaps. His days are squandered in worry and vexation. But he who trusts in G-d and prays to him at every step, and thanks Him for whatever he attains, then even if G-d bestows great wealth to him, he still stays with his trust and does not worry on account of his wealth.)

TISHREI 9

Another benefit for the one who trusts in the Al-mighty, is that his trust will lead him to the following:
- To not serve other than G-d
- To not hope in any man, nor expect from anyone (Micha 5:6).
- To not work to win their approval.
- To not flatter them.
- To not agree with them in what is not the service of G-d (ex. going to their time wasting parties - Pas Lechem)

TISHREI 10

- To not be afraid of their matters.
- To not be afraid of disagreeing with them (of not conforming to their ways - PL; "to not be afraid if they quarrel with him and outcast him" - ML).
- To divest himself of the cloak of their favors and free himself from the burden of expressing gratitude to them, and from the obligation of paying back their favors (and therefore he will not need to flatter them, or join them in what is not the service of G-d - TL).

TISHREI 11

(*Marpe Lenefesh*: He endeavors and does everything he can to not need others and to not enclothe himself in the favors of others. For this would place him under an obligation to toil to express gratitude to them and to also make a return, as it is proper and obligatory to pay back a benefactor with good, as mentioned earlier in the beginning of the third gate. Rather, he desires that G-d alone be his benefactor, and that he thanks only Him.)

TISHREI 12

Other benefits for the one who trusts in the Al-mighty, is that his trust will lead him to the following:

- If he rebukes them, he will not be afraid of slighting them.
- He will not shy from humiliating them (so that his rebuke is effective - Pas Lechem).
- He will not embellish their false ways (to them, but rather will denigrate it to them - *PL*)

As the prophet wrote: "But the L-ord G-d helps me, therefore shall I not be confounded; therefore have I set my face like a flint, and I know that I shall not be ashamed" (Yeshaya 50:7), "Do not fear them or their words" (Yechezkel 2:6), "And you, son of man, fear them not, and fear not their words" (Yechezkel 2:6), "fear them not, neither shall you be intimidated by them" (Yechezkel 3:9).

Another benefit: The trust in G-d will lead one to empty his mind from the distractions of the world, and to focus his heart to matters of service of G-d.

TISHREI 13

(*Marpe Lenefesh*: This is because the chief cause of mental agitation and confusion which prevents a man from learning Torah and devoting himself to religious service is - constant worry on his livelihood, how will he earn money and through what means. But one who trusts in

G-d will diminish his worry in this and increase his worry for religious service. And he will have tranquility of heart like the Alchemist, and even more...)

And he will be similar in his peace of mind, tranquility of heart, and few financial worries to the alchemist, one who knows how to transform silver to gold and copper or tin to silver through skill and procedures.

TISHREI 14

(*Pas Lechem*: the author used this trade as an example because many of the masses of his generation aspired to it, due to its making great wealth [Translator: In our times it is much easier to detect fake gold and so the trade has lost its appeal. Perhaps a modern day analogy of the alchemist would be one who owns a sophisticated counterfeit money machine.]

And the one who trusts in G-d will have the following 10 advantages over the alchemist:

(1) The alchemist requires special materials to perform his operation, without which he cannot do anything. These materials are not found at all times and in all places. But for one who trusts in G-d, his sustenance is assured and can come through any means of all the means of the world, as written "[And He fed you with manna, which you knew not, neither did your fathers know]; That He might make known to you that man does not live by bread alone..." (Devarim 8:3).

TISHREI 15

For at no time and in no place are the means of obtaining his livelihood withheld from him, as you know already from the story of Eliyahu and the ravens, or with the widow and the cakes and water (Melachim 17:9), or the story of Ovadia with the prophets, where he said "I hid among the prophets of G-d, 100 men, 50 in each cave, and I fed them bread and water" (Melachim 18:13) (i.e. Ovadia was a means to provide for the prophets - PL), and "Young lions suffer want and are hungry, but those who seek the L-ord lack no good" (Tehillim 34:11), and "Fear the L-ord, His holy ones; for there is no want to those who fear Him" (Tehillim 34:10).

TISHREI 16

(2) The alchemist must perform actions and follow procedures without which he cannot successfully complete his goal. It is even possible that the fumes and odors will cause his death, along with the long work and great effort with them day and night. But one who trusts in G-d is secure against mishaps, and his heart is assured against future (potential) bad things. Whatever comes to him from G-d, he will accept with joy and gladness and his livelihood comes to him peacefully, quietly, and happily, as written "He causes me to lie down in green pastures; He leads me beside still waters" (Tehillim 23:2).

TISHREI 17

(*Pas Lechem* commentary: "whatever comes to him from G-d gives him joy..." is an explanation of the previous statement "his heart is assured against bad things..." because certainly it cannot be taken literally, that for one who trusts in G-d, no bad things will ever happen to him, since what our eyes see contradicts this. Rather, after he trusts in G-d that He will not do to him anything that is not for his good, if so, "whatever comes to him from G-d, he will accept with joy and gladness, as the Talmud says in Berachos 54a, therefore it is correct to say that no bad things ever happen to him.

Translator: Later on in Gate #8 he says: "And when you do this (spiritual accounting) with a faithful heart and a pure soul, your mind will become illuminated, and you will see the path to all of the exalted qualities... and you will reach the status of one treasured by G-d... You will not part from a permanent joy in this world and in the next...")

TISHREI 18

(3) The alchemist does not trust anyone with his secret due to fear for his life. But one who trusts G-d does not fear any man on account of his trust, just the contrary it is a source of honor, as King David said: "in G-d I trusted, I will not fear, what can a man do to me?" (Tehillim 54:12).

(4) The alchemist must either prepare one large quantity of gold and silver for long term needs or must prepare small batches for short term needs. If he prepares a large quantity, all his days he will fear for his life that perhaps all the gold and silver will be lost in any number of ways (and he will be left penniless), and his heart will never quiet, nor will his mind be at peace due to fear of the king and of the people (finding his big stash of gold).

TISHREI 19

(*Matanas Chelko*: i.e. even if he is successful, he is in a constant state of worry. Likewise, in our times, we can observe that anyone who is successful in business is also worried about many factors - unless he trusts in G-d. Hence he is just like the Alchemist.)

But one who trusts in G-d, has strong peace of mind that G-d will provide for him at any time He wishes and in any place, just like He sustains the fetus in its mother's womb or the chick inside an egg, which has no opening to enter anything from the outside, and birds in the air, or fish in the sea, and the tiny ant despite its weakness, while the mighty lion some days cannot obtain food, as written "Young lions suffer want and are hungry, but those who seek the L-ord lack no good" (Tehillim 34:11), and "The L-ord will not starve the soul of the righteous" (Mishlei 10:3), and "I have been young, and now am old; yet I have not seen the righteous forsaken, nor his seed begging bread" (Tehillim 37:25)

TISHREI 20

(5) The alchemist is under anxiety and fear of everyone, from the greatest to the lowest of people as a consequence of his work, but one who trusts in G-d will be revered by great men and honorable people, even animals and stones seek to do his will (i.e. do not harm him - TL) as written in the entire Psalm "He who sits..." (Tehillim 91), and "In six troubles He will save you, and in the seventh no harm will touch you." (Iyov 5:19), until the end of the matter.

TISHREI 21

(6) The alchemist is not immune from sickness and disease which hinders his joy in being wealthy, and prevents him from benefiting from what he has and enjoying what he has acquired. But one who trusts in G-d, is immune from sickness and disease except as an atonement or to increase his reward, as written "Now youths shall become tired and weary, and young men shall stumble" (Yeshaya 40:30), "those who hope in G-d will renew strength" (Yeshaya 40:31), and "For the arms of the wicked (who trust in their strength - *TL*) shall be broken, but the L-ord supports the righteous" (Tehillim 37:17).

TISHREI 22

(7) It is possible that the alchemist will not be able to buy food with his gold and silver due to no food being available in the city at times, as written: "they shall cast their money in the streets" (Yechezkel 7:19), and "neither silver nor gold will be able to save them" (Tzefania 1:18), but for one who trusts in G-d, his sustenance will not be blocked at any time or in any place, as written "in famine He redeemed you from death" (Iyov 5:20), and "the L-ord is my shepherd, I shall not lack" (Tehillim 23:1), and "They will not be shamed in time of calamity, and in days of famine they shall still be satisfied" (Tehillim 37:19).

TISHREI 23

(8) The alchemist does not linger in one place too long due to fear that his secret will be discovered. But one who trusts in G-d feels secure in his land, and has peace of mind in his place, as written "Trust in the L-ord and do good; dwell in the land and be nourished by faith" (Tehillim 37:3), and "The righteous shall inherit the land and dwell forever in it" (Tehillim 37:29).

(9) The alchemist's skills will not accompany him in the afterlife, they may only provide him, in this world, security from poverty and from needing other people. But for one who trusts in G-d, the reward for his trust will accompany him in this world and in the next, as written "Many

are the pains of the wicked (in the afterlife - *PL*); but one who trusts in G-d will be surrounded by kindness" (Tehillim 32:10), and "how great is Your goodness that you hid away for those who fear You" (Tehillim 31:20.

TISHREI 24

(10) If the alchemist's work is discovered, it will become a cause for his death, because his work runs contrary to the natural order, and the Director of the world will allow someone to kill him when he fails to hide his secret (G-d won't save him at a time of danger. Alternatively, G-d will cause him to be caught when his time has come - *ML*). But for one who trusts in G-d, when his trust becomes known, he will be held in high esteem and honored by the public. They will feel blessed to be near him or to see him, and his presence will bring good fortune to the city and shield the people from troubles, as written "the righteous man is the foundation of the world" (Mishlei 10:25), similar to Lot in Tzoar (Bereishis 19, who saved the city by his presence there - *TL*).

TISHREI 25

Among the benefits of trusting in G-d regarding religious matters:

One who trusts in G-d, if he has wealth, will be quick to fulfill his monetary obligations to G-d and to men with a willing and generous spirit. If he does not have wealth, he will consider that lack of wealth to be among the favors of G-d to him, because he is exempt from the monetary obligations to G-d and men which wealth brings, and he is spared from the mental distraction of protecting and managing it, as one of the pious used to say: "may G-d save me from dispersion of the mind". They would ask him "what is dispersion of the mind?" He would answer: "to own property at the head of every river and the center of every town." And this is what our sages referred to in saying: "the more possessions, the more worry" (Avos 2:7), and they said: "who is wealthy? He who is content with what he has" (Avos 4:1).

TISHREI 26

One who trusts in G-d will receive the benefits of money, namely, his material needs, but without the mental distraction and constant worry of the wealthy, as the wise man said "The sleep of the laborer is sweet, whether he eats little or much, but the satiety of the rich does not allow him to sleep" (Koheles 5:11).

Another benefit, one who trusts in G-d will not diminish his trust on account of having much wealth because he does not rely on the money. He regards it as a deposit which he is ordered to use in specific ways, for specific matters and for a limited time. And if he stays wealthy for a long time, he will not become arrogant due to his wealth. He will not remind the poor person of his charity gifts since he was commanded to give to him, and he will not seek his gratitude and praises. Rather, he will thank his Creator who appointed him as a means for doing good to the poor person.

TISHREI 27

If his wealth is lost, he will not worry nor mourn his loss. Rather, he will thank his Creator for taking back His deposit, just like he thanked G-d when it was given to him. He will be happy with his portion, and will not seek to damage others (in order to gain benefit - *TL*). He will not covet other people's wealth as the wise man said "A righteous man eats to sate his appetite, [but the stomach of the wicked shall feel want]." (Mishlei 13:25).

TISHREI 28

(*Matanas Chelko*: This is analogous to a case of two poor neighbors. One of whom had a rich relative who came to visit him and gave him a huge donation of 1000 dollars then left. Upon hearing about the donation, the second neighbor begged his friend for 200 dollars but he refused. The neighbor pleaded for 100 dollars and this time his friend painfully agreed. But if from the beginning, the rich relative said to him, "I see you and your neighbor are both in great poverty. Take 800 dollars for yourself and take an additional 200 for your neighbor". Surely, he would have ran joyously to his neighbor without sadness or heavy feeling. This is because he never felt like the owner of that 200.. So too, one who has money beyond his needs must feel that it is not only for himself but for distributing also to others. Hence, one who trusts in G-d is always joyful in all situations for he knows and feels this secret.

TISHREI 29

Benefits of trust in G-d for worldly matters:

- Peace of mind from the worries of this world.
- Peace from the frenzy and drive to pursue the lusts of this world.
- Feeling calm, secure, at peace in this world, as written "blessed be the man who trusts in G-d, and G-d shall be his refuge" (Yirmiyahu 17:7), and "For he shall be like a tree planted by the water, that sends out its roots by the stream. [It does not fear when heat comes; its leaves stay green. It has no worries in a year of drought and never fails to bear fruit]" (Yirmiyahu 17:8).

Among them, peace of mind from the need to travel to faraway journeys, which weakens the body, and hastens aging, as written "my strength has weakened from the journey, my life shortened" (Tehillim 102:24).

Tishrei 30

It is said about a novice ascetic who travelled to a distant land in search of a livelihood. He met one of the idolaters of the city where he arrived and said to him: "how completely blind and ignorant you are to worship idols!". The idolater asked him: "And what do you worship?". The ascetic answered "I worship the Creator, the Omnipotent, the Sustainer of all, the One, the Provider of all, which there is none like Him". The idolater countered "your actions contradict your words!" The ascetic asked "How so?", the idolater said "if what you say were true, He would have provided a livelihood for you in your own city, just like He provided for you here, and it would not have been necessary for you to trouble yourself to travel to a faraway land like this." The ascetic, unable to answer, returned to his city and reassumed his asceticism from that time on, and never again left his city.

CHESHVAN 1

Another benefit, peace of mind and body, due to sparing oneself from pursuing grueling jobs, and wearying occupations, avoiding work of kings - mingling in their culture and dealing with their corrupt servants.

But one who trusts G-d, selects among the different occupations one which is easy on his body, allows him to earn a good reputation, does not consume his mind, and is best suited for fulfilling his Torah obligations and the principles of his faith, because the choice of occupation will neither increase nor decrease the income he will earn unless G-d decreed so, as it says "For it is not from the east or from the west, neither from the desert does elevation come. But G-d judges; He lowers this one and elevates that one." (Tehillim 75:7), and "He causes me to lie down in green pastures; He leads me beside still waters" (Tehillim 23:2).

CHESVAN 2

Another benefit, minimal aggravation in one's business dealings. If one's merchandise does not sell, or if he is unable to collect his debts, or if he is struck by illness, because he knows that the Creator is in charge of his life and knows best what is good for him, as written "Only to G-d should you hope, my soul, for my hope is from Him" (Tehillim 62:6).

Another benefit, joy in whatever happens to him, even if it is something difficult and against his nature, because he trusts that G-d will do only what is good for him in all matters, just like a mother has compassion on her baby in washing it, diapering it, and tying or untying it against its will, as David said "Surely I have behaved and quieted myself, as a child that is weaned of his mother: my soul is even as a weaned child" (Tehillim 131:2).

CHESVAN 3

(*Matanas Chelko*: This is the essence of trust - to feel like a baby in the hands of its mother. One should contemplate this matter of bathing the baby. The mother needs to do all sorts of things in order to cleanse it. And even though the baby does not sense the good in these things, nevertheless, the mother must do them since she knows it is for the baby's benefit. This is the conduct of G-d towards us, like a mother with her baby. All that He does and metes out to us is only for our good.

Since I have clarified the benefits of trust in G-d for religious and secular matters, I will now clarify seven topics on the matter of trust:

The Seven Chapters of the Gate of trust

1. What is trust
2   The criteria for trusting someone
3. The prerequisites to trusting in G-d
4. When trust applies and when it does not
5. The difference between one who trusts in G-d in earning a livelihood and one who does not.
6. Obligation to refute those who promote delaying the service of G-d until reaching sufficient material prosperity.
7. Things that damage one's trust in G-d, and a summary of the matter of trust.

CHESVAN 4

Chapter 1
What is Trust

What is trust?

Peace of mind of the one who trusts. That one relies in his heart that the one he trusts in will do what is good and proper for him on the matter he has trusted him with, according to his ability and his understanding of what will further his good.

But the main factor, which leads one to trust in the one trusted, and without which trust cannot exist, is for one's heart to be confident that the one trusted will keep his word and will do what he pledged, and that he will also think to do what is good for him even on what he did not pledge out of pure generosity and kindness (this will be explained).

CHESVAN 5

Chapter 2
The criteria for trusting someone

CRITERIA FOR TRUSTING ONESELF IN ANOTHER

There are seven factors which make it possible for one to trust in another (human being):

(1) Compassion, pity and love. When a man knows that his friend has compassion and pity for him, he will trust in him and be at peace with regard to troubling him with all of his matters.

CHESHVAN 6

(2) To know that his friend, besides loving him, is not forgetful or lazy in taking care of his needs. Rather, he knows that his friend is active and resolved to do it. Because if all of this is not clear, one's trust in him will not be complete, since one knows of his forgetfulness and laziness in attending to his needs.

But, when the one he trusts combines these two traits, great compassion for him and full attendance to his matters, he will trust in him without a doubt.

CHESVAN 7

(3) He is strong. He will not be defeated in whatever he desires, and nothing can prevent him from doing the request of the one who trusts him. Because if he is weak, one cannot fully trust in him, even though it is clear that he is compassionate and active, due to the many occasions in which he failed doing things. When one combines these three traits, trusting in him will be more fitting.

(4) That the one he trusts knows what is beneficial for him, both for his inner and outer life and also that none of the ways which benefit him or further his welfare are hidden to him. Because, if he does not know all of this, one will not be at peace in entrusting himself to him. But if he combines the knowledge of the ways which are beneficial to him, the ability to implement them, great attendance to them, and compassion for him, his trust will certainly be strengthened.

(5) That the one he trusts is under the exclusive care of him from the beginning of his existence, his development, babyhood, childhood, youth, adulthood, old age until the end of his days (i.e. that no one else has ever done to him any good except the one he trusts - *ML*). And when all this is clear to the truster, he is obligated to be at peace on his friend, and to rely on him, because of the many past benefits he already received from his friend and the constant favors he still presently receives. And this will obligate strengthening one's trust in him. (since he has been continuously benevolent to him from then until now, certainly he will not abandon him until his final end - *PL*)

(6) All matters of the truster are entirely in the hands of the one he trusts, and no one else can hurt him, help him, benefit him, or protect him from harm, as a slave chained down in a prison is entirely in the hands of his master. If the truster were in the hands of the one he trusts in this manner, it would be more fitting to trust in him.

CHESHVAN 8

(*Pas Lechem*: The fifth condition was that no one else ever benefited him. This sixth condition refers to ability - that the ability to benefit or harm him is only in his friend's hands. No one else has any ability to benefit or harm him... since this is the case, his heart will not look towards trusting others and he will place all of his trust on his friend)

(7) That the person he trusts is absolutely generous and kind (i.e. the most possible extreme of generosity and kindness - *TL*) to those deserving and to those who are not deserving, and that his generosity and kindness is continuous, never ending and without interruption.

CHESHVAN 9

(*Marpe Lenefesh* commentary: Otherwise, he will abandon hope from the favors of G-d, since he is in doubt whether he is worthy of them, and his trust in G-d will diminish. And through this, he will distance from G-d and His Torah. Rather, let him reflect that G-d is benevolent to the good and the bad, as written: "His mercy is on all of His creations" (Tehillim 145:9). And through this, he will come closer to G-d and repent and he will become worthy of the good.)

Whoever combines these traits, in addition to all of the previous traits has completed all the conditions that deserve trust, and would obligate the person who knows this to trust in him, to be at peace internally and externally, in his heart and in his limbs, and to give himself up to him and accept his decrees and judge him favorably in all his judgments and actions. (to presume that certainly everything is good and even what seems bad is actually good - *ML*)

CHESHVAN 10

When we investigate these seven conditions, we will not find them at all in the created beings, but we find them all in the Creator. He is compassionate to His creations as written "The L-ord is merciful and gracious" (Tehillim 103:8), and "Now should I not take pity on Nineveh, the great city" (Yonah 4:11).

(*Pas Lechem*: One may think that He is only merciful on those who are already in pain, but not before this, and therefore trust in Him will not help to be saved from future troubles. Therefore, the author brought the second verse from Nineveh, where G-d had pity on them even before the troubles came and annulled the decree...)

CHESHVAN 11

And that he never neglects us, as written "Behold the Guardian of Israel will neither slumber nor sleep" (Tehillim 121:4), that He is all-wise and invincible as written "He is wise in heart and mighty in strength; who hardened [his heart] against Him and remained unhurt?" (Iyov 9:4), and

"Yours, O L-ord, are the greatness, and the power, and the glory, and the victory, and the majesty" (Divrei Hayamim I 29:11) and "The L-ord your G-d is in your midst-a Mighty One Who will save" (Tzefania 3:17).

And that He alone is the one who guides a person from the beginning of his existence and development, as written "Is He not your Father who has acquired you? He has made you and established you." (Devarim 32:6), and "By You have I been upheld from birth: You are He that took me out of my mother's womb" (Tehillim 71:6), and "Did You not pour me out like milk and curdle me like cheese?" (Iyov 10:10), and the rest of the matter.

CHESHVAN 12

That one's benefit or harm is not in the hands of people but rather, only in the hands of the Creator, as written "Who has commanded and it came to pass, unless the L-ord ordained it? Out of the mouth of G-d, evil and good do not go out (of the boundary He has set - *PL*)" (Eicha 3:37), and "[All flesh is like grass, and all their kindness is as the flower of the field]; The grass shall dry out, the flower shall wilt, but the word of our G-d will stand forever" (Yeshaya 40:8), and "...surely the people are like grass" (Yeshaya 40:7), and we have already explained this sufficiently in the third gate of this book.

(*Pas Lechem*: (summary) First verse shows that decrees of G-d, whether for good or for bad, do not go out of the boundaries He has decreed, rather as He decreed - so shall it be.

Second verse: Perhaps one will think that only the beginning of the matter is from G-d, but it will not endure unless a man completes it and perpetuates it, therefore - "the grass shall dry out", i.e. every man, just like his existence is ephemeral, as he is like grass, which wilts and dies, so too the kindness man does is like a temporary flower, which passes but the "word of G-d will stand forever", i.e. just like He is eternal, so too His decrees and acts are eternal.)

CHESHVAN 13

That His generosity is universal and His kindness is all-embracing, as written "The L-ord is good to all, and His mercies are on all His works"

(Tehillim 145:9) and "Who gives food to all flesh, for His kindness endures forever" (Tehillim 136:25), and "You open Your hand and satisfy every living thing [with] will (i.e. the good He bestows is not in a stingy way, according to basic need, but rather like His will - *PL*)" (Tehillim 145:16).

But really, the intellect can infer that these 7 conditions exist in the Creator and not in the created beings (as he will explain next chapter - *TL*), and therefore I have brought these verses from scripture only as a remembrance.

CHESHVAN 14

(*Pas Lechem*: i.e. my intent was not as a proof otherwise I would have brought more verses, but rather only as a remembrance, namely, when these verses are constantly on a person's mouth - he will remember, through them, the 7 factors.

Translator: As the author wrote in the beginning of Gate #1: "that habitually having them on one's tongue always, brings one to *remembrance* of the heart...", see there)

CHESHVAN 15

When one clarifies this to himself, and his recognition in the true kindness of the Creator will be strong - he will place his trust in Him, give himself up completely to Him, and leave the guidance of his life to Him, never suspect Him in His judgments, nor be upset by what He has chosen for him, as David said (on the good - *TL*) "I will lift up the cup of salvation and call upon the name of the L-ord" (Tehillim 116:13), and (on the bad - *TL*) "I found trouble and sorrow and call upon the name of the L-ord" (Tehillim 116:3-4).

CHESHVAN 16

(*Pas Lechem commentary*: He first stated two general phrases:

1. "he will place his trust in Him" - for providing his needs.
2. "give himself up completely to Him" - this refers to a general consent and acceptance that G-d will do with him as He wishes, even for what appears bad to him.

Then he explained the two phrases:

*   and leave the guidance of his life to Him" is an explanation of (1).
*   never suspect Him in His judgments, nor be upset by what He has chosen for him" is an explanation of (2).

This latter subdivides to:

a. "never suspect Him in His judgments" - if G-d sentences him to some bad trouble which is specific and short term.
b. "nor be upset by what He has chosen for him" - if G-d choses for him a widespread life-long matter such as poverty or a bad wife, or the like.)

THINK GOOD AND IT WILL BE GOOD 143

CHESHVAN 17

Chapter 3
The preliminaries to trusting in G-d -

The introductions which must be clearly understood and the truth of which must be realized in order that a person's trust in G-d will be complete are five.

(*Pas Lechem*: When he understands them to their full depth and after this he verifies the truth of them in his heart to absolute truthfulness - then his trust in G-d will be complete)

FIRST INTRODUCTION TO BRING COMPLETE TRUST
To believe and clearly understand that all of the seven factors (in the previous chapter) which when combined make it possible to trust in someone apply to G-d. And I have already mentioned them and commented on them from verses that occurred to me.

CHESHVAN 18

THE SEVEN FACTORS AS THEY APPLY TO G-d
ONE: the Creator is merciful on a man more than any other merciful being, and all mercy and compassion that a man is shown from anyone besides G-d is really derived from G-d's mercy and compassion, as the verse says "He will give you compassion, and cause others to have compassion on you and multiply you" (Devarim 13:18).

(*Tov Halevanon*: i.e. even that which a person finds favor and compassion in the eyes of another human being - this is due to G-d's giving the person compassion on that human being towards him.

CHESHVAN 19

Matanas Chelko - for example, a man walks on the street and sees a poor man. He feels compassion for him and gives him what he needs. From where did this compassion come from? From the Master of the world. On his own, the man would have kept walking and ignored the poor man. And even if he had stopped briefly and helped him a little bit, he would not have done so properly. But since G-d has compassion on the poor man, He imparts of His compassion on this man so that the man will feel compassion for the poor man. Hence, since the compassion stems from G-d, it is ascribed to G-d alone. This is the meaning of "there is nothing but Him" (Deut. 4:35), there is nothing in the world but G-d.

TWO: none of the ways which benefit a man are unknown to the Creator. Logic necessitates this, since man is one of His handiworks. No one can know better than man's Maker the ways to further his making (i.e. biological conception in the womb - *PL*), and the ways of loss (where no conception will occur and the drop of semen will be lost - *PL*), and the possible damages which can occur (in the development of the embryo in the womb during the time of pregnancy - *PL*), and the ways it (the born child during his growth and development - *PL*) can become sick and healed.

CHESHVAN 20

And this is also true for human makers (who know best what damages or benefits their inventions), although they do not really create anything new, but rather merely make a new form from existing raw materials, since to create a new form from nothing is impossible to man.

And all the more so, He who has called into existence from nothing the basic elements of man, his form, his anatomy, and the order of his synthesis (of body and soul - *PL*). Obviously, He is the wise One who undoubtedly knows which matters benefit or harm man in this world and in the next, as written "I am the L-rd your G-d who teaches you for your benefit, who guides you in the proper path" (Isaiah 48:17), and also "G-d rebukes the ones He loves (to turn them to the proper path - *TL*), and like a father to a son He desires in" (Mishlei 3:12).

CHESHVAN 21

THREE: the Creator is the strongest of all the strong. His word reigns supreme and nothing can reverse His decree, as written "Whatever G-d wants, He does" (Tehillim 135:6), and "so shall be My word that goes out from My mouth; it shall not return to Me empty, unless it has done what I desire" (Yeshaya 55:11).

FOUR: He watches over and directs the lives of all men, He does not abandon any of them (from bestowing good or benefiting them according to their needs - *PL*) nor neglects any of them (from saving them from damages - *PL*). None of their matters, small or great are hidden from Him, and no matter can distract Him from remembering another matter, as written: "Why should you say, O Jacob, and speak, O Israel, 'My way has been hidden from the L-ord, and my judgment (i.e. my providence - *TL*) is passed over from my G-d'?" (Yeshaya 40:27), and "Do you not know-if you have not heard-an everlasting G-d is the L-ord, the Creator of the ends of the world; He neither tires nor wearies; there is no fathoming His understanding (i.e. on His providence of all the creations simultaneously - *TL*)" (Yeshaya 40:28)....)

CHESHVAN 22

(*Pas Lechem*: That which the latter verse ascribes the creation specifically to "the ends of the world", this is to convey that G-d's power is infinite, therefore the nature of His handiworks also must be boundless and immeasurable, as, in truth, they are [physically boundless] among the spiritual creations (souls,etc). However, when G-d's divine wisdom ordained to call into existence a world of finite character, He constrained His power in His handiwork and held it at a certain amount. And this is an amazing feat to the thinking person, and this is what the verse alludes to in saying: "there is no fathoming His understanding")

FIVE: No created being can benefit or harm either itself or any other creature without the permission of the Creator. (*Pas Lechem*: i.e. just like he cannot help himself, so too he cannot help others without the permission of the Creator.)

CHESHVAN 23

If a slave has more than one master, and each one has the power to help him, it is not possible for him to put his trust in only one of them, since he hopes to benefit from each master. And if one master can benefit him more than the others, he should trust proportionally more in him, even though he also trusts in the others. And if only one of the masters can benefit him or harm him, certainly he should put his trust only on that master, since he does not hope for benefit from the other masters. Similarly, when a human being will realize that no created being can benefit him or harm him without the permission of the Creator, he will stop being afraid of them or of hoping for anything from them, and he will place his trust in the Creator alone, as written "Put not your trust in princes, nor in mortal man who has no help" (Tehillim 146:3).

CHESHVAN 24

(*Pas Lechem*: the expression "nor in mortal man who has no help" alludes to both points simultaneously. (1) That if the generous man helps him, the help is not ascribed to him but rather to the Creator, since he cannot help him without the permission of the Creator. (2) The expression "who has no help" also alludes to that which the generous man also cannot even help himself. Both interpretations are true and simultaneously intended.

Tov Halevanon: That a generous man cannot help due to his own power, rather the help is from G-d and the man is just an agent, therefore it is more proper to trust in G-d.)

CHESHVAN 25

SIX: That one is conscious of G-d's abundant goodness to man, and how He brought him into existence out of abundant and pure benevolence and kindness, without man being worthy of this, nor because G-d has any need for him, but only out of generosity, benevolence, and goodness, as we explained in the Gate of Examination in this book, and like King David said "Many, O L-ord my G-d, are Your wonderful works which You have done, and Your thoughts which are toward us: they cannot be reckoned up in order to You; if I would declare and speak of them, they are more than can be numbered" (Tehillim 40:5).

CHESHVAN 26

(Translator: i.e. how do we know G-d brought man into existence out of pure benevolence and kindness? Because He does not need anything from man. This is logical because man is His creation and a creator does not need anything from His creation. As an illustration (heard from Rabbi Moshe Lazarus), close your eyes and think of a blue-colored orange fruit. You have just created that fruit in your mind. As long as you continue to think about it, it has a form of existence in your mind. Now, do you have any need for that orange? Of course not, it is just the opposite. The orange needs you for everything while you don't need it for anything. So too, we need G-d not the other way around. His "thoughts" are continuously giving existence to the universe (as brought down in the book Tanya, Shaar Yichud v'Emuna ch. 7: "G-d's Thought and Knowledge of all created beings encompasses each and every creature, for this is its very life-force and that which grants it existence from absolute nothingness."). Therefore, since He has no need for us, granting us existence is a continuous act of pure benevolence and grace. Note that this is just an analogy, not to be taken too literally for G-d is unknowable to us.)

CHESHVAN 27

SEVEN: That one clearly realizes that all existing things in this world, whether purposeful or accidental have predetermined limits which cannot be increased or decreased from what the Creator has decreed, whether in amount, quality, time, or place. It cannot be numerous if the Creator decreed it few, nor few if the Creator decreed it numerous, nor come late if decreed to come early, nor come early if decreed to come late. And if something appears to be contrary to this, really, it was already pre-decreed with foresight, only that all decrees [are implemented through] causes and means, which in turn have causes and means.

(*Tov Halevanon commentary*: i.e. That incident did not happen by itself, even though this incident is caused by another incident, and the other incident itself is caused by another incident, and so forth until the first cause - all of them came through a decree from G-d. He coordinated all the incidents in a controlled way.

CHESHVAN 28

For example: A boat whose crew wanted to go out to sea at this time tomorrow, the Sultan then falsely accused the captain of the ship and delayed him for some time period. During that time period, wars broke out in the sea. When the boat finally set out to sea, the crew feared the wars and wanted to escape through a different route. The boat wound up broken by boulders which were along that route in the sea and the entire crew drowned. The sea then carried a floating case filled with treasures towards the shore. At the same time, the Sultan of a nearby city falsely accused a Tzadik (righteous person) who ran away to the sea shore. At that moment, the case appeared floating near the shore. The righteous man found it and was able to obtain his livelihood from it for the rest of his life.

CHESHVAN 29

Behold, this that the first Sultan falsely accused the captain was the beginning of the initial cause of providing for the livelihood of this Tzadik, since if the crew went out to sea earlier, before the wars broke out, they would not have turned towards the dangerous route which broke the ship. The second incident was the breaking out of the wars at that specific time. The third incident, that which the case was able to float on the sea. The fourth incident was that which the sea current pushed the case towards this side of the shore. The fifth, the accusing of the righteous man by the Sultan at that specific time. The sixth incident, that which was put in his heart the idea to run away. The seventh incident, that which he ran away at that specific time and to that specific place.

KISLEV 1

Behold, all these matters did not happen accidentally, rather, G-d in His wisdom, coordinated that everything happen in its time and place. And even the breaking out of the wars and the drowning of the crew - everything occurred by decrees of G-d, each with its own reason, just that He coordinated in His wisdom to complete all of His will and decrees simultaneously. Strive to understand this because it is deep and this is the author's intent.

. . . And the final incident (of providing for the tzadik) preceded everything and was the first cause of all the causes which followed (relative to this decree) until this cause of providing for the righteous man materialized. And even so, all the events which preceded this did not occur incidentally, namely, that they did not occur merely for this small first cause which was accomplished. Rather, all these chains of events which accomplished this first cause (of providing for the tzadik), were planned by G-d with foresight, and every incident had its own independent reason and decree, something which is beyond our finite minds to grasp, how it is possible that all of these things are coordinated in unison, and each one is not accidental, rather everything according to its decree, without one matter contradicting another, and like the verse says: "for the L-ord is a G-d of all-knowledge, and by Him actions are weighed" (Shmuel 2:3).

KISLEV 2

Likewise, for the development of later causes, for example: When we see a torrent of water which flooded all the inhabitants of a city. It appears that due to the flood a single incident occurred to all those who were in that city. But this is not so, rather, there were other previous causes that occurred with G-d's coordination, so that all those who were decreed to die were assembled together in one place, due to many causes and chains of causes which preceded this cause of flooding, and everything occurring with G-d's foresight.

Translator: note that it was all planned with foresight from the creation of the world as explained in the story of R. Eleazar b. Pedat - Talmud Taanit 25a)

KISLEV 3

One who does not understand the matters of this world thinks that an immediate cause will force a change in matters, which in turn cause more changes (that present events constantly reshape the future). But really, a single cause is too weak to force a change by itself, as we see one grain of wheat can cause 300 ears of wheat to grow, which each contain 30 grains, so one grain would have produced around ten thousand grains. Can one hide the fact that one grain by itself is incapable of producing this amount? And likewise for other grains that one plants, and likewise we can say for a man or an animal from a drop of semen, or a huge fish from a tiny egg.

KISLEV 4

(*Lev Tov*: Rather, the true underlying power which causes the seeds to grow into ears of wheat is G-d's original decree from Genesis [that the seemingly biological life process driving the seed would unfold in this way]. And this pre-decree is what drives the matter to actuality through the available means.

Translator: Normally the effect does not exceed the capacities of the cause. Here it is clear that the effect (human being with spiritual soul) is beyond the powers of the cause (physical human seed). See Gate 1 for much more on this.)

KISLEV 5

To busy oneself in trying to bring early what the Creator decreed would come later, or to try to delay what was decreed to come early, or to try to make numerous what was decreed to be few or to try to diminish what was decreed to be numerous in worldly possessions, unless it causes strengthening of His service or accepting His Torah (since on religious matters G-d does not decree on a man, rather the free will is in man's own hands, as will be explained - *ML*), - all this is due to (1) weakness in the recognition of G-d's all-knowing understanding (of us and our needs - *PL*), and (2) foolishness in failing to understand the benevolent character of G-d's conducts.

(Pas Lechem: i.e. that all of G-d's conducts with His creations is for their benefit. Through realizing these two points, there will be trust.

KISLEV 6

The Madregos HaAdam wrote that one who worries and tries to earn more than what was decreed for him is like a man inside a moving train pushing the wall to make the train move faster.

The wise man has already hinted this when he said: "everything has a time and moment under the heaven" (Koheles 3:1), and afterwards he mentions 28 matters (corresponding to the 28 lunar positions which alludes to astrological fate - *TL*), as he says "a time to be born, and a time to die..", until "a time for war and a time for peace", and also: "for time and fate will overtake them all" (Koheles 9:11), and then he said: "[If you see oppression of the poor, and deprivation of justice and righteousness in the province], wonder not about the matter, for the Highest over the high watches over them, and there are higher ones over them" (Koheles 5:7). (that really it is not astrological "fate", but rather G-d is guiding everything behind the scenes through chains of causes according to His desire and decrees - *TL*)

KISLEV 7

(*Pas Lechem*: If you see oppression of the poor and deprivation of justice, etc., do not wonder, since certainly it has already been decreed on the wicked to get what they deserve, only that G-d will bring their retribution through chains of many causes (which are coordinated with everyone affected). Therefore, their retribution is delayed. But when the causes are finished, they will also be finished. This is what is meant by "for the Highest over the high watches over them, and there are higher ones", to teach that thus Divine wisdom decided to implement the divine decrees through many causes...

KISLEV 8

Pas Lechem: (earlier) And if you ask: if it is so that everything was pre-decreed, if so, why does this not happen right away from the beginning, for example, for an almond, why does it start as a bud, then blossoms into a flower, then sprouts a shoot, then a hull, then an almond shell, etc., why didn't ripe almonds grow from the beginning, as we see them now? On this, he answered that this is what Divine wisdom decided - that everything be implemented through chains of many causes and means in a natural looking progression.

KISLEV 9

Translator's note: the reason G-d made the world in such a way that His decrees are hidden behind "nature" is so that man can have free will to choose between good and evil. Let us consider what would happen if G-d would manifest His presence on the sky in His full power and glory to hit with lightning bolts all those who commit evil deeds. In such a situation virtually all people would start to live in terror and in fear. No man would have the courage to do anything for doing of which would not receive a direct order from G-d. Science and technology would collapse, as no-one would have the courage to research, investigate, or to just speculate - as everyone would be scared that this may act against G-d's intentions. Social life would collapse as no one would utter a word out of terror of saying the wrong thing. Medicine would fall down as doctors would be scared to heal thus breaking G-d's wishes. Most would be too scared to lift a finger for fear of sin and deserving a punishment. People would then live like forced slaves and soon the entire population would die out. In order to avoid such consequences and provide an arena for free will, G-d introduced several prevention measures to His coexistence with people.

KISLEV 10

Hence He almost never openly manifests Himself to living people. He always maintains people in ambiguity about His presence in order to maintain "free will" and the possibility of virtue. Therefore, everything that G-d does, He does in such a manner that it is ambiguous - i.e. that it can be explained in many different manners, etc., etc.

Note that this is only one minor aspect. There's a lot more to it than that. The primary reason (as heard from Rabbi Mordechai Kornfeld) is that it has lots in common with raising children (who is the better parent-the one standing ready with a stick and carrot, or the one hiding behind the door and letting his child grow?), coaching independence, and thus becoming akin to the Creator. The answer lies at the very root of the need for free will and the requisite amount of it, which is discussed by the Ramchal in Derech Hash-m (beginning of ch. 2 of the first section or so) and in Daas Tevunos (where he offers another, more familiar, explanation).

KISLEV 11

Related to this point, if G-d would manifest Himself openly to human beings, it would completely crush their egos. No man would be capable of thinking highly of himself due to perceiving just how utterly puny, weak, and insignificant he is compared to the infinite power, wisdom, and ability of G-d. This realization would render him completely and absolutely humble. In fact, this is exactly what happened to Moses. Despite all of his monumental achievements, he nevertheless became "the humblest man on the face of the earth" (Numbers 12:3) due to his open encounters with G-d.

KISLEV 12

Hence, it is necessary for free will that a natural order exists whose purpose is to provide a misleading appearance that the world carries itself. Therefore, when nature was created, with it came the loopholes for interpreting the world according to the atheistic views. It is essential for G-d's plan of free will. This is why the world appears billions of years old as a result of some cosmological accident, etc. etc. Likewise G-d created life forms in stages from simple to complex to make room for a naturalistic explanation, etc. etc. But the true truth seeker will see the marks of divine wisdom which are all around us and draw the correct conclusions, as explained in Gates 1 and 2.

KISLEV 13

Another reason is as the Ramchal writes (Daas Tevunos siman 40): "certainly G-d could have established the world through His omnipotent system, in such a way that everything would be totally incomprehensible to us, not before not after, without cause and effect. If He had done so, no one (atheist) would be able to open their mouths for we would not be able to understand anything whatsoever... but because He wanted us to understand a bit of His ways and attributes - on the contrary He very much wants us to exert ourselves on this..." end quote

KISLEV 14

Scientific progress has shown so far that all phenomena in the universe after the Big Bang is understandable to man. Even the weirdest, most bizarre quantum mechanics, black holes, etc. can nevertheless be fit into human-made mathematical models that we can understand and use to make predictions. Albert Einstein said: "The most incomprehensible thing about the world is that it is comprehensible." This indicates that it is all for man. It is a kind of ladder to come to know G-d's wisdom and ways.

The ways of judgments of the Creator are too deep, hidden and lofty for us to understand part of them, and all the more so to understand their general principles. And the verse already says: "As the heavens are higher than the earth, so are My ways higher than your ways and My thoughts [higher] than your thoughts" (Yeshaya 55:9).

KISLEV 15

SECOND INTRODUCTION TO BRING COMPLETE TRUST

(2) To know and clearly realize that the Creator is watching him, and neither one's private or public conduct is hidden from Him, nor his innermost being or outer appearance. He also knows whether a man's trust in Him is with a sincere heart or not, as the verse says "G-d knows the thoughts of the heart, that they are vain" (Tehillim 94:11) and "Does not He that tests the heart understand it?" (Mishlei 24:12), and "You alone know the hearts of all men" (Melachim I 8:39).

When this is clearly realized by the one who trusts, it is not proper for him to claim with his lips that he trusts in G-d (in the daily prayers in many places - *ML*), without trusting in Him in his heart and thoughts, whereby he would be in the category of he of whom the verse says "with their mouths and their lips they honor Me, but their hearts are far from Me" (Yeshaya 29:13).

KISLEV 16

(*Pas Lechem*: The reason the author counted this as one of the introductions/prerequisites to trust is only for the phrase: "He also knows whether a man's trust in Him is with a sincere heart or not", that through a man's remembering that G-d observes Him in all of his words and thoughts, he will also remember that included in this is G-d's observing whether or not his trust is sincere.

KISLEV 17

Marpe Lenefesh: When a man realizes that G-d knows the truth, whether what comes out of his lips is the same as what is in his heart, how could he then claim and say that he "truly trusts in G-d", when his heart is not with him. And then G-d will also remove His providence from him as mentioned in the beginning of the introduction to this gate ("..whoever trusts in something other than G-d, the Al-mighty will remove His providence from such a person..."), and then it will be a chillul H-ashem. And it is proper for us to put our eyes and hearts on the things which come out of our lips every day in our prayers, that we claim and say many times that we trust in Him and hope to Him, such as in Pesukei D'Zimra: "Nafshenu Chiksa L'H-ashem", "ki bshem kadsho batachnu", "yehi chasdecha..", and in Ahava Raba: "ki bshem kadshecha hagadol vehanora batachnu", and in the Shmonei Esrei "ve ten sachar tov lchol habotchim b'shimcha b'emes, vsim chelkenu imahem", "ki becha batachnu", and many others. It is proper for every man to put his eye and heart all of his days on the words of this gate, then "lo yevosh v'lo yikalem", not in this world and not in the next.

KISLEV 18

THIRD INTRODUCTION TO BRING COMPLETE TRUST
(3) That a person trusts in G-d alone for the things he is obligated to trust in (the things that one should not trust in G-d will be explained

later), and not to associate Him with anyone else by trusting in Him and one of the created beings because then his trust in G-d will be invalidated in that he associated someone else with G-d. You know what was said about Asa, despite all of his piety, when he relied on the doctors, as written "during his illness, he did not seek help from G-d, but only in the doctors" (Divrei HaYamim II 16:12) (i.e. he did not also pray), and he was punished for this. And the verse says "Blessed is the man who trusts in the L-ord; the L-ord shall be his refuge" (Yirmiyahu 17:7).

And it is known that one who entrusts two or more men to do a task, the matter spoils. All the more so, for one who trusts in G-d and man, that his trust in G-d will be ruined (since he equated G-d with a created being, which is a great demeaning of G-d's greatness - TL).

KISLEV 19

(*Pas Lechem*: The talmud says (Eruvin 50a) "a pot of partners is neither hot nor cold", i.e. that for two people who are entrusted with a task, even though they are of approximately equal worth, nevertheless, each one is not pleased with your trust in him since you also charged the second person to head the task and trusted in him. All the more so that it is hard on G-d to be pleased when you equate a servant with his Master.

Translator: The Rayatz Rebbe would say "bitachon (trust) is when a person finds himself in the middle of the ocean with nothing, not even a piece of straw". i.e. this is how one should view his situation. Heard from Devorah Leah Edison)

KISLEV 20

Furthermore, this will be the strongest factor for denying him the object of his trust, as written "cursed is the man who trusts in men,.. and turns his heart away from G-d" (Yirmiyahu 17:5).

(*Marpe Lenefesh*: Rather, let one reflect constantly that G-d is the Cause of all causes, and everyone and everything are merely His agents, as will be explained later on.)

FOURTH INTRODUCTION

That one is very careful and makes a great effort to fulfill what the Creator required of him in His service, to do his mitzvot and to guard oneself from what He has forbidden, just like he seeks that the Creator agrees to do with him in that which he trusts Him, as our sages said "make His will your will so that He will make your will His will, nullify your will to His will so that He will nullify the will of others to your will" (Avot 2:4).

KISLEV 21

(*Tov Halevanon*: i.e. nullify your taava (physical desires) so that they will not lead you to nullify a commandment of G-d, and separate from what is permitted to you, "so that He will nullify the will of others to your will", i.e. so that His providence on you will be greater than His providence on other people, and everyone in the world will yield for your sake, as the Talmud says (Berachos 6b) "the whole world was created for his sake only".)

KISLEV 22

And the verse says "Trust in the L-ord and do good; so shall you dwell in the land, and verily you shall be fed" (Tehillim 37:3), and "G-d is good to those who hope in Him, to one who seeks Him" (Eicha 3:25).

But, if one trusts in G-d and rebels against Him, how foolish is he, how weak is his intellect and his understanding! For he can see in this world that if an employer appoints a man to do something or refrain from doing something and the man disobeys the instruction, this will be the strongest factor in the employer's refusing to fulfill his side of the deal. All the more so, for one who disobeys the commandments of G-d, for which G-d Himself testified that one who trusts in Him and disobeys Him will have his hopes foiled and his trust will be considered hypocritical. Rather, he will be like that of who it is written "For what is the hope of the flatterer who deceives, when G-d casts off his soul? Will G-d hear his cry when trouble comes on him?" (Iyov 27:8-9), and "Will you steal, murder, commit adultery, swear falsely, offer up to idols, and follow other gods that you know not. And will you come and stand before Me in this house, upon which My name is called, and say, 'We are saved,' in order to commit all these abominations? Has this house upon which My name is called, become a den of thieves in your eyes? I, too, behold I have seen it, says the L-ord." (Yirmiyahu 7:9-11).

KISLEV 23

(*Marpe Lenefesh*: Even though G-d has compassion on all His creations, including the wicked, as he explained earlier, even so, for this, one should not think that G-d will forever tolerate him, and trust that G-d will continue bestowing good to him always despite his wickedness. And even though things are going well now, there is no escape from His judgments, and eventually, when He wishes, He will choose a time and place to collect His debt (of justice). Rather it is proper for a man to endeavor to fulfill all of G-d's commandments.

KISLEV 24

Matanas Chelko: Besides that one must realize that all powers are in G-d's hands, none can prevent Him from doing what He wishes, and further that G-d knows his thoughts, and it is impossible to trick Him. Hence, he cannot claim verbally that he trusts in G-d while he does not really trust Him in his inner being. Thirdly, that he should not associate anything or anyone else with G-d, as before. However, an extra condition is needed, namely, that this is in truth the will of G-d. For, one cannot place his trust in a strong person who can help him unless he knows that the person actually wants to help him. For example, if one tells a poor man: "such and such a person is a very rich man and is able to help you with all your needs.

KISLEV 25

The poor man still should not place his trust in the rich man since he does not know whether the rich man actually wants to help him. So too, by G-d, there is no doubt that He can perform signs and wonders for a person. But one cannot trust in this unless he knows that G-d truly wants to do so. The one and only way through which a person can know whether G-d wants to help and do for him is only if he himself does the will of G-d. Hence, necessarily, one of the pillars of trust is that he be a righteous person who does the will of G-d. And even though G-d also does the will of the wicked sometimes, nevertheless, they cannot trust in this because they cannot know for sure how long G-d will hold back retribution from them. Unlike the righteous, who can rest assured.

KISLEV 26

"make His will your will so that He will make your will His will" - the author is telling us that this mishna is the pillar of trust. He who wants to rest assured that G-d will do what he wants, let him do the will of G-d. Otherwise, how can he trust that G-d will do his wish? But if he exerts himself greatly to do the will of G-d, then he can hope and trust that G-d will likewise do his will... (Translator: see Gate 3 Chapter 7 where the author brings the minimum service whereby a person is assured of receiving continuous divine benefits.)

KISLEV 27

"Trust in the L-ord and do good; so shall you dwell in the land, and verily you shall be fed" - both things go together. If he wants to trust in G-d, he must do good, as before. And that which the wicked can trust in G-d's trait of kindness and compassion, this is only temporarily. As the Marpe Lenefesh commentary wrote (see above). Hence, the wicked should not trust that G-d's compassion and kindness will continuously bestow on him forever. Rather, he can trust temporarily on G-d's trait of kindness and compassion, that G-d will withhold retribution from him and continue to bestow life to him. But he must repent in the end and he can never know for sure when the time will come that G-d will collect His debt [of justice]. On the other hand, one who does the will of G-d can place his trust in G-d. For through this he is assured that G-d wants to help him and do what's good for him since G-d already promised this.

KISLEV 28

"Will G-d hear his cry when trouble comes on him?" - hence G-d testified that he does not wish to help and aid a person who transgresses His word. One who thinks to himself that G-d will help him even if he does not fulfill what G-d commanded him to do - this is the greatest folly. "Has this house upon which My name is called, become a den of thieves in your eyes?" - even though, of all places in the world, the Temple in Jerusalem is the place where prayers are most readily answered and for trusting in G-d, nevertheless, if it has become a den of thieves, already they should no longer trust in this, and they are not assured anymore that if they scream out in prayers that G-d will fulfill their request. (*translator*: for perhaps it is better for them to receive sufferings to atone for their evil deeds than to be saved)

KISLEV 29

Translator: nevertheless, one must know and trust that his repentance will always be accepted no matter how far he strayed and what he did etc. as the Marpe Lenefesh commentary explained earlier: "Otherwise, he will abandon hope from the favors of G-d, since he is in doubt whether he is worthy of them, and his trust in G-d will diminish. And through this, he will distance from G-d and His Torah. Rather, let him reflect that G-d is benevolent to the good and the bad, as written: "His mercy is on all of His creations" (Tehillim 145:9). And through this, he will come closer to G-d and repent and he will become worthy of the good.")

TEVES 1

An illustration of the causes: Consider the act of drawing up water from the depths of the earth using a wheel system to which buckets are attached and which raises the water from the well. The buckets are the near cause. The remote cause is the man who harnessed an animal to the wheel and compels the animal to move in order to raise the water from the bottom of the well to the surface of the earth.

FIFTH INTRODUCTION

A person should realize that every new thing that happens in this world after Genesis is completed in two ways:

First: By G-d's decree and His will that the matter should come into existence.

Secondly: Through intermediate causes and means - some near, some remote, some apparent, some hidden, all of which rush to bring into existence what was decreed, doing so with G-d's help.

(Ramchal: When a matter is decreed, a Bas Kol (heavenly voice) is proclaimed throughout the mystical worlds which summons and gives the power to the appointed forces needed to carry out the matter.)

TEVES 2

The intermediate means between the man and the buckets are: the animal, the mechanical contraption of interconnected wheels/gears which turn each other in series, and the rope. If a mishap were to occur to any one of the causes mentioned (i.e. the intermediate means or the close cause - TL), the intended purpose for which they were designed would not be accomplished.

And so it is for other things which come to existence. They cannot be produced by a man or anyone else, but rather, through the decree of G-d, and His preparing all the means through which the thing will be produced, as written "And by Him, causes are counted" (Shmuel I 2:3), and "Who is great in counsel and mighty in carrying it out" (Yirmiyahu 32:19), and "it was a cause from G-d" (Melachim I 12:15). And if the means are blocked, none of the actions which normally bring this matter into existence will succeed.

TEVES 3

(Pas Lechem: i.e. by Him are all the number of means which cause each and every thing to occur. And if one of the means were missing the thing would not occur. And since it is not so clear from the first verse that He is the First cause which prepares the other causes, one might think that they are merely known to Him in number. Therefore the author brought the second verse "Who is great in counsel and Mighty in carrying it out", which teaches that He is the Master of all causes and the one who carries them out... And if one is still stubborn and wants to say that there is no proof from these two verses. They only teach that the causes are attributed to Him since He is the Creator of everything, therefore the author brought the third verse which teaches that the matter was from G-d with specific intent for that thing.

TEVES 4

Matanas Chelko: even for making a loaf of bread, thousands of people are needed such as workers to plant, reap, mill, bake. And each stage requires machines built for sowing, reaping, etc. And the materials are transported through machines on roads and highways, etc. Hence even to make a piece of bread there are thousands of necessary details.. And even though we believe that G-d was behind everything, and that He can do it all without any intermediate means and can create ready to eat bread directly into our home, nevertheless, the author explains, that our eyes can see there is a nature and order that we must recognize and understand. Afterwards, he will explain why G-d wanted things to follow this order.)

TEVES 5

When we examine the need for a man to pursue means and exert himself to complete his needs, we can see with our own eyes that for one who needs food and proper food is served before him, if he does not exert himself to eat it by lifting the food to his mouth, chewing it, etc., he will not break his hunger. Likewise for someone thirsty, who needs water. And all the more so, if he has no food prepared, until he needs to exert himself through milling flour, kneading, baking, etc . And more so, if he needs to buy the food and prepare it. And even more still, if he has no money to buy them and will need even greater exertion to pursue means to earn the money or to sell the amount he needs from the objects he uses or his other possessions, or the like.

TEVES 6

WHY MAN MUST WORK FOR A LIVELIHOOD

There are two reasons why the Creator obligated a man to pursue means and exert himself for his livelihood and other needs.

(*Tov Halevanon*: Man does not find his food readily like other living creatures which do not need to pursue causes and means.

Matanas Chelko: "the Creator obligated a man..." - "hishtadlus" (exertion) is an obligation! It is an obligation to exert oneself to provide for himself and his family. Likewise for all the other things which we are forced to enter into the system of causes and means. It is for two reasons...)

TEVES 7

(1) Divine wisdom required the testing of man in the service of G-d or rebellion against Him. Therefore, G-d tests man with what demonstrates his choice in this - needs and lacking for external things such as food, drink, clothing, shelter, and sexual relations. G-d commanded man to pursue and attain them through the available means in specific ways (according to the Torah - *ML*) and at specific times.

(note: G-d knows already what each person will choose. The purpose of testing man is to give him an opportunity to elevate himself in the greatest possible way - by choosing good of his own free will, as explained in Gate 3)

Teves 8

What G-d has decreed that man will attain of them, man will attain fully after the completion of the prepared means. That which has not been decreed that he will attain - he will not attain, and the necessary means will be withheld. Through this process, his free choice of whether he served G-d or rebelled against Him will be demonstrated through his intention and choice, and the man will then deserve either reward or punishment, regardless whether or not he actually achieved his intentions.

TEVES 9

(*Pas Lechem*: the author said "through his intention and choice" because the status of the choice is according to the intention, namely, if he chooses good with bad intentions, such as choosing good with intent for flattery or boasting himself, or arrogance - he is evil. Likewise for the opposite, as our Sages taught us (Nazir 23b) from Yael)

TEVES 10

(2) Secondly, if a man were not forced to exert himself in seeking a livelihood, he would kick (become defiant) and chase after sin, and he would ignore his debt of gratitude to G-d for His goodness to him. As written: "And the harp, and the lyre, the timbrel, and flute, and wine, are in their feasts: but they regard not the work of the L-ord, neither consider the work of His hands" (Yeshaya 5:12), and "But Yeshurun grew fat, and kicked: you are grown fat, you are grown thick, you are covered with fatness; then he forsook G-d who made him, and lightly esteemed the Rock of his salvation" (Devarim 32:15). And the sages said "it is good the study of Torah with working for a livelihood because the toil in both removes thoughts of sin, and all Torah study without work will in the end be abandoned and bring to sin" (Avot 2:2). And all the more so for one who has no share in either Torah or work, nor directs his attention to any of these pursuits.

TEVES 11

(*Pas Lechem*: From here we see that indulgence in physical pleasures makes a man's heart coarse, thereby causing him to refrain from doing the commandments.

Tov Halevanon: If everything were prepared for man, he would be idle to chase after sin, also his body's nature and physicality would tend to kick and be ungrateful for the favors of G-d due to the delight in his heart, since everything would be ready before him. He would think that he is deserving of all this and he would not realize that it is from G-d.

TEVES 12

Marpe Lenefesh: If everything were prepared and ready before a man, he would not have any free choice. And he would remain forever at the same level and he would not deserve any reward or punishment...

TEVES 13

Matanas Chelko: In our times, people only want to work a little. Therefore, they lack the necessary exertion and they come to sin. The Creator's intent was that a man work so strenuously from morning until evening that when he returns to his home after a long day of work, he will not have strength to watch television. But, as we said, people do not tire themselves to this extent, so when they return home, they have strength remaining to sin and their evil inclination is still in its full power. The purpose of exertion is to weaken the evil inclination. This is what the sages said "it is good the study of Torah with working for a livelihood because the toil in both removes thoughts of sin".

TEVES 14

In truth, if a man would exert himself in Torah to such an extent that his evil inclination would be weakened, then he would have reached the intended purpose and would not need to also exert himself in earning a livelihood. But this path is only for special individuals. The vast majority need to exert themselves in both. Exertion in Torah alone is not enough for them. However, the intent for both is the same, namely, that the exertion weakens his strength until he is no longer capable of sinning. Hence, the purpose is not simply to learn Torah and work for if these two do not weaken him to such an extent that he can no longer sin, then he will still come to sin. Rather, the aim is to toil and strain in Torah and also in work until both exertions remove thoughts of sin.)

TEVES 15

It was out of compassion for man that G-d has compelled him to be occupied with matters of this world and the next for all of his days, and so that he does not seek that which he does not need and which he cannot understand with his limited intellect, such as matters of what was before the creation and of the final end (since these things do not further his perfection and on the contrary - they damage him - *PL*), as the wise man said "also the [toil of] the world He has set into their hearts, so that man should not seek the deed which G-d did, from beginning to end." (Koheles 3:11).

TEVES 16

WHEN G-D REMOVES THE BURDEN OF
EARNING A LIVELIHOOD FROM A MAN

If a man strengthens himself in the service of G-d, resolves to fear Him, trusts in Him for his religious and secular matters, steers away from reprehensible things (such as anger or arrogance - *PL*), strives for the good midot (character traits), does not rebel in prosperity nor turn towards leisure, is not enticed by the evil inclination, nor seduced by the witchery of this world - the burden of exerting himself in the means to a livelihood will be removed from him, since the two reasons mentioned above no longer apply to him, namely, to test him on his choice and to protect him from rebelling during prosperity. His livelihood will come to him without strain (of the heart - *PL*) or toil (of the limbs - *PL*), according to his needs, as written "G-d will not bring hunger to the righteous" (Mishlei 10:3).

TEVES 17

(*Tov Halevanon*: "the witchery of this world" refers to the worldly pleasures which spellbind the eyes of the one who gazes at them until he thinks they are good for him but he does not realize their ultimate end.

Pas Lechem: Since he no longer needs to be tested because his heart has already strengthened in the service of G-d, and he is full of fear and trust of Him, and also he is not liable to rebel, so why should G-d trouble him further?

TEVES 18

Matanas Chelko: This is another great principle. If a man thinks for whatever reason that he no longer needs to engage in the pursuit of a livelihood. This is only justified if he is clinging to G-d not because he trusts in G-d. Many people mistakenly think that the amount of hishtadlus (exertion for livelihood) is proportional to the amount of trust a person has. This is not correct. A man can have great trust but if he has not yet reached the level that he is straining himself as before or it is still necessary to test him whether or not he will do only the will of G-d, then even if he has much tranquility, he is still under obligation to exert himself in his livelihood....[see there at length]...In our times, if one learns in yeshiva or Kollel and has some sort of plan on how to support himself and his family - this is considered Torah study with work. For that which the sages said that one must combine Torah and work, their intent was not that every person must specifically work but rather that he has some sort of plan... nevertheless he is lacking the second reason, namely, that one must strain himself until he has no strength left to come to sin. Therefore, he is under duty to strain himself in Torah study to this extent.)

TEVES 19

If one asks: Behold we see some tzadikim (very righteous people) which do not receive their livelihood except after hard and strenuous toil, while many transgressors are at ease, living a good, pleasant life?

We will say: The prophets and the chasidim (extremely pious) already investigated this matter. One of them said "[Righteous are you, O L-rd, when I plead with You: yet let me talk with You of your judgments:] Why does the way of the wicked prosper? why are all they happy that deal very treacherously?" (Yirmiyahu 12:1), and another "Why do You show me iniquity and look upon mischief; and plunder and violence are before me; and the one who bears quarrel and strife endures." (Chavakuk 1:3), and "for a wicked man surrounds the righteous; therefore, justice emerges perverted." (Chavakuk 1:4), and "Why should You be silent when a wicked man swallows up one more righteous than he?" (Chavakuk 1:13), and another one said "Behold these are wicked, yet they are tranquil in the world and have increased wealth." (Tehillim 73:12), and "But for naught I cleansed my heart and bathed my hands with cleanliness" (Tehillim 73:13), and another said "And now we praise the bold transgressors, those who work wickedness are built up, they tempt G-d, and they have, nevertheless, escaped." (Malachi 3:15), and many more like this.

TEVES 20

But the prophet refrained from giving an answer because each specific case has its own particular reason (there is no general answer which includes everything - *TL*). Therefore Moshe Rabeinu commented on this in the Torah saying (Devarim 29:28) "the hidden things belong to G-d"..and the wise man said in connection to this "If you see the oppression of the poor, and perverting of justice and righteousness in a province, marvel not at the matter" (Koheles 5:7), and the verse says: "the Rock, His deeds are perfect for all His ways are justice" (Devarim 32:4). (i.e. ultimately, the matter is hidden and concealed by its nature and is beyond the powers of the human mind to grasp - *PL*)

TEVES 21

WHY THE RIGHTEOUS SOMETIMES SUFFER
Nevertheless, I saw fitting to attempt to clarify this matter that should be to some extent satisfactory (so that it won't be so difficult - *TL*).

The possible reasons why a tzadik is prevented from obtaining his livelihood without effort and must instead exert himself for it and be tested by it is as follows.

TEVES 22

1. A previous sin for which it is necessary to pay him for it, as written "the tzadik will pay in the land" (Mishlei 11:31)

(*Marpe Lenefesh*: As the sages said (Kidushin 39b): "He whose merits outweighs his sins is punished (Rashi: in this world to clean him from his sins, so that he receives complete reward in Olam Haba) and is as though he had burnt the whole Torah, not leaving even a single letter; while he whose sins outweighs his merits is rewarded (Rashi: to pay him the reward for his merits in this world so as to banish him in Olam Haba) and is as though he had fulfilled the whole Torah, not omitting even a single letter!")

TEVES 23

2. In the way of exchanging, to pay him more good in Olam Haba (the afterlife), as written "to benefit you in your end" (Devarim 8:16)

(*Marpe Lenefesh*: These are "Yisurim shel Ahava" (chastening of love) which are not due to sins, as the talmud says (Berachos 5a): "if he examined his deeds and did not find any sins let him be sure that these are Yisurim shel Ahava, as written (Mishlei 3:12): 'For whom G-d loves He chastens'", i.e. to increase his reward in Olam Haba more than his merits.

Pas Lechem: To exchange for him a fleeting world for an eternal world.)

TEVES 24

3. To demonstrate his good bearing and good acceptance of suffering in the service of G-d, so that others will learn from him, as you know from the matter of Iyov.

(*Marpe Lenefesh*: That he receives everything with a good countenance, and he does not rebel in sufferings so that others will learn from him and see him and notice him and desire to serve G-d even though they don't have all their lusts, and even though they are in poverty, hardship or in painful sicknesses as we find with Iyov (Job) and many other sages, who were in suffering yet did not stop from Torah and service, and as is known of Hillel who was extremely poor, and others who needed to labor for their livelihoods and nevertheless studied the Torah.

TEVES 25

Alternative explanation:

Pas Lechem: To show the world that the Tzadik bears the bad of this world, with good patience and a good countenance, and despite his suffering, he does not budge from the service of his Creator in order to ease the bad. Unlike the wicked, that even for something he is forced to bear, he bears it with an angry heart, and therefore he throws off the yoke of service in order to ease his troubles.

Tov Halevanon: He bears his sufferings and is not begrudging towards G-d and accepts them with a good countenance)

4. Due to the wickedness of his generation, G-d tests him with poverty, hardship, or sickness to demonstrate/contrast his piety and service of G-d unlike them, as written "Indeed, he bore our illnesses, and our pains he carried them" (Yeshaya 53:4).

TEVES 26

(*Pas Lechem*: Here G-d knows that the people of his generation won't learn from him and they will get no benefit from this. Nevertheless, G-d tests him in order to demonstrate his level and worth and contrast it with them. That even though they are in enjoyment and he is in a life of suffering, they are ungrateful towards G-d while he is good with Him and serves Him in truth and wholeheartedly. The intent in this is so that they will acknowledge G-d's justice in the end of days when they will see the exceedingly great reward of the Tzadik. And like our sages said in Pirkei Avot 5:3, "Avraham was tested with ten trials..to show his high esteem."

Marpe Lenefesh: Due to the wickedness of the generation, sometimes G-d sends suffering to a Tzadik to atone for the sins of the generation (to avert disasters or the like), and without a doubt, his reward will not be withheld and the wicked will be paid what they deserve, as Rashi explained on the verse he cited)

TEVES 27

5. Due to his not being sufficiently zealous in standing up for G-d, and exacting justice (i.e. protesting - *TL*) from men of his generation, as you know from the story of Eli and his sons, as the verse says "And it will be that everyone who is left in your house, will come to prostrate himself before him for a silver piece and a morsel of bread" (Shmuel 2:36).

TEVES 28

(*Pas Lechem*: As the talmud says (Shabbat 54b): "Whoever can forbid his household [to commit a sin] but does not, is seized (held accountable) for [the sins of] his household; [if he can forbid] the men of his city, he is seized for [the sins of] the men of his city; if the whole world, he is seized for [the sins of] the whole world")

TEVES 29

Translator: There is another general purpose to suffering for everyone including children as explained in Gate 2 ch.5. Here is an excerpt:

Later on he is subjected to illnesses and meets with painful incidents so that he recognizes the world, and that its nature is not concealed from him. Thus he is put on his guard against trusting in this world thereby permitting his lusts to rule over him, in which case he would become like the animals that neither think nor understand; as it is written *"Be ye not as the horse or as the mule which have no understanding"* (Tehillim 32:9).

Tov Halevanon: *"illnesses"* - such as chicken pox and measles. *"painful incidents"* - many weaknesses come in the boyhood years. PL - accidents such as stepping on a metal nail.

"Be ye not as the horse or as the mule" - they need to be leashed and muzzled, so too man. The painful incidents humble his lusts.

"so that he recognizes the world" - how a person's situation can change swiftly from contentment to pain so that he realizes not to trust in it and its tranquility - rather to always be afraid and to seek refuge in G-d's shadow.

SHEVAT 1

Marpe Lenefesh: If a human being had only constant good in this world, he would forget and not recall the matters of his final end, and he would trust (hope) in this world and follow the musings of his heart and his lusts for all of his days. Therefore, it was among the divine plan to send him sometimes bad illnesses, even during his youth in order that he recognize and know that there is no complete good in this world. And even if he is in a very good situation, the bad illnesses can come and ruin his joy, so that he won't trust in this world.

SHEVAT 2

Another reason for suffering explained by the kabbalists is to rectify something done in past lives. Most people are said to have lived previously in past lives (see shaar gilgulim). So for example, someone born into a life of misery and suffering for no apparent reason whatsoever - this may be in order to rectify something from a past life. For example, the Zohar states that the Jewish slaves in Egypt who born and died doing hard labor slavery work for Pharaoh were reincarnations of the generation of the builders of the Tower of Bavel.)

SHEVAT 3

WHY THE WICKED SOMETIMES PROSPER
Sometimes G-d sends good to the wicked for the following reasons:

1. A previous good deed he did, to pay him in this world, as written "And He repays those He hates to their face, to destroy them" (Devarim 7:10) which Onkelos renders: "He pays those He hates for their good deeds during their lives to destroy them".

2. As a temporary deposit, until G-d gives him a righteous son who is worthy of it, as written "he prepares but the tzadik will wear it" (Iyov 27:17), and "to the sinner He has given a preoccupation to gather and to accumulate, to give to him who is good in G-d's sight" (Koheles 2:26).

SHEVAT 4

3. Sometimes the money is the chief cause of his evil (in the next world) or death (in this world), as written "There is a grievous evil that I saw under the sun; riches kept by their owner for his harm." (Koheles 5:12) (such as Korach or Naval - *PL*).

4. Sometimes it is to give him time to repent and become worthy of it, as you know of the story of Menashe.

5. His father did good and it is fitting to benefit him in the merit of his father, as said to Yehu ben Nimshi "four generations of your descendants will sit on the throne of Israel" (Melachim II 10:30), and "He who walks innocently is righteous; fortunate are his sons after him." (Mishlei 20:7), and "I was young, and have aged, and I have not seen a righteous man forsaken nor his descendants begging bread." (Tehillim 37:25).

SHEVAT 5

6. Sometimes it is to test those who are deceptive or have an evil interior. When they see the wicked prosper, they quickly stray from the service of G-d and hasten to win the favor of the wicked and to learn from their actions. In this way it will be clarified the pure men to G-d and it will be demonstrated who was faithful to G-d in bearing at a time when the wicked rule and persecute him. He will receive reward from the Creator for this, as you know of the story of Eliyahu and Isabel or Yirmiyahu and the kings of his generation.

(*Pas Lechem*: The intended purpose of all this was so that the pure men "will receive reward from the Creator for this".

SHEVAT 6

Marpe Lenefesh: Through this it will be demonstrated who was of good, pure heart to G-d and faithful in His service. And even though the wicked were ruling over him and humiliating him, he bears everything and knows that their success is temporary and eventually G-d will collect His debt. And he doesn't learn from their ways and will receive reward for this. But if G-d were to punish the wicked immediately, and reward the righteous right away, there would be no room for free will (which was the purpose of creation), and everyone would hasten to do good and receive reward quickly and everyone would fear swift punishment.

SHEVAT 7

CHOICE OF OCCUPATION

Since it has been clarified the obligation for a man to pursue the means for a livelihood, now we will clarify that not every man is required to pursue every possible means.

The possible means are numerous. Some occupations are easy, requiring little strain such as shop keeping or light work with the hands such as sewing, writing, contracting businesses, hiring sharecroppers or workers, supervisors.

SHEVAT 8

Some occupations require hard physical labor such as tanning, mining iron or copper, smelting metals, heavy transport, constant travel to faraway places, working and plowing land, or the like,

For one who is physically strong and intellectually weak, it is fitting to choose an occupation among those that require physical exertion according to what he can bear.

He who is physically weak but intellectually strong should not seek among those which tire the body but should instead tend towards those who are light on the body and that he will be able to sustain .

SHEVAT 9

Every man has a preference for a particular work or business over others. G-d has already implanted in his nature a love and fondness for it, as He implanted in a cat's nature the hunting of mice, or the falcon to hunt smaller birds, the deer to trap snakes. Some birds hunt only fish, and likewise, each animal species has a liking and desire for particular plants or animals, which G-d has implanted to be the means for its sustenance, and the structure of its body and limbs is suited for that thing.

The long bill and legs of a fish catching bird, or the strong teeth and claws of the lion, horns of the ox and ram (i.e. for defense - *TL*), while animals whose sustenance is from plants do not have the tools to hunt and kill.

SHEVAT 10

Similarly you will find among human beings character traits and body structures suited for certain businesses or activity. One who finds his nature and personality attracted to a certain occupation, and his body is suited for it, that he will be able to bear its demands - he should pursue it, and make it his means of earning a livelihood, and he should bear its pleasures and pains, and not be upset when sometimes his income is withheld, rather let him trust in G-d that He will support him all of his days.

(*Pas Lechem*: For example, one for who the trait of compassion dominates him should distance from becoming a butcher. And likewise, the sages said: "a kapdan (impatient/overcontrolling) should not be a teacher" (Pirkei Avot 2:5), and similarly for other traits.)

SHEVAT 11

INTENTIONS WHEN WORKING FOR A LIVELIHOOD
And he should have intention when his mind and body is occupied with one of the means of earning a living to fulfill the commandment of the Creator to pursue the means of the world, such as working the land, plowing and sowing it, as written "And G-d took the man and placed him in Gan Eden to work it and to guard it" (Bereishis 2:15), and also to use other living creatures for his benefit and sustenance, and for building cities and preparing food, and to marry a woman and have relations to populate the world.

SHEVAT 12

He will be rewarded for his intentions in heart and mind to serve G-d whether or not his desire is accomplished, as written "If you eat from the toil of your hands, you are praiseworthy, and it is good for you" (Tehillim 128:2), and our sages of blessed memory said "Let all your actions be for the sake of Heaven (to serve G-d)" (Avot 2:12).

In this way, his trust in G-d will be intact, undamaged by the toiling in the means to earn a livelihood, as long as his intention in heart and mind is for the sake of Heaven (to do the will of G-d that the world be populated and built up).

SHEVAT 13

(*Tov Halevanon*: It will not damage that which he is made idle from Torah study and service of G-d since this too will be considered for him as righteousness and service)

One should not think that his livelihood depends on a particular means and that if these means fail, his livelihood will not come from a different means. Rather, trust in the Al-mighty, and know that all means are equal for Him. He can provide using whatever means and at any time and however He so wishes, as written "for with the L-ord there is no limitation to save with many or with few" (Shmuel I 14:6), and "But you must remember the L-ord your G-d, for it is He that gives you strength to make wealth, in order to establish His covenant which He swore to your forefathers, as it is this day." (Devarim 8:18), and "Not by might nor by power, but by My spirit, says the L-ord of Hosts." (Zecharia 4:6).

SHEVAT 14

Chapter 4
- When trust applies and when it does not

The concerns for which the believer is obligated to put his trust in G-d are of two categories. (1) matters of this world, and (2), matters of Olam Haba (afterlife). And matters of this world subdivide to two divisions.

1. matters of this world for the benefit of this world. (2) matters of this world for the benefit of the afterlife.

SHEVAT 15

The matters of this world for the benefit of this world subdivide to three parts:

2. what is beneficial for the body only.
3. what contributes to one's maintenance or enables one to gain wealth, and various possessions.
4. what is beneficial for [dealing with] one's household, wife and relatives, for his friends and enemies, and for those above and below him among the various classes of people.

SHEVAT 16

Matters of this world that will secure benefit in Olam Haba subdivide to two parts.

1. duties of the heart and limbs which relate to oneself only, and whose actions do not result in benefit or damage to others.
2. duties of the limbs which cannot be done without association with another, where one of them is active and the other is passive. For example, giving charity, acts of kindness, teaching of wisdom, instructing others to do good or to refrain from evil.

Matters of the afterlife subdivide to two parts.

1. The reward that is deserved.
2. That which is a special kindness which the Creator bestows to the pious and to the prophets, in Olam Haba.

SHEVAT 17

THE 7 CATEGORIES TO TRUST IN

Therefore all things for which one trusts in the Creator fall into 7 categories:

1. matters of the body alone.
2. matters of one's possessions and means of earning a livelihood.
3. matters of one's wife, children, relatives, friends, and enemies [and for those above and below him].

4.   duties of the heart and limbs which only benefit or damage oneself
5.   duties of the limbs which affect others as well, whether benefiting or harming.
6.   reward in the afterlife according to one's conduct in this world.
7.   reward in the afterlife from the Creator in the way of kindness on His trea-
     sured ones and those who love Him (i.e. to increase their reward due to their
     love and clinging to G-d - *TL*), as written "How great is Your goodness that
     You have hidden away for those who fear You; You have done for those who
     trust in You before the sons of men!" (Tehillim 31:20)

SHEVAT 18

Since I have explained the fundamental introductions (in chapter 3)
which make it possible for one to place his trust in the Al-mighty, it is
proper for me to follow them with an explanation of the proper way of
trust in each of the seven categories, through which one should trust in
G-d and in something besides Him.

(*Tov Halevanon*: i.e. To explain which is the proper way of trust, that
can be called complete/flawless trust in G-d versus the trust which is
mixed with trusting in something besides G-d such as one who trusts in
G-d and also in some means, which would not be a proper and just trust.

Marpe Lenefesh: Namely, if he regards them as means between himself
and G-d, and that they are merely agents from G-d as will be explained)

SHEVAT 19

FIRST CATEGORY - MATTERS OF THE BODY ALONE

For the first category, matters of the body alone, these are: his life
and death, his income for obtaining food, clothing and shelter, his health
and illness, his traits. The proper way of trust in the A-lmighty for all of
these matters is to submit oneself to the course the Creator has decreed
for him in these matters, and to place one's trust in G-d and to know that
none of these matters can come to be unless it was previously determined
by G-d that this would be the most proper situation for his matter in this
world and in Olam Haba (the afterlife), and ultimately the greatest good
for him(even if right now it appears to his eye to be not good, certainly,
it is the best thing for him for his ultimate end - *PL*), and that the Creator

has exclusive, total control over all of these matters. In none of them can any created being advise any plan, or exercise any control except through His permission, decree, and judgment.

SHEVAT 20

(*Pas Lechem*: (on the 3 terms: permission, decree, judgment) To not think that some human being's advice can possibly be beneficial unless it is through the permission and decree of the Creator. For example, regarding the healing of a sick person, the talmud expounds [on the verse shmos 21:19]: "from this we learn that permission has been given to the physician to heal". The power in nature to heal through medicinal means is a permission of the Creator. This is a universal matter. And this is combined with the decree of G-d who decreed that this illness be healed through this specific doctor, as the talmud says (Avoda Zara 58a) "through such and such a doctor, using such and such a medicine". This is for the good category. On the bad category, if a man planned to harm him and succeeded, or that he led him in the bad path, and caused him to stumble, certainly, this judgment was sentenced by G-d, otherwise, he would not have succeeded.

SHEVAT 21

Matanas Chelko: For all matters of this world, such as the things relevant to his body, home, or livelihood - everything was already pre-decreed by the Creator, and no man has any power or authority on these matters. This is one of the foundations of trust - that no man has any power in this. Therefore, there is no need to fear other people for none of them can benefit or harm him in any way.

And just like one's life and death, health and sickness, are not in the hands of others, so too, one's livelihood, clothing and other bodily needs are also not in their control.

SHEVAT 22

With clear faith that his matters are given over to the decrees of the Creator, and that the Creator's choice for him is the best choice, it is also his duty to be engaged in means which appear to be beneficial to him and to choose what seems to be the best choice under the circumstances, and the Al-mighty will do according to what He has already pre-decreed.

(*Pas Lechem*: The author specifically stated the passive form of the verb "to be engaged" (in means...) instead of the active form "to engage" (in means...) since we are talking about a person who fully believes that all his movements are given over to the hands of the Creator, and if he does some thing, he is not doing it, rather it is being done to him by G-d, like an ax in the hands of a woodchopper.

SHEVAT 23

Translator: In Gate 3 chapter 8 the author explains this in more details and notes that it is beyond the ability of human understanding to grasp. see there with the commentaries essential reading.)

An example of this: Even though a human being's end and length of his days are determined by the Creator's decree, nevertheless, it is a man's duty to pursue means to survive such as food and drink, clothing, and shelter according to his needs, and he must not leave this to the Al-mighty, and think: "if the Creator has predecreed that I will live, then my body will survive without food all the days of my life, therefore I will not trouble myself in seeking a livelihood and toiling in it".

SHEVAT 24

Likewise, one should not put himself in danger while trusting on the decree of the Creator [that he will live a set time], drinking poisonous drink or going to battle lions or other dangerous animals without necessity, or to cast himself into the sea or into fire, or other similar things that a man is not sure of them and puts his life in danger. And the verse has already warned us in saying "You shall not try the L-ord, your G-d" (Devarim 6:16), because either one of two things will happen.

(*Matanas Chelko*: "to battle lions or other dangerous animals without necessity" - the [extra] words "without necessity" come to hint that if one was attacked by a lion, he should not give up hope and think he has no chance of being saved. Rather, he should trust in G-d to save him, similar to what David did (Samuel 17:36-37).

SHEVAT 25

Either he will die, and it will be considered as if he killed himself, and he will be held accountable for this just as if he had killed another man, despite that his death in this fashion was a decree of the Al-mighty and occurred with His permission.

(*Tov Halevanon*: i.e. even though this person died by putting himself in danger and it was already predecreed by G-d that he would die through this danger and at that time. Nevertheless, he will be punished like one who murders another person, despite that the other person's death was predecreed. Even so, the murderer is guilty [since he had free will, and the decree of death could have been fulfilled through another way - Translator].)

SHEVAT 26

And we have already been commanded not to murder another human being in any form from the verse "do not murder" (shmot 20:13). And the closer the murdered is to the murderer, the more the punishment should be severe, as written "on pursuing his brother with a sword, corrupting his mercy" (Amos 1:11). And similarly the punishment for one who kills himself will undoubtedly be very great.

This is like a slave whose master commanded him to guard a place for a fixed time, and warned him not to leave the place until his messenger will come. When the slave saw that the messenger was late in coming, he abandoned his post, and the master became furious at him and punished him severely. Similarly, one who causes his own death (by doing dangerous things) moves out of the service of G-d and into rebellion against Him, by putting himself in mortal danger.

SHEVAT 27

This is why you will find Shmuel say (to G-d) "And Shmuel said, "How shall I go? For, if Saul hears, he will kill me." And the L-ord said, "You shall take a heifer with you, and you shall say, 'I have come to slaughter (a sacrifice) to the L-ord." (Shmuel I 16:2). And this was not considered a lack of trust in the Al-mighty, and the answer from G-d to him shows that his zeal in this was appropriate (since G-d does not do public miracles without great necessity - *TL*), and He answered him "You shall take a heifer with you, and you shall say, 'I have come to bring an offering to the L-ord." (Shmuel I 16:2), and if this were considered a lack of trust G-d would have answered him "I cause death and grant life. I strike, and I heal" (Devarim 32:39), or something similar, as He answered Moshe when Moshe claimed "But I am slow of speech and slow of tongue" (Shmos 4:10), answering him "Who has made a man's mouth? Who makes a man mute or deaf, seeing or blind". And if Shmuel, with his perfect righteousness did not find it a light matter to put himself to a slight risk of danger, and even though he would be doing so by the command of G-d, as He commanded him "Fill your horn with oil, and go, I shall send you to Jesse, the Bethlehemite, for I have seen for Myself a king among his sons" (Shmuel I 16:1), all the more so for someone not commanded by G-d, that this would be considered reprehensible.

SHEVAT 28

(*Pas Lechem*: If you ask: "why was it considered a lacking by Moshe but not by Shmuel?". The answer is that Moshe was commanded "go and speak...", therefore certainly he will be granted the power of speech and he will be able to speak, therefore [G-d rebuked him]: "Who has made a man's mouth?.." However, by Shmuel, his question was not against the command. It was possible for him to fulfill the command to anoint David and afterwards for Saul to kill him.)

SHEVAT 29

(The second possibility) is that he will be saved by G-d's help. Then his merits will be annulled and he will lose his reward, as our sages said on this matter (Shabbat 32a): "a man should never put himself in danger thinking that a miracle will be performed for him, because maybe no miracle will be done for him, and even if a miracle is done for him, his merits are reduced". And Yaakov our forefather said "I am not worthy from all Your kindnesses" (Bereishis 32:11), to which the targum explains: "my merits have diminished due to all of Your favors and kindnesses."

SHEVAT 30

PROPER TRUST IN MATTERS OF EARNING A LIVELIHOOD
What we have explained for matters of life and death, also applies to the duty to pursue means for health, food, clothing, shelter, good habits and distancing from their opposite - (to engage in them) while firmly believing that the means to these things do not help at all in attaining them, without the decree of the Creator. Then, when a farmer must plow his field, clear it from weeds, and to sow it, and water it, when rainwater is not available, let him trust in the Creator to make it fertile, and to protect it from plagues, to increase and to bless the crops. And it is not proper to leave the land unworked and unsowed and to trust G-d and rely on His decree that it will grow fruit without being sown first.

ADAR 1 (For a leap year, repeat each day for two days)

Matanas Chelko: This is a powerful illustration from farmers. For everyone can see that the farmer cannot claim it was all his own making, for even after all the work of plowing, sowing, etc., he must still rely on G-d for rain, and that the rain be not too much and not too little. This is a tremendous illustration on the ways of faith from which one can apply to all matters.

ADAR 2

Translator: Another illustration: The Jews in the Sinai desert received manna daily for 40 years. Based on a person's spiritual level, the manna would arrive daily either far away in the desert or directly at his doorstep.

Thus even though the person was forced to exert himself to search in the desert, nevertheless, he knew that the portion he eventually found as well as the amount of exertion he had to do was pre-decreed for him from the beginning. So too, a person must exert himself according to what he needs, but at the same time, he must realize that the amount he eventually earns was designated for him by G-d from the beginning and that his exertion did not increase or decrease this amount - Translator)

ADAR 3

And likewise workers, merchants, and contractors are under a duty to pursue their livelihood while trusting in G-d that their livelihood is in His hands and under His control, that He guarantees to provide a man (as the verse "who gives sustenance to all flesh" - PL) and fully provides for him through whatever means He wishes. One should not think that the means can benefit or harm him in the least.

ADAR 4

If one's livelihood comes through one of the means he worked on, it is proper for him not to trust in this source, rejoice in it, intensify in it, and turn his heart to it, because this will weaken his trust in the Al-mighty. It is improper to think that this source will be more beneficial to him than what was pre-decreed from the Creator. He should not rejoice for having pursued and engaged in it. Rather, he should thank the Creator who provided for him after his labor, and that He did not make his work and struggle result in nothing, as written "If you eat the toil of your hands, you are praiseworthy, and it is good for you" (Tehillim 128:2).

ADAR 5

(*Matanas Chelko*: hence, the labor and the livelihood are two unconnected things. The labor is a kind of tax payment, and if through this he receives his livelihood and eats, he is also under duty to thank G-d for the food.

Translator: I once asked a taxi driver in Israel if he makes good money driving. He corrected me saying "the taxi driving is my tikun, and the money is from G-d. The two are not connected. They're separate things."

A pious man once said: "I am amazed of he who gives to another what the Creator decreed for the latter, and afterwards reminds the latter of the favor he did for him, and seeks to be thanked for this. And I am even more amazed by one who receives his livelihood from another who is forced to provide for him and then submits himself before him, pleases him and praises him."

ADAR 6

(*Marpe Lenefesh*: i.e. the recipient does not give praise and thanks to G-d who provided his livelihood through the donor, and appointed the donor as a caretaker of him. Rather, he submits only to the donor, and flatters him as if the donor provided him of his own...and likewise he wrote later on "if only they realized that no human being has the power to give or prevent anything except to he who the Creator decreed - they would not hope to anyone other than Him, etc". And he wrote this again several times. This seems to be a contradiction (since the donor had free will whether or not to give to him). The answer to this is that the completion of something is not in man's hands, rather, only the free will and resolve to do it, and G-d is the one who brings all things to completion . . .

ADAR 7

Therefore this is the explanation here - a man is under a duty to choose and resolve to separate from his money according to his generosity in order to give charity to the poor or to this poor man, and when the Creator desires to provide for this poor man through this donor, he arranges that they meet in one place and this donor will give to this poor man, and sometimes to another according to His wisdom. Or if the man is not good before Him, G-d will make him stumble with bad people or other mishaps. But the main thing is that one tries to do the duty that is placed on him - to give charity and to do kindness. And if he is prevented, then he did his side and will receive full reward from G-d. Likewise for all mitzvot and all acts in the world as he will explain later on... And with this you will understand what he wrote earlier in the beginning of chapter 3: "and all mercy and compassion that a man is shown from anyone besides G-d is really derived from G-d's mercy and compassion", see there. That G-d puts in the heart of this one to give to that one. With this introduction many difficult things are clear in the details of G-d's guidance of His world and through this you will understand most of this gate, with G-d's help.

ADAR 8

Rabbi Yaakov Emden: Nevertheless, it is certainly a duty to thank and praise one's benefactor and not to think that one is exempt since the good came from G-d.... see there in Masoret Yisrael edition for more

Matanas Chelko: the recipient should not feel inferior and smaller thereby submitting himself towards the rich man and speak to him like a poor man...)

ADAR 9

If one's livelihood fails to come through the means he has worked on, it is possible that the money allocated to him for the day has already reached his hands (and that he doesn't realize it - PL) or that it will come through other means.

However the case, it is proper for him to engage in the means of earning a livelihood and not to be lax in pursuing after them, provided they are suited to his traits and physical abilities, as I previously explained. And all the while, he should trust in G-d, that He will not abandon him (in providing his needs - PL), neglect him (regarding his physical health - PL), or ignore him (in whatever trouble befalls him - PL) as written "The L-ord is good, a stronghold on a day of trouble and knows (Rashi - the needs of) those who trust in Him" (Nachum 1:7)

(*Pas Lechem*: The first half teaches that G-d does not ignore his troubles while the second includes the other two matters, that G-d does not abandon him nor neglect him)

ADAR 10

PROPER TRUST IN MATTERS OF HEALTH AND SICKNESS

Similarly, we will say regarding health and sickness. A man is placed under a duty to trust in the Creator in this, while working on maintaining his health according to the means whose nature promotes this, and to fight sickness according to the customary ways, as the Creator commanded "and he shall surely heal him" (shmos 21:19). All of this, without trusting in the means of health or illness that they could help or hurt without the permission of the Creator.

And when one puts his trust in the Creator, He will heal him with or without a means, as written "He sends His word and heals them" (Tehillim 107:20).

ADAR 11

(*Pas Lechem*: From this verse we see that it is really His word, namely, His decree that heals - not the means.

Translator: Rabbi Avigdor Miller would say that in ancient times bloodletting was a popular medical procedure. Today it is neither accepted nor effective. This does not mean that it was not effective back then. Actually it was. The science of the times had logical reasons why it should work, and people believed in those reasons, therefore G-d healed them through the bloodletting. So too today, medical technology makes us believe certain medicines and medical procedures should work, and therefore G-d heals us through those.)

ADAR 12

It is even possible that He will heal him through something that is normally very harmful, as you know from the story of Elisha and the bad water, that he healed their damaging properties with salt (Melachim II 2:19), and similarly "And G-d showed him a tree and he tossed it into the waters [and the waters became sweet]" (Shmos 15:25), And the midrash tanchuma there explains that this was a bitter, oleander tree. Another example, "let him smear crushed figs on the boils, and he will heal" (Yeshaya 38:21) (and figs normally damage even healthy flesh - *PL*). And you already know of what happened to the pious king Asa when he trusted in the doctors, and removed his trust in G-d regarding his illness, the sharp rebuke he received for this (i.e. because he did not pray to be healed). And the verse says: "For He brings pain and binds it; He wounds, and His hands heal." (Iyov 5:18).

ADAR 13

SECOND CATEGORY - POSSESSIONS AND MEANS OF EARNING A LIVELIHOOD

(Previously he spoke on trusting in the livelihood itself, that certainly it will come through whatever means employed. Now he will speak on proper trust when engaging in the means themselves. understand this. - *PL*)

For the second category, the matters of man's possessions, means of financial gain in his various pursuits, whether in commerce, skilled trades, peddling, business management, official appointments, property rentals, banking, work of kings, treasurers, contracting, writing work, other types of work, going to faraway deserts and seas, and other similar things, from what people toil in to amass money, and increase the superfluous. The proper way of trust in the Al-mighty for this is to engage in the means which G-d has made available to him to the extent necessary for his maintenance and sufficient for his needs of this world (i.e. his minimum necessary needs only - *TL*).

ADAR 14

And if the Creator will decree for him more than this, it will come to him without trouble or exertion, provided he trusts in the Al-mighty for it and does not excessively pursue the means nor inwardly trust in them in his heart.

And if the Creator has not decreed for him more than his sustenance, even if all those in heaven and earth were to try to increase it, they would not be capable by any way nor by any means. And when one trusts in G-d, he will find peace of mind and tranquility of spirit, confident that

G-d will not give over his portion to someone else, nor send it to him earlier or later than the time He decreed for it.

ADAR 15

(*Pas Lechem*: A man's nature is to desire to indulge a bit in luxuries beyond his subsistence needs. Only that, he should not squander his time in occupying himself in this, since it is not essential. Rather, let one trust in G-d that he will find his desire also in this [i.e. in living at subsistence level], because "He will fulfill the desire of them that fear him" Tehillim 119:15)

ADAR 16

PROPER TRUST FOR THE WEALTHY

Sometimes the Creator directs the livelihood of many men through one man. This is in order to test that man whether he will serve G-d or rebel against Him. And G-d will place this to be among the man's most difficult tests and sources of temptation. For example, a king who provides for his army and servants, or princes, ministers of the king, important officials, all of who are surrounded with groups of their servants, attendants, officers, wives, and relatives. They exert themselves to obtain money for those dependents through all types of means, regardless whether they are good or bad means.

ADAR 17

(*Pas Lechem*: the Creator will make this thing a strong means to test him. A man is tested in this more than any other test, because the magnitude of a test is measured by the greatness of the temptation of the evil inclination, and certainly the temptation of the evil inclination in this is exceedingly strong, to close one's hand from providing for the poor and destitute, and to not be concerned about providing their needs, thereby diminishing his wealth, as written in Devarim 15:9: "Guard yourself lest there be in your heart", and this is what he meant by "tests and sources of temptation". And likewise "wives and relatives" *is referring to all men* [i.e. every man is master of his household and provides for his wife, children, elderly parents, etc.])

ADAR 18

And the foolish among them will err on three fronts.

(1) In acquiring money, he will use bad and degrading means to take what the Creator has decreed he will take. And if he had sought after his wealth with proper means, he would have reached his desire, and both his religious and secular affairs would have succeeded, and he would not have received any less from what the Creator had decreed for him.

ADAR 19

(2) He thinks that all the money that reaches him is for his own support. He does not understand that the money consists of three parts: one part, for the food he needs for his own body alone, and this is something G-d assures to all living creatures to the end of its days. The second part, for the food of others, such as his wife, children, servants, employees, and the like. This (extra money) is not assured by G-d to all people (that his business will prosper to the extent that his wife and children won't themselves need to engage in some means - PL), but rather only to a select few, and under special conditions, and this opportunity presents itself at certain times but not at others, according to the rulings of the Creator's system of kindness and justice. Third, money to hold on to. This is money which has no benefit for the man. The man guards it and accumulates it until he bequeaths it to another or that he loses it. The foolish person thinks that all the money decreed for him by the Creator is for his own sustenance and physical maintenance, and so he eagerly pursues it and exerts much effort to acquire it; and it is possible that he is amassing wealth for his widow's next husband, his stepson, or for his greatest enemy.

ADAR 20

(3) The third error is that he provides money to those (dependents) as the Creator decreed this would happen through him, but he reminds them of his favors as if he were the one who provided for them and did them a kindness, and he expects them to thank and praise him richly, and that they serve him due to them, and he becomes arrogant, haughty, and inflated of heart. He neglects to thank G-d for them (that G-d appointed him as a means to bestow good on others whereby he would be an agent for this and receive reward for it - TL). He thinks that if he did not give this money to them, it would remain by him, and that if he did not provide for them they would not have any money. But really, he is the poor man, who will toil for nothing in this world and will lose his reward in the next world.

ADAR 21

(*Marpe Lenefesh*: One can explain this to also be referring to one who realizes that it is the decree of G-d that these be provided through him, but he thinks that if there were not a decree that he provide for the poor, the abundant money would remain by him. But he errs in his outlook, because a rich man is like a funnel, if it pours down below, then we pour more up above. But if it is clogged below, we stop pouring above.)

The wise man, however, conducts himself in these three ways according to what will be proper for his religious and secular pursuits.

ADAR 22

(*Marpe Lenefesh*: i.e. He acquires money in good and honest ways, and he is not in a rush to become rich. And if he does have wealth, he will distribute it to all those who it is fitting to distribute to. He is easy-going (vatran) with his money. If he gives he is not arrogant on account of this. He doesn't desire to be praised for it, and he gives praises and thanks to G-d who appointed him as a caretaker of many people)

And his trust in what is in G-d's hands is greater than his trust in what is in his own hands because he does not know if the money in his hand is meant for his own benefit or is merely placed in his care. And thus he will gain honor in this world and receive rich reward in Olam Haba (afterlife), as written in the psalm (112) "Haleluy-a praiseworthy is the man who fears G-d." until the end of it.

ADAR 23

(*Matanas Chelko*: The author did not discuss how much money one should leave for himself and did not mention the halachos (laws) we find in the shulchan aruch on this matter. In truth this is one of the greatest trials of a rich person. For he does not know exactly how much he must give to tzedaka and how much to keep for himself.... What the Sages said of the amount of chumash (one fifth), this was said regarding every person. For even one who is not rich can give this amount. Likewise, what they wrote "one who distributes his money should not distribute more than one fifth" (Kesuvos 50a), refers only to average people. But one who is very rich, certainly he was not given money so that it sits in the bank, but rather to distribute it to the poor. The Gedolim have said that all the segulos of tzedaka such as "tzedaka saves from death" or that it "atones for one's sins" - this is only after one has already given a fifth. For, a fifth is a duty placed on every person. Therefore, only that which one gives with mesirus nefesh (self-sacrifice) has these special merits and segulas. The amount to save in the bank for a time of need depends on each person and what is the proper amount according to the way of the world... [see there are length].

ADAR 24

WHY THE MASSES ARE FORCED TO WORK ENORMOUSLY

There are some classes of people who busy themselves in acquiring money and amassing wealth only for the love of being honored by other people, and to make a name for themselves, and no amount of money is ever enough for them. This is due to their ignorance of what will bring real honor in this world and in the next. The reason they make this error is because they see the masses honoring the wealthy, but really, this honor is motivated by a desire for what they possess and to try to get some of what is in their hands.

ADAR 25

(*Pas Lechem*: His intent is that there are two causes why the masses honor the wealthy. (1) Because they are hoping, seeking, and longing all of their days to attain that which will bring them wealth, and since these things are very important in their thoughts, they also regard the wealthy as important. (2) Because the masses hope to draw from their hands and benefit from them, therefore they flatter them. [similarly for other things which the masses honor such as popularity, power, etc - translator])

If the masses reflected and understood that the wealthy do not have the capability nor the power either to give or to hold back to someone except to whom the Creator decreed, they would not hope to anyone besides G-d.

ADAR 26

(*Marpe Lenefesh*: If it was decreed for this person that his money will not come from that person, then that rich person does not have the ability to give to him. Even though man has free will, the completion is not in man's hands, as written earlier. Likewise, the rich man cannot prevent this, if the Creator decreed the money will be his. G-d will arrange that the rich man will lose the money, or some other means that will cause the money to reach the hands of that person.)

Nor would they find anyone worthy of honor except for he who the Creator has distinguished with praiseworthy qualities, for which he is worthy of the Creator's honor, as written "Those who honor Me, I will honor" (Shmuel I 2:30).

ADAR 27

(*Pas Lechem*: i.e. he who is worthy of the Creator's honor due to his praiseworthy traits. And since man's worth is extremely puny to be conceivably worthy of the Creator's honor, he brought a proof from the verse "Those who honor Me, I will honor". [note: simultaneously, the verse also teaches on what will bring true honor - translator])

And because the masses, in honoring the wealthy, were foolish in the causes of real honor, the Creator added to their foolishness in the causes of their requests [for money] (that they constantly seek to become rich - *TL*). And so they fell into great effort and tremendous toiling all of their days, while they abandoned that which is their duty to busy themselves with and to which they should hasten, namely, fulfilling their duties to the Creator, and to thank Him for the good He bestows on them, whereby their desire (for honor - *TL*) would have undoubtedly been closer to them in this way, as written "long life is in its right, in its left wealth and honor" (Mishlei 3:16), and "wealth and honor is from You" (Divrei Hayamim 29:12).

ADAR 28

There exists among those who seek wealth, one who reaches all his heart's desire through the means we mentioned (commerce, skilled trade, etc), to another it came through an inheritance or the like, and he thinks it is due to the means, and without them, he would not have received anything, and he praises the means and not their Cause (i.e. the Creator who orchestrates all the means - *PL*).

How similar is he to a man in the desert, thirst weighing on him, who finds unclean water in a pit, and becomes full of joy. He quenches his thirst from them. And afterwards, he moves a bit further, and finds a well of pure water. He regrets on what he did previously, of drinking and quenching his thirst from the unpure water.

ADAR 29

Similarly, for the man who became wealthy through a certain means. If this means would have failed, he would have attained it through other means, as we explained earlier and as the verse says: "nothing can prevent G-d from saving, whether through many or through few" (Shmuel I 14:6).

(*Pas Lechem*: If so, all of the bitter and wearying toil he exerted himself in this means was for nothing, because it could have come to him through a light and easy business. Alternative explanation: One who acquired wealth though distasteful means could have employed honest means and attained the same amount - *ML*)

NISSAN 1

PROPER TRUST IN TIGHT FINANCIAL TIMES

And the proper way for one who trusts in G-d, when his livelihood is withheld for some day is to say in one's heart: "He who took me out (from the womb) to this world at a fixed time and moment, and did not take me out to it earlier or later, He is the One who is withholding my livelihood for a fixed time and a fixed day, because He knows what is good for me."

NISSAN 2

Likewise, when one's livelihood comes very exactly, no more than the amount for basic food, it is proper for one to reflect in his heart and tell himself: "He who prepared my sustenance at my mother's breast, in my beginning, according to my need, and what was sufficient for me day by day, until He replaced it for me with something better, and (the milk's) coming exactly did not damage me at all, so too I will not be damaged now at all, by His sending me my food in the limited, exact amount, until the end of my days.

NISSAN 3

He will be rewarded for this, as the Creator told our ancestors in the (Sinai) desert, whose matter was in this way: "The people shall go out each day and gather what they need for the day" (Shemos 16:4), and "go and call out to the ears of Jerusalem and say 'I remember for you the kindness of your youth, the love of your betrothal, when you followed Me in the wilderness, in a land that was not sown'" (Yirmiyahu 2:2).

NISSAN 4

(*Tov Halevanon*: The sages expounded on the reason - so that a man will always hope to G-d day by day that He will provide his daily bread [and his trust in Him will be strengthened])

Likewise, if one's livelihood comes through one means but not through any other means (that he would have preferred - *PL*), or in one place and not in any other place, or through one person and not through any other person, let one say in his heart: "He who created me in a certain form, shape, characteristics, and measure and not through any other, for my purpose and benefit, He has chosen that my livelihood come through ways suitable to my purpose and benefit, and not through any other ways." And, "He who brought me into this world at a fixed time, and through two specific people, and not through other people of the world, He has chosen for me my livelihood from a specific place and through a specific person, He made him the means to my livelihood for my benefit", as written "G-d is righteous in all His ways" (Tehillim 145:17).

NISSAN 5

THIRD CATEGORY - SOCIAL MATTERS

The explanation of the third category, matters of one's wife, children, household members, relatives, friends, enemies, acquaintances, those higher or lower than him among the various classes of people, the proper ways of trust in G-d is as follows. A man is necessarily in either one of two situations: either he is a stranger or he is among his family and relatives.

NISSAN 6

PROPER TRUST FOR ONE LIVING ALONE

If he is a stranger, let his companionship be with G-d during his time of loneliness, and trust in Him during his period of being a stranger. And let him contemplate that the soul is also a stranger in this world, and that all people are like strangers here, as the verse says "because you are strangers and temporary residents with Me" (Vayikra 25:23). And let him reflect in his heart that all those who have relatives here, in a short time, will be left a solitary stranger. Neither relative nor son will be able to help him, and none of them will be with him. (see Gate 8 ch.3 way #30 for more on this - Translator)

NISSAN 7

(*Marpe Lenefesh*: i.e. he should reflect in his heart that it is for his benefit that he has no relatives or friends that he can enjoy with, and it is good for him so that he makes his companionship with G-d and places his trust in Him alone since he has no one else to trust due to his being a stranger. Furthermore, all of us are strangers because the soul, which is of divine origin, is in this world like a stranger in a strange land. And in truth, the essence of man is his soul... and further in a short while he will leave this world, and certainly then he will lay there alone without relative or savior.

NISSAN 8

Tov Halevanon: One surrounded by family will benefit from this for only a short time, since either he will have a long life and will see the death of his children and relatives and will be left lonely and in painful solitude or if he will not live a long life, what need does he have for relatives? And this is worse than the first case.)

NISSAN 9

And afterwards, let him consider that as a stranger, he is freed from the heavy burden of maintaining relatives and fulfilling his duties towards them. He should consider this to be one of the kindnesses of the Creator towards him, because if he needed to pursue a livelihood for providing his material needs, his exertion would be lighter without a wife and children, and their absence is peace of mind for him and it is good. And if he is concerned about his interests in the next world, his mind will undoubtedly be clearer and freer when he is alone.

NISSAN 10

And therefore the ascetics would leave their relatives and homes and go to the mountains, in order to focus their hearts in the service of G-d. Likewise, the prophets, during the era of prophecy, would leave their homes and live in solitude to fulfill their duties to the Creator, as you know from the story of Eliyahu's meeting with Elisha, which it is said of Elisha "twelve pairs of oxen were before him, and he was with the twelfth" (Melachim I 19:19). And as soon as Eliyahu hinted to him a small hint (to come with him), he understood him and said "Let me, please, kiss my father and my mother, and I will go with you", and afterwards, "and he went after Eliyahu and ministered to him".

NISSAN 11

(*Tov Halevanon:* he left behind all of his work and separated from his mother, father, and all of his relatives and went after Eliyahu.

note: such extreme asceticism is not in accordance with the teachings of Judaism and only sanctioned when practiced by such exceptional characters as Eliyahu the prophet - Rabbi Moses Hyamson,*zt"l* [see also Gate#9])

NISSAN 12

It is said about one of the ascetics, who traveled to a country to teach its inhabitants the service of G-d. He found them all dressed in the same manner and adorned in the same way. Their graves were near their homes, and he did not see among them any women. He asked them about this and they answered him: "the reason we are all dressed alike is so that there's no noticeable difference between a rich man and a poor man, and the rich man will not come to arrogance for his wealth, and the poor man will not be embarrassed of his poverty, and so that our matter above the earth should be in our eyes like our matter below the earth (i.e. in the grave where everyone is dressed the same way - *TL*). It is said of one of the kings that he would mix with his servants, and there was no noticeable difference between him and them, because he would conduct himself in the way of humility in his dress and adornments.

NISSAN 13

(Rav Yaakov Emden: i.e. the king would dress like them "so that his heart will not be haughty over his brothers" (Devarim 17:20), this is the way of the Torah provided he does not become frivolous before them and that his fear is over them.)

As to the reason why the graves of our dead are near our homes, they said, this is so that we encounter them and prepare ourselves for our deaths, and that we prepare our provisions for the afterlife. As to your noticing that we separated ourselves from women and children, know that we prepared for them a village near here. When one of us needs something from them, he goes to them and after obtaining his wants, returns to us. This we did because we saw how much distraction of the heart, great loss, and great exertion and strain there was when they were among us, and the great peace of mind from all of this, in separating from them, to focus on matters of the afterlife and to be repulsed by matters of this world. And their words found favor in the eyes of the ascetic, and he blessed them and commended them on their matters.

NISSAN 14

(*Pas Lechem*: He specified 4 points (distraction of the heart, great loss, great exertion and strain), the first two is the harm from desiring them, namely, when they are near, the eye sees them and the heart desires and he becomes always distracted from them, on this he wrote "distraction of the heart". And inevitably the constant desire will bring him to habitually have marital relations with them always. This causes great loss to a man's strength and health as the Rambam wrote in Hilchos Deos 4:19, on this he wrote "great loss". The latter two are the damages which come from providing for their needs (ex.big house). That when they are near, they persuade their husbands and act playfully and seek luxuries which brings to two harmful things, namely, "great exertion" in exerting oneself to provide for their needs and "strain" of the mind in the mental distraction of providing their needs. And the Sages already said (Sotah 47a): "yetzer, child, and woman, let one's left hand push away while the right hand draws near".

NISSAN 15

Afterwards, he wrote: "to focus on matters of the afterlife and to be repulsed by matters of this world", because in distancing from them, the heart is free to think on matters of the afterlife, and also through being repulsed by this powerful lust, the heart of a man will habituate in being repulsed by the other lusts of this world.)

NISSAN 16

PROPER TRUST FOR ONE'S WIFE RELATIVES, FRIENDS, AND ENEMIES

If the one who trusts in G-d has a wife, relatives, friends, enemies, let him trust in G-d to be saved from them.

THINK GOOD AND IT WILL BE GOOD   201

(*Tov Halevanon*: i.e. to be saved from their burdens, namely, all those things mentioned above that a stranger is saved from.

NISSAN 17

Marpe Lenefesh: To be saved from them by fulfilling his duties towards them.

Tov Halevanon: Here he added the term "enemies", something he did not mention earlier regarding the man who is solitary or a stranger, because this is the normal way of the world, that the solitary man or the stranger/foreigner due to little worldly association and his low stature has no enemies, unlike the man with a wife, sons, relatives, friends, who has much association in the world and develops enemies due to jealousy. . .)

NISSAN 18

He should strive to fulfill his duties to them (provide their necessities - *PL*), to do their wishes (to also provide them with a bit more than the necessities like the nature of the world - *PL*), to be wholehearted with them (to provide their needs willingly not like one forced to do so - *PL*). He should refrain from causing any harm to them, try to promote what is good for them. He should deal faithfully towards them in all matters, and teach them the ways that will be beneficial for them in their religious matters and the secular ways [which will benefit them] in the service of the Creator, as written (Vayikra 19:18) "you shall love your neighbor as yourself..", and "do not hate your brother in your heart" (ibid). Do not do this out of hope for future benefits from them or to pay them back for past benefits. Nor should you do this out of love of being honored or praised by them, or out of desire to rule over them - but rather with the sole motive to fulfill the commandment of the Creator, and to guard His covenant and precepts over them. (i.e. to see to it that they guard the covenant of G-d and His commandments - *TL*)

NISSAN 19

The person, whose motive in fulfilling their wishes is one of the [reprehensible] motives we mentioned above, will not obtain what he wants from them in this world. He will tire himself for nothing, and will lose his reward in the afterlife (since his intent was not l'shem shamayim - *PL*). But if his sole motive is to serve G-d, the Al-mighty will help them to make a return to him in this world, and G-d will place his praise in their mouths and they will hold him in high esteem, and he will reach the great reward in Olam Haba (afterlife), as the Al-mighty said to Shlomo "also what you did not ask, I will give you, also wealth and honor" (Melachim 3:13).

NISSAN 20

(*Pas Lechem*: Corresponding to "do not do this out of hope for future benefits, etc.", he wrote: "the Al-mighty will help them to make a return to him".

Corresponding to "Nor should you do this out of love of being honored or praised by them", he wrote: "and G-d will place his praise in their mouths".

Corresponding to "(nor should you do this) out of desire to rule over them", he wrote: "and they will hold him in high esteem", that he will seem great and awe-inspiring in their eyes and automatically they will do whatever he says.

Therefore without intending to, indirectly, he attained all of their benefits in this world, similar to what our sages said (Nedarim 62a): "study the Torah out of love, and in the end, the honor will come". And his primary reward will be in Olam Haba)

NISSAN 21

PROPER TRUST FOR BENEFITING FROM OTHERS

But the ways of trust in G-d in dealing with those above him or below him in the various classes of men is as follows. The proper way to act when one needs to request some benefit of someone above or below him is to trust in G-d, and to consider them as means of obtaining what he needs, just like one makes the working and sowing of the land a means of obtaining his food. If G-d wishes to support him through it, He will make the seeds sprout, grow, and multiply, and one does not thank the land for this, but rather, he thanks the Creator alone. And if the Al-mighty will not desire to supply him through it, the land will not produce, or it will produce but be struck by damaging things, and one does not blame the land.

NISSAN 22

So too, when he seeks something from one of them, it should be equal in his eyes whether the person he asked is weak or strong, and he should trust in G-d for its completion.

(*Pas Lechem*: i.e. that he does not trust in his heart more that his request will be completed if he asked a strong person than if he had asked a weak person since he believes that the man is only an intermediary and that G-d is the one actually doing it.)

NISSAN 23

And if it was completed through one of them, let him thank the Creator who fulfilled his desire, and thank the person through whom it was done, for his good will towards him, and that the Creator brought his benefit through him, and it is known that the Creator does not bring good except through the tzadikim (righteous), and it is rare that He brings a loss through them, as the sages said "merit occurs through the meritorious and guilt through the guilty" (Bava Basra 119b), and the verse "No wrong shall be caused for the righteous" (Mishlei 12:21 - Rashi "No sin will chance before him inadvertently").

NISSAN 24

(*Tov Halevanon*: i.e. perhaps you will say, if the matter is so (that G-d is doing it and the person is only an intermediary) why should I thank a person who benefits me, since he is forced by G-d and does good to me without choice due to the decree of G-d? (Answer:) you are obligated to thank him nevertheless since he is the one G-d chose to cause the good and G-d brings good through the righteous and faithful before Him...)

And if his request is not accomplished through them, one should not blame them, and not consider it due to their being lax in it, rather he should thank the Al-mighty who chose what is best for him in this, and praise them according to his knowledge of their efforts to fulfill his will, even though the matter was not completed according to his and their desire. Similarly, one should act with his acquaintances and friends, his business associates, employees and partners.

NISSAN 25

If someone higher or lower than himself requests from him to do something for them, he should wholeheartedly use every means to do it, and apply his mind to do the matter, provided one is capable of doing it and that the person who requested it is worthy that he exerts himself on his behalf (but if the person is wicked, refrain from it as he wrote in the end of gate #3 - *ML*). And after this, he should trust in the Al-mighty for its completion. If G-d completes it through him, and makes him the cause for benefiting another, he should thank G-d for this privilege. If G-d withholds this from him, and he is not capable of doing it, he should not blame himself, and he should inform the person that he was not lax in doing it, provided that he indeed exerted himself to do it.

NISSAN 26

PROPER TRUST FOR DEALING WITH ENEMIES

But for one's enemies, those jealous of him, those who seek to harm him, he should trust in G-d regarding their matters. He should bear their contempt, and should not treat them back in the same way.

(*Marpe Lenefesh*: As the sages said (Yoma 23a see rashi Rosh Hashana 17a): "he who forgoes his honor when it is slighted will merit that all his transgressions be forgiven")

NISSAN 27

Rather he should pay them back with kindness, and to try to benefit them as much as he possibly can, and to remember in his heart that only G-d has the ability to benefit or harm him.

(*Translator*: I once heard a lecture by Rabbi Nissan Kaplan of the Mir Yeshiva where he said that this method is the most powerful way to work on trust. In order to internalize trust, one must do physical actions in this world, namely paying back evil with good. He says that getting into the habit of doing this, is what builds trust in the most effective way.

NISSAN 28

If his enemy becomes a means to harm him, he should judge them favorably and suspect that it is due to himself or his past deeds from his bad start in life towards G-d. He should plead to the Al-mighty and seek from Him to atone for his sins, and then his enemies will become his friends, as the wise man said "when G-d is pleased with a man's way, even his enemies will make peace with him" (Mishlei 16:7).

NISSAN 29

(*Matanas Chelko*: the main trust in these matters is as the Chazon Ish wrote: "to abstain doing [bad] things to those who did bad to him" (Emuna U'Bitachon 2:2). For the primary denial of trust is to do [bad] against one who did bad to him or vexed him, as written in the Sefer Hachinuch regarding the commandment not to exact revenge which is one of the roots of faith. Therefore, the author wrote that it is included in the commandment of "love your fellow as yourself". For denial of G-d is recognized and manifest when one exacts revenge on someone who did bad to him. He forgets the great principle of the Ramban (end of parsha Bo): "if he does G-d's commandments, G-d will reward him with success, but if he transgresses them, G-d will afflict him with punishments - everything is from divine decree."

NISSAN 30

Rabbi Yaakov Emden, *zt"l*: This matter requires great investigation. We find many verses supporting this such as "Do not say: 'I will repay evil'; but wait on the L-ord, and He shall save you" (Mishlei 20:22), "If your enemy is hungry, give him bread to eat; and if he is thirsty, give him water to drink" (ibid 25:21). Likewise, we find by King David especially with Saul in the cave and with his garment, and like Saul said to him (Shmuel 24:19): "And you have shown today how you have dealt well with me, how the L-rd delivered me into your hand, and you did not kill me; For when a man finds his enemy, does he send him away safely? And may the L-rd repay you with goodness for what you have done to me on this day". And in Tehillim (35:13) "But as for me, when they (my enemies) were ill, my clothing was sackcloth", and (ibid 38:14) "Thus I was as a man that hears not, and in whose mouth are no reproofs (when others were mocking me)", and (ibid 37:7) "Be silent before the L-ord, and wait patiently for him: fret not yourself because of him who prospers in his way, because of the man who brings wicked devices to pass", and (ibid 62:5) "My soul, wait you only upon G-d; for my expectation is from Him", and many more like this.

IYAR 1

On the other hand, we find many verses which contradict this, especially by King David for he sought to exact furious revenge from Naval merely for refraining from doing good to him. Likewise, he pleaded G-d to exact revenge on his enemies, as he said: (ibid 41:11) "be gracious to me and raise me up, so that I may repay them", and (ibid 28:4) "Give them according to their deeds and according to the evil of their endeavors", and he complained (119:84) "How many are Your servant's days? When will You execute justice upon my pursuers?", and many more like this. He even praised revenge in saying: (58:11) "The righteous shall rejoice when he sees the vengeance".

IYAR 2

And his overlooking of Shimi in saying (Shmuel II 16:10) "G-d told him to curse" is not an indication since he was then in great troubles, and he humbled himself and accepted the humiliation as an atonement, thereby bearing the pain in exchange for the punishment fitting for him for the event with Batsheva. And in the end when Shimi sought forgiveness it was fitting for him to pardon him, due to the need of the time and also since one who admits and repents is treated with mercy (by G-d). Even so, David guarded the matter and paid him back through his son Shlomo. And it does not appear correct to say that whenever scripture praises revenge it is referring to the gentile enemies of G-d and His people (who come to wage war, etc.). Likewise, Yirmiyahu pleaded for revenge from the men of Anatot, who were Kohanim of his own family, in saying (Yirmiyahu 15:15) "avenge me of my perse-cutors; take me not away in your longsuffering". We must answer all this by saying that everything varies according to the severity of the matter and the greatness of the wrongdoing. [translator - and the author here is speaking about most cases which are usually petty matters]) Afterwards, he wrote: "He should plead to the Al-mighty and seek from Him to atone for his sins", similar to what David did in the event with Shimi, then "his enemies will become his friends" as what happened with Yaakov and Esav or the tribes with Yosef, and obviously with Shimi.

IYAR 3

FOURTH CATEGORY - Duties of the heart and limbs which don't affect others

PROPER TRUST IN THE FREE WILL TO SERVE G-d

The explanation of the fourth category, matters of duties of the heart and of the limbs which only benefit or harm oneself, for example, fasting, praying, dwelling in a sukka, taking a lulav, wearing tzitzis, observing the sabbath and the holidays, refraining from sins. This category also includes all of the duties of the heart since their performance does not affect others, and whose benefit or harm is limited only to oneself and is not shared by others. The proper way of trust in the Al-mighty in all of these, I will explain, and I ask the Al-mighty to teach me the truth, in His mercy.

IYAR 4

(*Pas Lechem*: In his examples, he first wrote "fasting" and "praying", since these mitzvos are logical, and were practiced before the giving of the Torah. Adam also fasted and prayed for his sin. Afterwards, he gave the examples of received mitzvot, and started with "sukka" since of all the mitzvot which apply today, it is the reminder of the clouds of glory in the desert (i.e. the exodus from Egypt), and lulav before tzitzis since it is preceded in the Torah... [see there for more details]

IYAR 5

Matanas Chelko: "I ask the Al-mighty..." it seems from the author's words that the following branch of trust is the most difficult to explain. Since we don't find that he uttered a prayer like this anywhere else in the book when explaining trust. Perhaps, it is because he is explaining the foundations of free will.)

IYAR 6

Any human action which is either service [of G-d] or sin can only take place if three factors occur. (1) the choice in heart and mind (i.e. a thought that it is fitting to do this thing - *ML*). (2) The intent and resolve to do what one chose. (3) The endeavoring to complete the act with one's physical limbs and to bring it into actuality.

IYAR 7

[Of these three factors,] two are not beyond our control, namely, (1) the choice of service or sin and (2) intent and resolve to carry out the choice. For these, trusting in G-d would be a mistake and a foolishness, because the Creator left free choice in our hands whether to serve Him or rebel against Him, as written "...[life and death I have set before you] and you shall choose life" (Devarim 30:19).

IYAR 8

(*Tov Halevanon*: If a man does not choose to pursue doing good and to refrain from sins, and instead trusts in G-d that He will prepare that good deeds will come his way and that G-d will distance from him the causes which lead to sins - this is a great mistake.)

But the bringing out of the act into actuality, He did not leave in our hands, but rather, made it depend on external means which sometimes are available and sometimes are not.

IYAR 9

(*Tov Halevanon*: For example, fasting and prayer, perhaps his body will be too weak, or sukka and lulav, perhaps he will not be able to obtain the sukka wood or the lulav... Or to give charity he needs to have money, and to encounter a proper poor man, etc. These external means are not in our free choice nor in the desire of G-d, but rather occur by encounter and opportunity. Only that for good deeds, there is a bit of siyata dishmaya (Divine assistance) as our sages taught (Shabbat 104a): "if one comes to purify himself, he is helped", but "if one comes to defile himself, he is given an opening" (ibid 104a), i.e. that the means are left to chance [Translator: not that G-d pushes him to defile himself but rather He withdraws His providence and leaves the person to chance as written in the introduction to this gate])

IYAR 10

If in choosing to serve the Al-mighty, one would trust in Him and think to himself: "I will not choose the service of G-d nor attempt to do any part of it until He chooses what is good for me of it" - he has already strayed from the straight path, and slipped his feet away from the proper way, because the Creator has already commanded us to choose in matters of His service, and to intend and make efforts towards it, with complete, wholehearted resolve for the sake of His great Name, and He has informed us that this is the proper way for our welfare in this world and in the next.

IYAR 11

(translator: His great Name refers to G-d as He manifests Himself to us. This is explained earlier in gate#1. We use the term "His Name" because G-d Himself is too beyond for us to even speak about.)

If the necessary means are available to us, so that we are capable of accomplishing the work in G-d's service which we chose to do, then we will receive the great reward for choosing it, for the intent and resolve to do it, and for completing the actions by our physical limbs. But if its accomplishment with the physical limbs is withheld from us, then we will receive reward for our choice and intent to do it, as we previously explained (in ch.3), and similarly for punishment of sins.

IYAR 12

(*Tov Halevanon*: And if you ask, how can this be a mitzvah if there was no act done yet? For this he said that the completion of the act is not essential to the mitzvah. Even though the mitzvah is not accomplished, he will receive reward from the choice and resolve to do it. But if the act is completed, the reward is greater, and likewise for punishments of sins.)

IYAR 13

The difference between the service of G-d and secular activities in this world, regarding trust in G-d, is as follows. For secular matters, it was not revealed to us which one of all the means is best and most beneficial for us nor the ways in which some course is more harmful and worse than other courses. We do not know which particular trade is best suited for us and most fitting for us in obtaining money, preserving health, and for general well-being. Nor do we know which business sector, which journey to undertake, or which other worldly endeavors will be successful if we engage in them.

IYAR 14

Therefore, it follows that we must put our trust in the Al-mighty that He will help us choose and carry out what is the best choice for us, provided that we apply ourselves (in the means which are fitting to attain this thing - *PL*) and that we plead to Him to arouse in our hearts to make the good and proper choice for ourselves. (then after these two things we can have in our hearts the trust mentioned - *PL*)

IYAR 15

(*Tov Halevanon*: Lest you ask: "if so, (that in the choice and resolve in the service of G-d, I must not trust in G-d) then also I must not trust in Him for matters of my livelihood. If so, why did the author say earlier that one should "submit himself to the course the Creator has decreed for him. . . ". On this he answered, that there is a big difference between the two. . .

Marpe Lenefesh: He gave a reason for this difference, namely, "it was not revealed to us which means is best...", and we don't know what to do, whether engaging in this trade or that business will be best for us or maybe in something else. And as the sages said (Berachos 33b) "everything is in the hands of Heaven (G-d), except for fear of Heaven")

IYAR 16

But the service of G-d is not like this, because G-d has already taught us the proper ways for it, commanded us to choose it, and gave us the ability to do it. If we then plead to Him in the choice we should make, and trust in Him that He will reveal to us what is good for us, we will be mistaken in our words (of prayer) and foolish in our trust, because He already taught us the proper way which will be good for us in this world and in the next, as written "G-d has commanded us to fulfill all of these statutes, to fear the L-ord, our G-d, for our good, all of our days". And regarding the reward in Olam Haba "we will be rewarded, if we are careful to observe" (Devarim 6:25).

IYAR 17

Furthermore, in secular matters, sometimes a good means changes to become a bad means and vice versa, while for service of G-d and transgression it is not so, matters of good and evil do not switch positions and never change.

(*Marpe Lenefesh*: Furthermore, how can we charge our mind to choose this business or this trade? Many times we find one person becomes rich through this business or trade and it is good for him, while another person does not profit at all from it and it is bad for him. If so, there is no way for us to know, rather only that which G-d puts in our hearts [to choose] is for our good. We find many verses which teach this such as (Mishlei 19:21) "There are many plans in a man's heart but the counsel of the L-ord - that shall stand", and "A man's heart plans his way: but the L-ord directs his steps" (Mishlei 16:9), and (ibid 20:24) "A man's steps are directed by the L-ord; how then can anyone understand his own way", and many more verses. But the actions in the service of G-d, that which is good, namely, fulfilling the commandments - this is good forever and never changes. Likewise the negative commandments are always bad. (another explanation)

IYAR 18

Tov Halevanon: That even though it appears good, it is possible that in the end it will lead to destruction, and the opposite, what appears evil and bitter in one's eyes may turn out in the end to be a great salvation. And like our sages said (Berachos 54a): "a person should bless on the bad, like he blesses on the good...")

IYAR 19

Hence, for religious acts, trust in G-d is proper only in the completion stage of the act. After choosing it wholeheartedly and faithfully and after the second stage of resolving and making efforts to do it with a pure heart , and with intent to do it for the sake of His great Name. With this, we are obligated to beseech Him to help us in it, and to teach us on it, as written "lead me in Your truth and teach me" (Tehillim 25:5), and "lead me in the path of Your commandments for I desired it" (Tehillim 119:35), and "I have chosen the way of truth, I have placed Your ordinances before me" (Tehillim 119:30), and "I have clung to Your testimonies; O L-ord; put me not to shame" (Tehillim 119:31), and "And take not the word of truth utterly out of my mouth; for I have hoped in Your judgments" (Tehillim 119:43).

IYAR 20

(*Rabbi Yaakov Emden*: "we are obligated to beseech Him to help us in it" also against the Yetzer (evil inclination) since (Kidushin 30b): "every day a person's evil inclination rises powerfully against him and seeks to slay him...Were it not for the Holy One blessed be He who helps him, a man would not be able [to contend] with it".

Pas Lechem: "after choosing it" means: to make a strong decision in his mind to not budge from it.

"wholeheartedly" means: not hesitantly.

"faithfully" means: choosing to do it without outside interests.

"with a pure heart" means: making efforts to do it without outside interests but rather "for the sake of His great Name".

IYAR 21

Tov Halevanon: "and with intent to do it for the sake of His great Name" - i.e. with all this, everything goes by the intent as our sages said (Nazir 23b): "a sin lishma (for the sake of G-d) is greater than a mitzvah that is not lishma

"to teach us on it" means to remove the veil of foolishness from our eyes and to strengthen our choice towards Him so that we may also know the ways of His service and by which way we should seek it.)

IYAR 22

All these verses demonstrate that the psalmist's service of G-d was his own choice. He prayed to G-d for two things only:

(1) To wholly devote his heart and to strengthen his choice in the service of G-d by distancing the distractions of the world from his heart and eyes, as he said "unite my heart to fear Your Name" (ibid 86:11) and "uncover my eyes that I may gaze at the wonders of Your Torah" (Tehillim 119:18), "turn away my eyes from beholding vanity" (ibid, 119:37), "incline my heart towards Your Torah and not to unjust gain" (ibid, 119:36), and many more.

IYAR 23

(*Pas Lechem*: "To wholly devote his heart" means: that his thoughts be only in G-d's service, not in the vain worldly desires and to strengthen his choice that it be enduringly set and firmly established

IYAR 24

Matanas Chelko: "to strengthen his choice" - prayer is to strengthen one's choice, i.e. before the act is completed. For example, one who has decided to go learn Torah in the synagogue. It is possible that he will be met with many distractions along the way. He may see some event or hear something, or some idea enters his mind. Each of these can potentially change his plan or weaken his resolve so he does not learn properly. Therefore, one must pray even after the decision and resolve in order to strengthen one's choice against the distractions. This is the important principle our teacher is teaching us - the purpose of prayer for spiritual things is to strengthen one's will.)

IYAR 25

(2) To strengthen him physically to be able to complete the acts of service of G-d. This is what is meant "lead me in the path of Your commandments" (119:35), "support me and I will be saved" (119:117), and many more like this. And I will explain in this gate which factors help and harm these things, and the proper path in it, with G-d's help.

IYAR 26

Matanas Chelko: To summarize, in matters that one does not know the proper path, and with what should he engage in, he should trust in G-d and pray to G-d that He will put in his heart the will of what to do and how to do it. On the other hand, for things which he already knows are proper and that he should do them, such as the study of Torah and performance of commandments, it is not proper to beseech G-d to give him the will to do them, but one can beseech G-d to strengthen his will in them, remove the obstructions from doing them, and ask Him that he merits to accomplish his good choice to fulfill them. A note on the matter of free will: Our teacher, included in his words the foundation of what is free will. Those who think free will means that a person can do what he wants - are mistaken. For behold, whether for physical or spiritual matters, one does not have the ability to do what he wants - for everything is done solely by divine decree. And even for doing a commandment or a sin - even though he wants to do it, it is possible that sometimes G-d will prevent him from doing it. Rather, free will means the will to do. A person has free will to choose what he wants to do. But to bring this thought to actuality is only in G-d's hands.

IYAR 27

If we go deeper in this, we will see that in truth, even the will to do something is not "free will". For behold, even an animal has the will to do what it wants. The animal wants to eat, sleep, kick - and does it. So too, a man wants to eat, sleep, etc. and does it [with G-d's consent]. If so, what is the difference between man and animal? The answer is that a man's free will is that he has the ability to refrain from doing what he wants. This is the difference between man and animal. The animal cannot refrain from doing what it wants. That which its nature wants to do, it does. It does not have the power to refrain from doing what it wants.

IYAR 28

But a man has been granted the ability to refrain from doing what his nature wants to do. If an animal lusts for something, it does not have the ability to restrain itself from fulfilling this lust and will. A human being on the other hand, can lust for physical things, but he has the power to refrain from fulfilling that will and lust which his nature pushes him to do. This is true free will - to form in his being, through his intellect, the will and desire to overcome his natural desires. The root of free will is fear of G-d. That which the Torah says "you shall choose life" (Deut. 30:19), which implies man has free will, this refers to the free will to acquire fear of G-d, to form in his being the will to fulfill the will of G-d, instead of pursuing the fulfillment of his natural will. This is free will. All the other things he does, stem from the tendency of his nature, just like an animal.

IYAR 29

Hence, it is possible for a man to spend his entire life without ever using his free will even once! Because free will is that which a person creates and forms by himself, through fear [of G-d] a new will to stand up against his animalistic and natural will, in order to fulfill the will of G-d. This is what our sages said (Berachos 33b): "everything is in the hands of Heaven except the fear of Heaven". For only through the power of fear of G-d that a person has, can he overcome and stand up against what was already decreed from Heaven, namely, his natural will and powers.)

SIVAN 1

FIFTH CATEGORY - *Duties of the limbs which affect others*

The fifth category, physical duties which affect others whether beneficially or harmfully, such as giving charity, maaser (tithes), teaching wisdom, commanding others to do good, warning them against evil, returning loans on faith, keeping a secret, speaking well of others, good activities, honoring parents, bringing the wicked back to G-d, instructing/advising others what will be good for them, pitying the poor and treating them with mercy, patiently bearing their contempt when arousing them to the service G-d, inspiring them to hope for the reward [in doing good], and instilling in them fear of punishment [for doing bad].

SIVAN 2

The proper way of trust in G-d for these, is for one to keep in mind all these and similar acts, resolve and make efforts to practice them, according to what we previously explained in the fourth category, regarding the duty when choosing (in these things -PL) to have the sole intent of drawing near to G-d alone; not for acquiring a name or honor among human beings, nor out of hope to receive reward from them, nor to try to rule over them. And afterwards having done his utmost - to trust in G-d in the completion of the acts which he undertook, according to what G-d wants from us (that we do His will, accordingly He will help us to complete what we undertook - *ML*).

SIVAN 3

In all of this, one should be careful to hide his deeds as much as possible from those who do not need to know. Because if it is kept hidden, the reward will be greater than if it becomes known. And that which he is unable to hide, let him remember the important general principle which we explained, namely, that neither benefit nor harm can come from the created things, except by permission of the Creator.

SIVAN 4

(*Pas Lechem*: If he cannot hide it and therefore, he is afraid lest the yetzer put in his heart ulterior motives, as before, then let him remember...
Manoach Halevavos: If he is unable to hide it, and he thinks he will be mocked by the mockers, or that he will be obstructed from completing it due to their hampering him, or that the poor man he benefits will receive shame, do not be concerned thereby refraining from the good

deed, rather "remember the important general principle...", and that it is not in the ability of others to obstruct him, or hamper him, and the mockery will not damage him. Likewise, the shame of the poor man will not harm him, with G-d's help.)

SIVAN 5

When the Creator completes a mitzvah (commandment) through him (that G-d benefits another person through him - *PL*), he should consider that this is a favor bestowed on him from the Creator. He should not rejoice if other people praise him for doing it, nor desire that they honor him for it, since this will bring him to become proud in his actions, and his purity of heart and motive towards G-d will be ruined, thereby his deeds will be spoiled and his reward for it will be lost. I will explain this later on in its proper Gate (in #6 the gate of submission - *PL*) with G-d's help.

SIVAN 6

(*Pas Lechem*: "his deeds will be spoiled" - G-d will not accept his deeds and also he will lose his reward.

Marpe Lenefesh: "his reward for it will be lost" since he had pleasure and praise for his deed, he already received his reward for this.)

SIVAN 7

SIXTH CATEGORY - *reward in this world and the next*

The explanation of the sixth category, regarding the reward in this world and the next which one merits for his good deeds in this world, is divided into two parts. (1) Reward in this world only. (2) Reward in the next world only. Sometimes one merits reward in both worlds for one act.

This was not explained to us clearly, however the Creator guaranteed to His people a general reward for general good behavior, but He did not specify the details of reward in this world for each act of service like He did regarding the punishments in this world for transgressions. For example, He specified which offences warrant capital punishment

by stoning (i.e. falling from a height), burning, decapitation, or strangu-
lation, or 40 lashes, death (through G-d's providence), premature death
(karet), monetary fines - two, four or five fold, monetary damages by ox,
pit, tooth, fire, damaging a man, embarrassing by seizing, slander, and
other offences. But regarding the reward and punishment in the afterlife,
the prophet [Moshe] did not explain anything for several reasons.

SIVAN 8

One of these is that the semblance of the soul without the body is
foreign to us, and even less known is what the soul in that state would
take pleasure in or suffer from. However, this was explained to one who
understood such things, as G-d spoke to Yehoshua (the high priest)
(who G-d granted special understanding into divine matters - *PL*) "I will
give you a place to walk among these (angels) that stand" (Zecharia 3:7),
and this was not referring to when the soul is joined to the body, but
rather was a hint to what would happen after death, where the soul, in
its simple, ethereal state, divested from and no longer using the body,
resumes the form of the angels, after it had been purified and made
radiant when its deeds were good in this world.

SIVAN 9

(*Pas Lechem*: "the soul in its simple, ethereal state":
"simple" - in that it is divested of the entanglement of its physicality.
"ethereal" - in that its essence is extremely fine in spiritual constitution.
"after it had been purified and made radiant when its deeds were
good in this world" - i.e. the soul will attain this through purifying itself
in this world. He specified two terms "purified" and "made radiant"
because there are two evils which the soul is susceptible to from the
entanglement and sickness of physicality. One, that the physicality defiles
it by causing it to do bad deeds and sins. Two, the defilement from the
superfluous desires (for excessive food, speech, tranquility, etc. see Gate
3). Even though the latter does not cause "corrosion" on it as much as
much as sins do, nevertheless, it will not escape from some defilement
and filth which it absorbs from the physical...

SIVAN 10

Marpe Lenefesh: The above account of Yehoshua Kohen Gadol was entirely a spiritual vision, as it is written there: "And he showed me Yehoshua the high priest standing before the angel of the L-ord..." Certainly those standing there are spiritual beings, and when he will "walk among them", certainly it means without a physical body.

Tov Halevanon: I will give you a place to walk among these (angels) that stand" - means that he will have kiyum (ability to exist) in the world of angels.)

SIVAN 11

Another reason is that the explanation of reward and punishment in the next world was received by the people from the prophets, and can be derived by the wise (in every generation, in addition to the transmitted tradition - *PL*), and it was left out of books as much of the explanation of the positive and negative commandments were left out, relying on the transmission from the oral tradition.

(*Marpe Lenefesh*: The prophets would explain it to them by heart, just like most of the Torah and the explanation of the commandments were transmitted orally by heart, due to many sound reasons.

SIVAN 12

Marpe Lenefesh: "can be derived by the wise" - since obviously the main reward and punishment is in the next world, since, behold, in this world life is short and its good does not last, and there is not one person in the world who is completely in enjoyment, without any sadness, worry, or fear to hinder his joy. If so, one who does the will of G-d in this world will certainly be rewarded according to His infinite ability and goodness, which cannot be imagined in this world, and certainly this is in the next world which is eternal and all good. See the Sefer Hayashar for a detailed explanation of this.)

Another reason is that the people were foolish and of little understanding (when they left Egypt) something which is not hard to see in the verses.

SIVAN 13

(*Pas Lechem*: Their foolishness was to such a great extent that it was not hard to see from what is written in the Torah, namely, their hearts' craving for the desires such as asking for meat and other complaints, and little understanding in fundamental matters of purpose, as we see from the incident of the golden calf or their complaints regarding the spies and the congregation of Korach.)

SIVAN 14

The Creator conducted Himself with them like a father who has mercy on his young son, when he wants to discipline him slowly and gently (so as not to overload him, so too the Creator did not want to inform them of the punishments in the afterlife which are very harsh - PL), as written "Yisrael is a child, and I loved him" (Hoshea 11:1). When a father wants to educate his young son in the wisdom with which he will attain exalted levels, and the youth is not capable of understanding them at that time, if he tries to induce him, saying "bear the hard discipline and the learning, in order that you later reach the great levels", the son would not have the patience to bear this, and would not listen to his father, because he does not understand them.

SIVAN 15

But if the father promised him with what is pleasurable right away, whether food and drink, fine clothing and a nice wagon, or the like, and warned him [that if he did not heed he would suffer] what will cause him immediate pain such as hunger, nakedness, spankings or the like, and gave him clear proofs and tangible evidence, so as to impress these promises and warnings in his son's mind and the truth of his statements, it will be easy for the son to bear the strain of the discipline and to endure its tedious work.

SIVAN 16

And when he becomes a young man and his intellect strengthens, he will understand the intent of the discipline he was put through (the exalted levels - *PL*) and turn towards them. He will think little of the sweetness of pleasures which he had earlier been so eager to run towards. This kind of education was a kindness toward him. (i.e. this conduct to motivate him initially through sweet things, etc. as before, was due to the father's mercy on him - *PL*)

SIVAN 17

(*Pas Lechem*: Two forms of strain are needed in the study of [Torah] wisdom. One, that a person is required to be imprisoned in the prison of the study halls of wisdom, to be constantly entrenched at the feet of the sages, as the talmud says: "it (the Torah) is not to be found among merchants and dealers" (Eruvin 55a), and likewise in Shabbos (120a) on the verse "I will not be a chovesh (binder up)" [the talmud expounds:] "I will not be of those who shut themselves up in the Beit Hamidrash (house of Torah study)". Two, the strain of the learning itself, as the talmud says (Sanhedrin 26b): "why is the Torah called tushia (in Isaiah 28:29)? Because it weakens the strength of man [through constant study]". Corresponding to these two the author used two expressions "(1) bear the hard discipline and (2) the learning", and correspondingly he wrote two expressions: "(1) the son would not have the patience to bear this, (2) and would not listen to his father", "because he does not understand them" - he does not understand the exalted levels which this will lead him to.

Afterwards he wrote: "it will be easy for the son to bear the strain of the discipline and to endure it's tedious work" corresponding to these two.)

SIVAN 18

Similarly, the Creator encouraged his people with promises of rewards and threatened them with punishments that would come soon [i.e. in this world - PL] because He knew that after they would be strongly established in the service, their foolishness regarding reward and punishment here on earth would shed (i.e. that which they served primarily for reward in this world [would shed] - *PL*) and their intent in the service would be to Him, and they would direct their conduct for Him. And in this way, we can explain all of the physical forms ascribed to the Creator in scripture.

SIVAN 19

(*Pas Lechem*: "and their intent in the service would be to Him" refers to the intent in each specific act, that they would direct their intent to G-d in every act that they do. And for the general conduct in the service he wrote: "they would direct their conduct towards Him", that all of their aspirations in their conduct would be to cling to Him.

Marpe Lenefesh: That which scripture ascribes physical form to G-d, such as "the hand of G-d" (Shemos 9:3), "the eyes of G-d" (Devarim 11:12), is also for this reason - so that everyone will understand together, the wise man and the fool, that there is a Creator and Master, as explained at length in Gate #1 chapter 10)

SIVAN 20

Another reason, is that a man does not become worthy of the reward of Olam Haba (the next world) due to his good deeds alone (since the reward is infinitely great - *TL*). Rather he is deemed by G-d worthy of it due to two things besides his good deeds. (1) That he teaches other people the service of G-d, and guides them to do good, as written "they who bring merit to the public shall be as the stars forever" (Daniel 12:3). And also, "to them that rebuke shall be delight, and on them will come the blessing of the good" (Mishlei 24:25). And when the industrious man will combine the reward for those who he brought merit, with the reward for his own good deeds, and the reward for the faith in his heart and patient acceptance [of G-d's will] - he will be deemed by the Creator worthy of the reward of Olam Haba. (i.e. if he also brings merit to others in addition to his own piety, then certainly he is worthy of the reward, as written: "to them that rebuke shall be delight" - *ML*)

SIVAN 21

(*Tov Halevanon*: (from Gate#8 end of ch.3) those who rebuke others on their wickedness, the delight of G-d and the blessing of G-d will come on them, and certainly for one who rebukes himself for his wickedness, his reward will be greater and more intense.

Matanas Chelko: To merit entering the world to come, one must have earned the mitzva of bringing merit to the public. After he has merited to enter there, his state and level will be according to his specific service of G-d. But one who properly performed the commandments and became a tzadik but did not bring any person to Torah, he does not have the key to the world to come. (See there at length for an explanation. A summary is that one can be paid all his reward in this world for all commandments but not for sanctifying G-d's Name which comes through bringing others close to Torah. see there.)

SIVAN 22

(2) The second factor is a kindness from the Al-mighty, and generosity and goodness, as written "to You, G-d, is kindness, for You pay a man according to his deeds" (Tehillim 62:13) (i.e. even if one has only his own good deeds [and did not bring others to the good], G-d will bestow on him good reward in Olam Haba - *TL*).

SIVAN 23

The reason for this, is that even if a man's good deeds are numerous like the sand of the seashore, it would not weigh enough to cover even one favor the Creator had bestowed on him in this world. All the more so, if he has committed any sins, because if the Creator will hold a man strictly to account for his obligation of gratitude, all of his good deeds would be cancelled and wiped out by even the smallest favor the Creator has done for him, and that which the Creator owes him will not amount to anything. Hence, that which the Creator rewards a person for his good deeds is to be regarded as a Divine grace to him.

SIVAN 24

(*Tov Halevanon*: "it is a kindness of the Almighty" - i.e. to bestow good reward (Olam Haba) to a tzadik due to his own good deeds alone, even if he does NOT teach others and rebukes them. Even though, justice demands that a person be held accountable for the sin of his fellow since "all of Yisrael are arevim (responsible) for each other" (Shevuot 39a) for visible matters (provided one can effectively rebuke the other person) and also since we have been commanded to teach others and rebuke them as a positive commandment. Nevertheless, from the abundant kindness of G-d which has intensified on us, G-d does not withhold his reward in Olam Haba. Likewise, even if one teaches others and rebukes his fellow back to the good, it is still, [strictly speaking,] not enough to merit the reward of Olam Haba which is infinitely great, were it not for His kindness... Hence the Torah and the prophets did not mention the rewards of Olam Haba in the section of the covenant and the rebuke (Parsha Bechukosai, Ki Tavo, Shema) since, according to justice, a man does not deserve this reward, and it is sufficient to give man reward in this world. Hence, the Torah only mentioned what is proper according to justice. Similarly, our sages taught: "prophecy was asked 'what should be the punishment for the sinner?', It replied: 'the soul which sins shall die'. 'The Torah was asked, etc.', it replied: 'let him bring an Asham (offering) and be atoned', G-d was asked, etc. He replied: 'let him come and do teshuva'. Understand this. And since the Torah did not mention the rewards, it likewise did not mention the punishments despite that it is a debt he must pay according to his sins.

SIVAN 25

Marpe Lenefesh: The Sh'la wrote (page 52b): "Consider an analogy of one who [severely] broke his leg or blinded an eye, and a great doctor came and through his great expertise, healed him for free, or even for pay. Wouldn't he love him greatly all of his days, and nothing the doctor asked of him would be difficult for him? Behold, G-d gave a person hands, feet - all of his limbs, and sustains him and watches over him, and gave him a soul so that he can come to immortality..." see there for more.

And the author already wrote in Gate#2 ch.5 on some of the favors that G-d did to us from our first existence in this world until today. He who places them always before his eyes - then, his heart will become fiery (impassioned) towards G-d, yisborach.)

SIVAN 26

The punishment in both worlds, however, is through truth and justice, and it is a debt a man must pay. Yet here too the Creator's loving-kindness is extended to us in both worlds, as written "to You, G-d, belongs loving-kindness" (Tehillim 62:13), and "the compassionate One will atone for sin, and will not destroy" (Tehillim 78:38).

(*Tov Halevanon*: G-d's kindness here means that G-d waits for him always in this world and gives him time to repent, and if he repents, even if it is just before his death, G-d will exempt him from the punishments of Olam Haba (i.e. but if not, then no sins are overlooked and must be punished in order to pardon the person as will be explained later. - Translator)

SIVAN 27

Marpe Lenefesh: The kindness is that He pays man some punishment in this world with easy suffering (instead of paying him in the next world with far worse suffering), and also slowly, slowly one at a time, not in furious wrath, as written: "Only you did I love above all the families of the earth; therefore, I will punish you for all your iniquities" (Amos 3:2) as our sages expounded in Avoda Zara 4a. Otherwise [if one thinks G-d's kindness means He will overlook his sins], behold they said: "if a man says 'G-d will overlook my sins, his life will be overlooked", unless it is through [the system of] teshuva (repentance) and this is also a kindness.)

SIVAN 28

Another reason, is that good deeds are of two categories.

1. Those concealed from others, and visible only to the Creator, like the duties of the heart, and other similar duties.

2. Those visible in the limbs and not concealed from other creatures.
3. For the fulfillment of the visible duties of the limbs, the Creator rewards with visible reward of this world. While for fulfillment of concealed duties, He rewards with hidden reward, namely, in Olam Haba. Therefore, King David, spoke of this with words which hint to this matter, as written "how great is Your goodness which You hid away for those that fear You; [which you have done for them that take refuge in You before the sons of men]" (Tehillim 31:20). And likewise, the way of punishments for hidden and revealed misdeeds, is similar to the way of reward.

SIVAN 29

(*Pas Lechem*: The above verse mentioned "fear" which is concealed in the heart of a person, and ascribed to it concealed reward [in future tense]. Afterwards, the verse continues that those who "take refuge" in Him, i.e. who cling to Him in acts which are visible before the eyes of "the sons of men", and on these G-d already payed the reward, hence "which you have done" is in past tense.)

The proof for this view is as follows. G-d has guaranteed to His people that for their visible service, He would give them visible and swift reward in this world. This is explained in parsha *Bechukosai*"If you will go in My ways.." (Vayikra 26), and likewise, for visible sins, visible and swift punishment in this world, because the masses understand only that which is visible not that which is hidden, as written: "the hidden things belong to G-d, but the revealed things belong to us and to our children, forever"(Devarim 29:28). And the verse says "if the people will turn their eyes away from the [evil] acts of this man and his family, I will turn My face to this man and his family" (Vayikra 20:4). Hence, the reward and punishment for the fulfillment or transgression of the duties of the heart belongs to the Creator. Therefore, Scripture omitted an explanation of their reward and punishment in the next world. (see Tov Halevanon for more details)

SIVAN 30

Another reason why rewards and punishments mentioned in scripture are limited to those in this world only is because the prophet is addressing worldly people. On the other hand, since Yehoshua (kohen gadol) was in the mystical world of angels (i.e. his soul was divested of his body at that time and was in the spiritual world - *PL*), G-d told him, "I will give you a place to walk among these (angels) that stand" (Zecharia 3:7). The proper way of motivating with hope and fear should be in accord with the time and place. Understand this.

TAMMUZ 1

(*Marpe Lenefesh*: During the giving of the Torah at Sinai, the Jewish people were in this world. Hence it is proper to inform them of the reward and punishments of this world, since a man does not fear that which is not tangible to him and that he does not understand.

Tov Halevanon: "the prophet is addressing worldly people" means according to their attachment to physicality and physical pleasures which their hearts constantly turn to and seek the good of their bodies and fear what is harmful to it, while the spiritual pleasure or pain which their soul will be subject to in the next world is worth nothing to them compared to the physical pleasure or pain [in this world]. This is like in the Kuzari 1:104 ..... Therefore, G-d mentioned the rewards and punishments in this world according to what they hope for and fear from while they are alive here, namely, while they are attached to the physicality of the body and standing in this lowly world. But Yehoshua Kohen Gadol was an exceedingly wise man, pure, and already divested of the desires of physicality and elevated himself to the level of the spiritual. For him, the main reward was spiritual pleasure and he desired it even while still in this world, as explained in the wisdom of truth (Kabala). For this he wrote "Understand this". [i.e. the plain meaning as in Marpe Lenefesh, and the deeper meaning here. Both are correct.])

TAMMUZ 2

Another reason is that the purpose of reward in Olam Haba is essentially clinging to G-d, and drawing near to His supernal light, as written "your righteousness will go before you, the glory of G-d will gather you in" (Yeshaya 58:8), and "the wise will shine like the radiance of the firmament" (Daniel 12:3), and also, "To bring back his soul from the pit (i.e. Gehinom see below Tov Halevanon), to be enlightened with the light of the living" (Iyov 33:30). And no one can reach there except he who the Creator finds favor in, and the favor of the Creator is the root of the reward, as written "his anger is but a moment, in His favor is life" (Tehillim 30:6). And there are hints in parsha bechukosai that pleasing the Al-mighty [is the greatest reward], this is what is written "My soul will not abhor you" (Vayikra 26:11), and "I will turn to you and be unto you a G-d and you will be unto Me a people" (ibid, 26:9).

TAMMUZ 3

(*Tov Halevanon*: "the purpose of reward" - The intent of this answer is that the spiritual reward is only clinging with G-d, and we will attain this when we minimize tending towards the bodily desires and purify our souls by fulfilling His commandments, yisborach. And then, our souls will be fitting and capable of clinging to the spirituality of G-d. And then G-d, in His kindness, will "conceal us in the shadow of His hand" (Yeshaya 49:2), even though we are not deserving of this reward from [the merit] of our deeds, but rather by "His kindness which prevailed over us" (Tehillim 117:2). But when a man turns towards the physical desires in rebelling against the Divine wisdom, then his soul is stuck in the darkness of the physical, and it is impossible in any way to draw close to Him, yisborach, except by its cleansing itself from its tuma (spiritual impurity), in purifying itself from its physicality in Gehinom, as known to the sages.

TAMMUZ 4

And according to this, reward and punishment in Olam Haba is not according to judgment and justice, like the reward and punishment in this world. Rather, they follow (1) a kind of nature (i.e. purity from the bad effects of physicality) and (2) also a desire of G-d for those who fulfill His will, both of these two things simultaneously. This is the difference between this answer and the previous one "a man does not become worthy of the reward of Olam Haba due to his good deeds alone... but rather it is a kindness..." [previous answer focused only on (2)]. Understand this.)

TAMMUZ 5

TRUST IN THE REWARD AND PUNISHMENT

Trusting in G-d regarding the reward in this world and in the next, which He promised to the righteous man for his service, namely, that He will pay reward to one who is fitting for it, and mete out punishment to one who deserves it, is incumbent on the believer, and is an essential part of perfect faith in G-d, as written, "and he believed G-d, and it was counted to him as a righteousness" (Bereishis 15:6), and "had I not believed to see the goodness of G-d in the land of the living" (Tehillim 27:13).

TAMMUZ 6

(*Tov Halevanon*: "that He will pay reward to one who is fitting for it" - One who has perfected his soul by purifying its physical and has become fitting to draw near to the spiritual light should trust that G-d will desire in Him, and will draw His kindness on him in the reward of Olam Haba, even though he does not deserve it due to his deeds.

TAMMUZ 7

"and mete out punishment to one who deserves it" - i.e. punishment comes on him through the aspect of justice and is a debt which he became obligated in [and must pay].)

It is not proper for one to trust in his own good deeds, and assure himself that he will receive reward in this world and the next due to his good deeds. Rather, he should strive and exert himself [to do good] and make efforts to thank G-d and be grateful for His constant kindnesses to him, and not be motivated by hope of future reward for his deeds. Rather he should trust in G-d and try his best to pay his debt of gratitude for His great favors towards him, as our sages have said "Do not be like servants who serve their master on condition of receiving reward, rather be like servants who serve their master without the condition of receiving reward, and let the fear of Heaven be upon you" (Avos 1:3)

TAMMUZ 8

(*Matanas Chelko*: This matter is subtle. Even though one must know that he will receive reward in the next world, nevertheless, the cause of doing the commandment should not be the receiving of the reward. Rather, one should do them because G-d commanded it and even if one did not receive any reward, he would do them anyways. He does the truth because it is the truth... Only that in this knowledge that he will receive reward, he rejoices more in fulfilling the will of G-d. (see there for more)

TAMMUZ 9

Tov Halevanon: "and let the fear of Heaven be upon you" - i.e. don't think that just like reward in the next world goes only by the grace and desire of G-d, so too the punishments of Olam Haba are not according to his deeds but only according to the desire of G-d... On this he wrote: "and let the fear of Heaven be upon you", i.e. the fear of punishment from above should nevertheless be upon you since punishment is according to Din (justice) in this world and in the next - not from the aspect of "desire".

TAMMUZ 10

Translator: Nevertheless, the Ramchal explains that even punishment is rooted in kindness, since the whole purpose of punishment is not as a revenge but rather in order to be able to pardon the person afterwards. Here is the excerpt:

Introduction to Divine Punishment by Rabbi Moshe Chaim Luzzato (Ramchal), zt"l

—excerpt from Kalach Pitchei Chachma, petach #2

The desire of the Creator is only [to bestow] good. It is impossible to say that the Divine will desired that there could be other forces which can prevent Him [from bestowing good] in any manner whatsoever. Because the Divine will wants solely and exclusively to bestow good, [and if it were the case that other forces could prevent this] then it would certainly not be good that His goodness not be capable of spreading over His creations.

And if you ask: "[Perhaps] this is good, namely, the bestowing of good to the righteous and the punishing of the wicked [is good]?"

TAMMUZ 11

Behold, it is written: "I will have mercy upon whom I will have mercy" (Shemos 33:19), [which was expounded to mean:] "even though he does not deserve it" (Berachos 7a), and it is written: "[In those days, and in that time, says the L-ord,] the iniquity of Israel shall be sought for, and there shall be none; [and the sins of Judah, and they shall not be found: for I will pardon them whom I preserve]" - behold G-d desires to bestow good also to the wicked.

Perhaps you will ask: "But all this is only after the long exile and the receiving of their punishments?".

I will answer you: "on the contrary, this is a support. If so, behold, the Divine will coordinates the matters so that in the end, all will be meritorious (see Derech H-shem part 2 ch.2-4). This demonstrates that the Divine will is truly and solely to bestow good, only that it is necessary to go with each person according to his way. For the wicked it is necessary to punish them in order to pardon them afterwards. If the intent [in punishing the wicked] was to expel them, then they should have been completely banished - not that they be punished in order to make them meritorious afterwards. This is a clear proof, because behold the end of a matter reveals the intended purpose of all the parts of that matter. And the end of the matter for every human being, whether the righteous or the wicked [after they are rectified] is to bestow on them good. If so, the intended purpose is to bestow good on all. Hence, the Divine will is solely good. Therefore, nothing will endure except His good.

TAMMUZ 12

Now that we have reached this point, namely, that the Divine will is only to bestow good, it is necessary that the matters do not go on like this indefinitely. Explanation: if the Divine will did not abhor destroying the wicked, then we would say that punishment is not something evil, rather "Evil pursues sinners" (Mishlei 13:21), and this is the way it is. But since we have said that the way is not like this, but rather, it [the punishment] is in order to afterwards bestow good on him, if so the punishment is evil and must be temporary, not eternal so that the sinner can be released from it. And since it is evil - it is against the Divine will. However, since it is against the Divine will, just like for each person, it is impossible for it to be eternal, so too for the world in general it is impossible for the existence [of evil] to be eternal. (just like G-d wants to rectify every wicked person, so too He wants to rectify the entire world, and nullify the existence of evil.)...

TAMMUZ 13

Now let us see if punishment, which precedes the [good] end for the wicked is [in actuality] good or not. A thing whose final end is different than its beginning - its beginning and end are not of the same kind. The process which will act on the wicked will be different in the end from what it was in the beginning. If so, the beginning of this process and the end of it are not of the same kind. The end is good, and this was what the active [Divine] will wanted in the beginning. The means, i.e. that which is before the end is not of this kind. If so, then what preceded the end is not good, and was not the desire of the active will.

We will answer this: If so, why did it change? Rather, since it is impossible to reach the end without this. But if it were possible without this, it would not be proper for this means to exist. The summary of all this is that punishment is evil, and it is the opposite of the desire and intent of the Divine will, but its existence is necessary to be created in order to reach from it to the ultimate purpose. If it were possible without this, it would have been deemed better by the Divine will... [see there for more])

TAMMUZ 14

One of the pious said "if one takes strict account of what he is obligated to the Creator for His kindness to him, no man would ever be worthy of the reward of Olam Haba for his deeds. Rather it is only as a kindness of the Al-mighty, therefore do not trust in your deeds." And King David said of this "to You, G-d, is kindness, for You pay a man according to his deeds" (Tehillim 62:13) (i.e. even the paying of a man for his deeds is only a kindness)

TAMMUZ 15

SEVENTH CATEGORY - trust in G-d for the special grace to His treasured ones

The seventh category - trust in regard to G-d's special grace to His elect and treasured ones on whom many favors which are indescribable will be bestowed upon in Olam Haba. The proper way of trust in G-d is as follows: To exert oneself in the means which bring one to the high levels of the pious who are worthy of this special grace from G-d. This entails conducting oneself in the ways of the ascetics who loath worldly pleasures, and to uproot from one's heart the love of them and desire for them and replace these with the love of the Creator, and to devote oneself to Him, to delight in Him, to be desolate/astonished from the world and its inhabitants (see commentary), and to follow the ways of the prophets and the pious, and to trust that the Al-mighty will show him favor as He will do with them in the afterlife.

TAMMUZ 16

(*Tov Halevanon*: To transform the love of this world and its great longing, which is the way of people to long greatly for matters of this world and its pleasures, and transform it with the love of G-d in this way of love. [i.e. not to extinguish the normal great love of this world and its superfluous things, but rather to channel this love to the love of G-d]

TAMMUZ 17

Matanas Chelko: ...without a doubt, we are talking here about a very lofty spiritual level. Nevertheless, we must understand that whenever a man loves someone or something, it is impossible for him to have perfect and complete love of G-d and of Olam Haba. This is the author's intent here. If one does not loath this world, he cannot love G-d at this level. Likewise, if one has love for worldly pleasures and matters in his heart he cannot love Olam Haba perfectly. Therefore, to reach this level, it is necessary to remove all love of this world from his heart and to loathe it.

TAMMUZ 18

Marpe Lenefesh: "to be desolate from the world and its inhabitants" - to not have any contentment in joining in the company of people, rather to distance from their conversations and social gatherings. (see gate #8)

Pas Lechem: that the remembrance of the affairs of this world and the ways of its inhabitants be desolate and absent from his heart. Or, the intent is that one is astonished and wonders in his heart from the world and its inhabitants, how they busy themselves without a [true] purpose, and "follow the vanities, etc." (Melachim II 17:15) and to abhor their affairs, as in (Daniel 8:27) "I was appalled by the vision; it was beyond understanding".

TAMMUZ 19

Matanas Chelko: i.e. that he has no contentment or pleasure from this world or its inhabitants

"to trust G-d will show him favor in the afterlife" - "trust" means to trust in the kindness of G-d. For according to strict justice, there is no place for trust... nevertheless, there is a distinction between trust in worldly matters and trust in matters of the hereafter. For matters of this world, one can trust that G-d will do him favors even if he does not engage in the means of a livelihood, [for special scholars] such as Rabbi Shimon bar Yochai. But for matters of the next world it is impossible to trust in this manner. Because if one does not toil and do, if he does not love the next world and make it primary, but instead his love and desires are of this world, he cannot trust that G-d will grant the [bliss of the] afterlife to him as a kindness. It is impossible to attain the afterlife without hishtadlus (exertion). Only by exertion and strain in doing the will of G-d can one trust that he will receive good reward from the Creator in the afterlife. But without this, it is not trust but folly. This is what the author continues . . .

TAMMUZ 20

But one who trusts that G-d will thus favor him without the means of performing good deeds is a fool and a simpleton. He is like those of whom it is said "they act like Zimri and expect the reward of Pinchas" (Sota 22b). Some signs of those who have reached this high level are those who: (1) teach servants of G-d on the service (due to the love of G-d in all their being, they cannot hold themselves back from remaining silent on the falling short in the service of G-d in other people - *TL*), (2) demonstrating patient bearing and accepting in times of trial and difficulty, (3) regarding everything else as insignificant compared with the fulfillment of the commandments of G-d, as we see by the test of Avraham (bereishis 22:1), or of Chananya, Mishael, and Azarya who were thrown in the fiery furnace (Daniel 3:13), or Daniel who was thrown in the lion's den (Daniel 6:13), or the 10 martyrs.

TAMMUZ 21

WHO IS WORTHY OF THE BLISS OF THE AFTERLIFE
Whoever chooses to die in the service of G-d, rather than rebel against Him, whoever chooses poverty rather than riches, sickness rather than health, suffering rather than tranquility, submits to the Creator's judgment, and desires in His decrees - such a person is worthy of the Divine grace of the Creator in the bliss of Olam Haba, of which it is written "That I may cause those that love Me to inherit substance; and I will fill their treasures" (Mishlei 8:21), and "no eye has ever seen, O G-d, beside You, what He has prepared for him that waits for Him" (Yeshaya 64:3), and "How great is Your goodness that You have hidden away for those who fear You" (Tehillim 31:20).

TAMMUZ 22

(*Marpe Lenefesh*: The reason is that every mitzvah is not worthy of reward, as he wrote earlier in the sixth category, because as our sages said on: "Who has given Me anything beforehand, that I should repay him?" (Iyov 41:3) that first G-d bestowed all good to a person and afterwards man performs commandments to make a return. But one who offers his life and soul, and all that is his for G-d, out of love, then all the good of this world is worth nothing to him compared to his love of G-d. If so, how could he not be worthy of the good reward of the righteous and the just? This is clear.

Translator: i.e. one who does not live for himself, but rather is "working" for G-d, then all the favors G-d does for him are "on the house" and in fact, even his mundane activities are considered as religious service as explained in Gate 3 chapter 9. See that entire gate at length with the commentaries for essential reading on properly understanding this gate.)

TAMMUZ 23

Chapter 5

The differences between one who trusts in G-d and one who does not with regard to employing the means for earning a livelihood, I say, are seven:

(*Marpe Lenefesh*: i.e. both are engaged in the means, whether in a handicraft or in a business, and even so, there is a big difference between them)

TAMMUZ 24

(1) One who trusts G-d accepts His judgment in all his matters, and thanks Him for good as well as for bad, as written "G-d gave, G-d took back, blessed be His Name" (Iyov 1:21), and as written "of kindness and of judgment I will sing to You" (Tehillim 101:1), which the sages explained "if kindness, I will sing, if justice I will sing" (Berachos 60b) (Rashi: when You bestow kindness upon me, I will praise you [with the

blessing:] "Blessed be He Who is good and does good", and when You perform judgment upon me, I will sing, "Blessed be the true Judge." In either case, to You, O Lord, I shall sing), and they also said: "a man is under duty to bless G-d on the bad (with joy - *ML*) just like he blesses on the good" (Berachos 54a).

TAMMUZ 25

But one who does not trust in the Al-mighty boasts on the good (saying "it is due to my might and ingenuity, etc" - *PL*) as written "For the wicked boasts of his heart's desire" (Tehillim 10:3), and he becomes angry on the bad as written "And the one who passes therein shall suffer hardships and hunger, and it shall come to pass,] that when he shall be hungry, he shall be enraged, and curse his king and his [idolatrous] god, and he will turn to Heaven" (Yeshaya 8:21).

(*Marpe Lenefesh*: He will curse them since he sees they are of no substance (*ein bo mamash*).

Rashi: *"And the one who passes therein"* - in abandoning the Holy One, blessed be He and relying upon the kings of the nations.

"and he will turn to Heaven": to beseech the Holy One, blessed be He, but He will not heed, for the verdict will have been sealed.

TAMMUZ 26

Matanas Chelko: one who trusts in G-d realizes that the results of all his efforts are only according to the will of G-d. Therefore, he thanks G-d whether he succeeds or not... but one who does not trust thinks that the exertion causes the success. And when he is not successful, he becomes angry at G-d or has some claims against Him [for not helping him].

In truth this is very strange, for if he has claims against G-d, then he recognizes that it is all from Him. Therefore, when he is successful why does he attribute this to his own strength and ingenuity? Why does he not also question G-d as to why he received such success?.. the answer is that he feels he is deserving of this success and is worthy of it. Only when bad things happen does he start to wonder what he did to deserve such bad things [why did G-d not help him] and he feels he did nothing wrong. All this stems from lack of trust. But one who trusts also wonders when he receives a great good that perhaps he does not deserve this, etc.)

TAMMUZ 27

(2) One who trusts in the Al-mighty has tranquility of spirit and a heart at ease regarding bad decrees, knowing that the Creator will arrange them for what is his good in this world and the next, as King David said "my soul, wait you only on G-d; for my expectation is from Him" (Tehillim 62:6). But one who does not trust in G-d, even when he is prosperous, is always pained and in a state of continual anxiety. He is saddened and grieving, because he is little satisfied with his situation, and yearns to augment, increase, and hoard in. And likewise in bad times because he is disgusted by it, and it is contrary to his desires, nature and traits. So too, the wise man said "all the days of the poor are evil" (Mishlei 15:15)

TAMMUZ 28

(*Matanas Chelko*: i.e. even if it is not good for him in this world, he knows and believes that it will be good for him in the next world. Therefore, he is not at all worried.

Tov Halevanon: "*all the days of the poor are evil*" - "poor" refers to one who is not content with what he has, as the sages said: "who is wealthy? One who is content with his portion." (Pirkei Avot)

TAMMUZ 29

Pas Lechem: "*yearns to augment, increase, and hoard in*" - corresponding to these three terms, he earlier wrote three terms denoting pain, namely:

(1) "*he is always pained*" - to augment. corresponding to love of pleasure, that whenever he is enjoying something, he is "pained" for augmenting the enjoyment from that thing.

(2) *state of continual anxiety* - to increase. corresponding to love of beneficial things, namely, money and possessions, he will "worry" always to increase his money

AV 1

(3) *"saddened and grieving"* - to hoard in. corresponding to what he already possesses but which is spread out here and there and causes him mental distraction, he will be mourning to hoard it in. Likewise what his land produces and is outside in his field, he is saddened in that it is not assured from damages until he can bring it to his domain.

All this is during the times of prosperity. But during bad times, he is very pained and disturbed, *"because he is disgusted by it"* - corresponding to his taava (love of pleasure), whereby a person is disturbed and repulsed by the matter, either:

AV 2

(1) because of absence of extra things, and on this he wrote: "it is contrary to his desires", or

(2) because of absence of necessary things, and this subdivides into two general categories:

(a) "nature": That the matter disturbs his nature. For example, one who is of cold nature (i.e. he needs to stay cool), he is disturbed by bearing things which are too warm or vice versa.

(b) "traits": That the matter disturbs his traits. For example, one who is hot-tempered is irritated by those who act brazenly against him. And the opposite, one who is of calm nature, is irritated by the company of the hot-tempered.

So too, the wise man said "all the days of the poor are evil": that one who is not a baal bitachon (firmly trusts in G-d), is always poor in his mind, as above)

AV 3

(3) One who trusts in G-d, even while he is engaging in the means for earning a livelihood, his heart will not rely on them, and he will not hope to receive profit or loss from them unless it is the will of G-d. Rather, he engages in them as part of his service of G-d who commanded us to occupy ourselves with the world, to maintain it and make it more

habitable. If these means will yield him profit or help him avoid a loss, he will thank G-d alone for this, and he will not love and cherish the means more for this, nor will he rely more on them on account of this. Rather, his trust in G-d will be strengthened, and he will come to rely on Him and not the means. And if the means do not yield any benefit, he knows that his livelihood will come to him when G-d wants, and through whatever way He wants. Therefore, he will not reject the means because of this, nor abandon employing them, and thus he will serve his Creator (as above - *TL*).

AV 4

But one who does not trust in G-d, engages in certain means because he places his trust in them, confident that they will yield him a profit and protect him against a loss. If they yield a profit, he will praise them and himself for his exertion in them and choosing of them, and he will not try other means. But if they do not yield him a profit, he will abandon them and reject them, and lose interest in them, as written "Therefore he sacrifices to his net (through which he succeeded in his actions - *TL*), and he burns incense to his trawl, for through them he lives in luxury and enjoys the choicest food" (Chavakuk 1:16).

AV 5

(*Matanas Chelko*: besides that he has no peace of mind in everything he does, he must also constantly change the means and strategies from one task or job to another. Through this he causes himself mental dispersion contrary to the peace of mind and tranquility of the one who trusts.

(4) One who trusts in G-d, if he has more money than he needs, he will spend it in a way which pleases the Creator (charity, etc.) with a generous spirit and a good heart, as written "everything is Yours, and from Your hand we have given to You" (Divrei Hayamim I 29:14). (since he knows and understands that everything is from G-d, and he is giving G-d of His money, certainly he will give with a generous spirit and a good heart - *PL*)

AV 6

But one who does not trust in G-d, does not regard the entire world and everything in it as enough for his maintenance and sufficient for his needs. He is more concerned with saving his money than fulfilling his obligations to the Creator and to his fellow men, and he won't feel anything (of the causes which will suddenly strike his money - PL), until all of his money is lost and he is left destitute, as the wise man said: "There is one that scatters, and yet increases; and there is one that withholds more than is right, but it leads to poverty" (Mishlei 11:24).

(*Pas Lechem*: the intent of the verse is that even though both extremes are bad, because even excessive scattering (donating) is not proper, as the sages said in Ketuvot 50a, since sometimes one will become poor through this. Nevertheless, some do not become poor [by excessive donating], on the contrary he will increase from what he had, but "one that withholds more than is right" this leads only to poverty.

AV 7

Matanas Chelko: the truster does not hold on to the extra money which remains after he has purchased his needs so that if, G-d forbid, he does not have enough money in the future, he will be able to sustain himself with this money. Rather, he gives it to others and spends it generously in the will of G-d, such as for tzedaka, or maaser. He knows that in truth everything is His, it all comes from Him, and G-d is fully capable of providing for him in the future for all of his needs. [i.e. he does not save beyond what is reasonable]

AV 8

(5) One who trusts in G-d engages in a means of livelihood, in order to also prepare provisions for his end, and needs for his appointed home (in the afterlife). Only a means of livelihood which is clear to him that it is safe for fulfilling his Torah study and fulfilling his religious service will he engage in it. But a livelihood which will bring any loss of Torah

observance or mislead him to rebel against G-d, he will not engage in, so as not to bring on himself spiritual sickness instead of healing.

AV 9

(*Pas Lechem*: "*to also prepare provisions for his end, and needs for his appointed home*" - the word "provisions" applies to what a man will use on a journey, as written (in the exodus from Egypt) "nor had they prepared any provisions for themselves" (Shmos 12:39), or "Prepare provision for yourselves, [for in another three days you will cross this Jordan...]" (Joshua 1:11), and when the soul leaves this world until it reaches its place, it will need provisions, as Rabbi Ploni said (before dying) "the provisions are scanty and the road is long" (Kesuvos 67b). And when the soul arrives to its appointed place, it will be sustained there forever and ever with what it prepared, and on this he wrote "needs for his appointed home")

But one who does not trust in the Al-mighty, trusts in the means, and relies on them, and he won't refrain himself from employing any of them. He will engage in good means as well as bad means (i.e. those permitted to him as well as those forbidden to him - *TL*), and he won't think about his final end, as the wise man said, "the wise man fears and avoids evil" (mishlei 14:16).

AV 10

(*Matanas Chelko*: he is always mindful that all matters of this world are only means to reach in the future to the afterlife. Therefore, he is always thinking that he must prepare provisions for his afterlife.

Marpe Lenefesh: He will have provisions for the afterlife.

Translator: In his youth, the Novhardok Rabbi asked Rabbi Yisrael Salanter why he should learn Torah, saying "but what will I live with?". To which Rabbi Yisrael countered: "but what will you die with?")

AV 11

(6) The one who trusts in G-d is beloved by all classes of people, and they feel at ease with him, because they feel secure that he will not

harm them, and their hearts are at peace with regard to him. They are not afraid of him that he will take their wives or their money (etc, as in the tenth commandment, do not covet your fellow's wife, etc - *PL*), and he also is not worried about them because he realizes that it is not in any created being's power or control to benefit or harm him. Therefore, he does not fear harm from them nor expects any benefit from them. And since he is assured from them and they are assured from him, he will love them and they will love him, as written "he who trusts in G-d will be surrounded by kindness" (Tehillim 32:10).

AV 12

But he who does not trust in G-d, has no [true] friend, because he is always coveting others, and jealous of them, and he thinks that any good that reaches others is a loss to him (as if it was in his hand and left from him to them - *PL*), and that their livelihood is taken from his own, and (1) any preventing of attaining his desires is caused by them, and that (2) others are capable of helping him to obtain his desires, and (3) if some harm comes to his money or his children, he will think they caused it, and (4) that they are capable of removing the harm and problems from him, and since his thinking is based on these principles he will [come to] despise them, slander them, curse them, and hate them. And he is the disgusting one in both worlds, regarded as a disgrace in both abodes as written "a crooked heart will not find good" (Mishlei 17:20).

AV 13

(*Pas Lechem*: He thinks *"any preventing of attaining his desires is caused by them"*, or he thinks that even though they did not cause him to be prevented from attaining his desires, but nevertheless, since it is in their ability to assist him to attain his desires and they don't assist him - he will hate them.

Pas Lechem: *"he will despise others, slander them, curse them, and hate them"* - He specified four types of denigration corresponding to these four previous divisions.

Corresponding to: (1) *"any preventing of attaining his desires is caused by them"*, he wrote: *"he will despise them"*.

Corresponding to: (2) that they don't want to assist him in attaining his desires, he wrote: *"slander them"*, since he is upset with them because of this and he speaks bad of them calling them mida sdom (cruel and apathetic), or the like.

Corresponding to: (3) *"if some harm comes to his money or his children, he will think they caused it"*, he wrote: *"he will curse them"*.

Corresponding to: (4) that they don't want to save him from his troubles, he wrote *"and hate them"*, since according to his view they hate him and rejoice on his troubles, therefore he also hates them.

AV 14

Matanas Chelko: Trust is a foundation of all commandments between man and his fellow. For perfection in fulfilling these commandments and in the commandment of "love your fellow..." comes through trust in G-d. The reason a man is not so much able to love his fellow is because when he sees that he is not succeeding as much as his fellow, he imagines that this is due to his fellow. But the truster realizes that it is all from G-d and His decrees. Through this he can feel only love for each and every person.... As we brought earlier from the Sefer Hachinuch (mitzva 241) on the commandment of not exacting revenge which is based on trust that everything occurs solely through the will of G-d, see there. But with this thought (of trust) it is impossible for him to hate his fellow or have complaints against him. Likewise, for jealousy. It cannot occur in one who trusts in G-d. Hence, all matters of commandments between man and his fellow are rooted in the trait of trust.

AV 15

(7) The one who trusts in G-d will not mourn if his requests are denied, or if he loses something he loves, and he will not hoard possessions nor be troubled by more than his day's needs (see below commentaries). He does not worry about what will be tomorrow since he does not know when his end will come. He therefore trusts in G-d to prolong his days, and provide his sustenance and needs during this time. He neither

rejoices nor grieves about the future (i.e. he does not rejoice in hoping for a future good which is coming up and likewise, he does not grieve or worry on any future bad thing coming up - *PL*), as written "do not delight in tomorrow because you don't know what today could bring" (Mishlei 27:1), and Ben Sira said "do not anguish about the troubles of tomorrow because one doesn't know what today could bring, perhaps tomorrow he will be no more (i.e. perhaps you will not live to see tomorrow - *ML*), and he had anguished on a world that is not his" (Sanhedrin 100b). Rather, his worry and mourning is on his lackings in the fulfillment of his obligations to G-d, and he tries to make up as much as he can of them, of his external (actions - *PL*) and internal duties (of the heart - *PL*), because he thinks of his death and the arrival of the day of ingathering, and the fear that death may come suddenly increases his efforts and zeal to prepare provisions for his end, and he won't be concerned about preparing for this world, and this is what was said "repent one day before your death" (Avos 2:10). They explained on this (Shabbat 153a): "repent today, perhaps you will die tomorrow, therefore let all your days be in repentance, as written 'at all times let your clothing be clean'" (Koheles 9:8).

AV 16

(*Pas Lechem*: "*he thinks of his death and the arrival of the day of ingathering*" - "thinks of his death", the intent is on the death of the body and the nullification of his [worldly] desires. Thinking of "the arrival of the day of ingathering", the intent is on the ingathering of the soul to its place. Both contemplations are necessary because in remembering the death of the body, he will be repulsed by its desires, while by remembering the ingathering of the soul, he will worry on his sins, which prevent the ascent of the soul to its place.

AV 17

Rabbi Yaakov Emden: "*nor be troubled by more than his day's needs*" - i.e. he does not ask of G-d more than his day's needs, as written: "[give me neither poverty nor riches,] but give me only my daily bread" (Mishlei 30:8), he will not trouble himself much for that which is not already

arranged for him, for example, if he rents out things or works at a handicraft he will not worry about whether he will find a renter or a buyer
tomorrow. Rather, he will trust that G-d will provide his daily bread, as
written: "[Behold, I will rain bread from heaven for you;] and the people
shall go out and gather a certain portion every day" (Shmos 16:4). And
our sages said: "he who has what to eat today and asks 'what will I eat
tomorrow?' is of those who are little in faith" (Sotah 48b).

However, one whose work is for a set duration and at a set period
(of the year) such as farmers - certainly he must exert himself on the
day and period (season of the year) which will be good for many days
and for difficult times, as written: " He that gathers in summer is a wise
son" (Mishlei 10:5), and he exhorted us to learn from the ant: "Go to the
ant, you sluggard; consider her ways, and be wise...it stores its provisions
in summer and gathers its food at harvest" (Mishlei 6:6), to learn from
its ways and be wise to prepare during times available. And likewise,
one who engages in business must journey to markets and fairs or the
like. There is no prohibition to fill storehouses and to rely on them for
years of famine, or to save cattle and properties from the extra that G-d
has made available to him, so that it be ready for the time of need, and
thus it is written in the Torah: "But you must remember the L-rd your
G-d, for it is He that gives you strength to make valor" (Devarim 8:18),
which the Onkelos renders: "He gives you counsel to acquire wealth",
and the wise man said: "The wealth of the rich is the city of his strength;
the destruction of the poor is their poverty" (Mishlei 10:15), when it
is wealth that was earned justly - take care of it, and do not kick at the
blessing of G-d. Also, one is not obligated to scatter it all [to tzedaka,
etc.], but rather through certain conditions. The intelligent person will
arrange his matters according to the way of nature in accord with the will
of G-d who arranged for him an order to seek his livelihood at certain
times, with a perfect and faithful heart that trusts in G-d.

AV 18

Matanas Chelko: "nor be troubled by more than his day's needs" -
there is no doubt that the author is speaking about very lofty levels of
trust, really (mamash) the greatest possible extreme of the trait - that

one does not worry about tomorrow. Nevertheless, reason also necessitates that it be such. For when one contemplates on what happened yesterday and further back, he will see that he always had what to live on and what to eat, and everything was only through G-d. Then too, he had nothing for tomorrow. Therefore, even today he can also rely on G-d for tomorrow. But the imagination deceives him and tells him that it is not comparable for in those past times he certainly had enough for the next day. But in truth, it is not so. Therefore, one needs to work on feeling this level of trust and live in this way.

AV 19

"since he does not know when his end will come" - this is a different point. The truster is not a dreamer. On the surface it seems that the wicked is more assured than the truster. For behold, the truster always worries that perhaps he will die tomorrow, as Rabbi Eliezer told his disciples "repent today for tomorrow you may die" (Shabbat 153a) But the wicked does not live by this idea. But in truth, it is not so (that the wicked is more assured) for the end of every human being is death. This is not a thought of sadness. On the contrary, it is proper and beneficial.

AV 20

A man should constantly contemplate that he is given a fixed amount of time to live and work in this world. But the wicked does not contemplate this thought to repent for perhaps he will die tomorrow. Rather, he trusts that certainly tomorrow and the day after he will still be among the living. This is a bit amazing for most people see through television or the like many murders, and that people do die, but they don't take to heart that it is possible they will also die like them. Rather, whenever they start to think about their deaths, they fall into great sadness. They feel so assured that they will be alive tomorrow and the day after that they don't even worry about this. It is known what the Chafetz Chaim said on how a man goes to a funeral and sees that people die, but does not reflect that perhaps he will also die tomorrow. Rather, he thinks that just like there is chevra kadisha (funeral worker group), so too there is chevra of the dead, and he is not part of this group and is not counted among them. In truth, this is just repressing of the eye.

AV 21

For one must reflect on the time of his end in this world. This is not a matter of sadness [to avoid] but rather like a farmer working on his field who still has much work to do. If his friend tells him to finish everything quickly before nightfall for then he will not be able to work, certainly he will not answer him: "don't speak to me about night, for it is sad and dark". Likewise for death, which is the time of nightfall for a man. Therefore, one must and is under duty to reflect on one's time for work in this world.)

AV 22

But one who does not trust in G-d, mourns greatly the constant troubles of the world that befall him, that his wishes and the things he loves are taken away or denied from him (he worries constantly that these things will be lacking to him - TL). He tries to amass much wealth of this world, as if he were assured from passing on (that his situation passes from this world to the next - TL), and the fear of death has left him, as if his days are unlimited and his life will never end. He does not consider his end, occupied only with this world, unconcerned about his religious matters, making no provisions for the hereafter, and his eternal abode. His trust in prolonging his days in this world is a cause for his perpetual desire for his worldly affairs and for his little desire in matters of his final end.

AV 23

(*Matanas Chelko*: "his trust in prolonging his days..." - in truth this is a great wonder. One who does not trust in G-d, trusts in only one thing - that he will not die and will live forever. For everything else he relies on his own strength and ingenuity, and that he has the power to decide and succeed. But regarding life and death, which everyone knows and recognizes that it is in G-d's hands - on this he trusts that he will live forever! This is what we wrote in the beginning of this gate, namely, that really every person trusts in something, and it is impossible to live otherwise. The difference is whether a person trusts in G-d, human beings, or in himself. For example, one who rides an airplane trusts in the mechanics that no failure will occur, and likewise on the pilot who knows how to drive the airplane. Likewise, he trusts that the baker did not put poison in the bread, and similarly for every thing. The reason is that this is the nature G-d implanted in man - to trust. For without this, it is impossible to live. One would be worried on every little thing, be it the baker or the workers, etc. [The proper way is that] in every thing it is proper to place one's trust in G-d (not the baker, etc.), but in things one does not know what will be such as death, one must prepare for himself provisions for the journey.

AV 24

When the preacher rebukes him or the teacher instructs him saying "how long will you avoid thinking about preparing provisions for your final journey and for matters of your eternal abode?"

He will answer "when I will have enough money for my needs and for the needs of my wife and children until the end of our days. Then I will have peace of mind from my worries of this world, and I will take time to pay my debts to the Creator, and will think about preparing provisions for my final end."

AV 25

Chapter 6

I saw proper to expose the foolishness and error in this way of thinking in 7 ways. I will reveal the greatness of their mistake, and if our words prolong, this is because there is much to shame and rebuke proponents of this outlook.

(*Pas Lechem*: *"foolishness and error"* - Some of the matters he will bring demonstrate to the person that he is a complete fool, similar to one

of the boorish people who have no human understanding. Other matters
he will bring do not demonstrate his foolishness so much but rather
show that he is mistaken, such as the fifth, sixth, and seventh. Afterwards, he wrote: "there is much to shame and rebuke..." corresponding
to these two "foolishness and mistake", because a man is shamed when
he is called a fool, and on the "mistake", he wrote "and rebuke", namely,
to clarify his mistake to him.)

They are a class of "security pledge seekers", similar in their practice
to merchants who sell goods on credit to someone he does not trust, and
will demand a security pledge at the time of sale, because he minimally
trusts his client or fears the client will not be able to pay him.

AV 26

(1) The first of the possible ways to answer him: we tell him "You, the
man who doubts the decree of the Creator, and doubts His [Almighty]
power, you whose light of intellect has obscured, whose candle of understanding has extinguished due to being overwhelmed by the darkness of
material desires. You deem proper to seek a security pledge from a client
who has no dominion over you, and cannot give you orders, however,
for a worker who seeks to be hired by an employer, it is not proper for
him to seek a security pledge of his wages before he starts to work. All
the more so, it is not proper for a slave to seek a security pledge of his
food from his master before working for Him, and even more so, for a
created being to seek a pledge from his Creator before fulfillment of the
service he owes Him!

AV 27

It is a wonder! For a slave to undertake service to his master with
a precondition that the master pay him a wage after his service is
completed would be regarded as a disgrace (since the owner boards,
lodges, and clothes him and provides for all his needs - Rabbi Hyamson,*zt"l*), as the sages said "be not like servants who serve their master
on condition to receive reward, but rather like servants who serve their
master even without condition of receiving reward" (Avos 1:3). And how

much more so if he were so brazen as to demand a pledge for his maintenance from his master before he even starts work. On similar to this it is written "Is this how you repay the L-ord, you disgraceful, unwise people?! [Is He not your Father that has acquired you? has He not made you, and established you?]" (Devarim 32:6).

AV 28

(*Pas Lechem*: *"who doubts the decree of the Creator"* - you are of those of little faith, who doubt the decree of the Creator, i.e. who doubt whether or not all of a man's guidance and needs are governed exclusively by the decree of the Creator

"and doubts His [Almighty] power" - you doubt His power, and the scope of His providence which spreads from the highest heavens (spiritual worlds) until the depths of our [physical] world, since the doubt on the providence [of G-d] in this world stems from their imagining and picturing the remoteness of the physical from His glorious holy place.

AV 29

Marpe Lenefesh: *"whose light of intellect has obscured, whose candle of understanding has extinguished due to being overpowered by the darkness of material desires"* - i.e. since the darkness of his material desires has overpowered him, therefore "the light of intellect has obscured, and the candle of understanding has extinguished", to the extent that he does not understand even self-evident things which no man is capable of denying.

Tov Halevanon: *"even the work of a slave to a master on condition to be paid after the work is regarded as a disgrace"* - that which he does not know his owner (a reference to Isaiah 1:3 "The ox knows his owner...but Israel does not know"), who acquired him with his money on condition that he serve him. And all the more so, the Holy One BB'H who is our Father, He acquired us, and it is proper for us to serve Him on account of the multitude of favors He has already bestowed on us, as the author wrote in the previous chapter.)

AV 30

(2) One who takes a security pledge from a client receives a definite amount and his request is limited. But for the proponent of this thinking, there is no end to what he seeks, because he does not know how much money will suffice for his and his family's needs and luxuries for the rest of their lives, and even if he obtained money many times his needs, he would not be at peace, because the time of their end is hidden, and the number of their days is not known, and he is foolish in what he seeks because there is no end by him and no measure.

(*Pas Lechem*: "*no end by him*" to the amount of his needs since he does not know how long he will live, and corresponding to the desire for luxuries, he wrote "no measure" since there is no measure for luxuries.

Translator: since he does not know his end, he imagines and conducts his life as if he will live forever as The Zohar wrote (Nasso 126):"A man walks in this world and he thinks that it will be his forever, and that he will remain in it for all time".)

ELUL 1

(3) One who takes a security pledge from his fellow, only does so if there are no previous debts that he owes the fellow, and the fellow has no claims against him, only then is he justified to request a pledge. But if he has outstanding debts to the fellow, and knows the fellow has legitimate claims against him, he has no business whatsoever in seeking a pledge, and it is not proper for him to accept it even if the fellow volunteered the pledge.

All the more so, for the Creator who has such legitimate claims on man, so that if the service of all human beings who ever lived could be accumulated and credited to a single man, their total would not be sufficient return to cover the debt of gratitude that a man owes for even one of the benefits the Creator bestowed on him (such as bringing him to existence from nothingness).

ELUL 2

(*Pas Lechem*: This is because the intent in the word "return" is: the receiving of a favor that the benefactor receives in return from the one who he benefited. But for G-d, it is completely not applicable to render to Him any favor from His creations. Therefore, it cannot be considered a "return".

Matanas Chelko: As written (Job 41:11) "Who has given Me anything beforehand, that I should repay him?", i.e. no man has ever done any commandment without having first received countless benefits from G-d. His life, possessions, and all matters - everything comes from G-d. The reason man cannot repay G-d is twofold. First, in truth, G-d does not get anything whatsoever from the fulfilling of His commandments. Hence, the fulfilling of a commandment cannot be considered a payment for all that one received. Secondly, all that a man does is worth less than a drop in the ocean in comparison with the gift of life which G-d has graced to man. All that he does shabbat, tefilin, talit, etc. is not payment for even one second of life.)

ELUL 3

And how can this brazen faced person not be ashamed to ask from the Creator big favors on top of previous favors thereby increasing his debt to Him. (the man seeks from G-d more favors, and that they be bigger than the favors He bestowed on him until now - *PL*) And maybe he will not even be able to fulfill the service that he says he will do (after he acquires wealth) because his days will have passed and his end will have come.

ELUL 4

(*Pas Lechem*: "*his days will have passed and his end will have come*" - two expressions corresponding to two categories of a person's death. One, that the number of days allotted to him from the time of his birth have passed, as is known, that every person has a fixed number of days allotted to him. Two, due to a heavenly decree because of some sin for which he incurred a death sentence.)

One of the pious would say to people: "Gentlemen, is it conceivable that the Creator would demand payment today for debts that are not due until tomorrow? And likewise, would He demand payment today for debts that are not due until next year, or many years from now?"

ELUL 5

They answered him, "How is it possible to claim from us payment of future debts when we don't even know if we will be living at the time when the debt is incurred? Rather, we are only bound to perform a definite service for a definite time and when the future comes, we will perform the service that is due then."

He would answer them: "So too, the Creator guarantees for you for every definite period its needed livelihood, and in return for this, you are indebted a great service (in that time period - PL). Just like He does not demand from you the special service before its appointed time, so too you should feel ashamed to ask for income before the time for it has arrived. Why do I see you seeking from Him income for several years in the future when you don't even know if you will live to reach those days. Furthermore, you ask Him to provide you with maintenance for a wife and children which you don't even have yet. You are not satisfied with the livelihood provided in the present and you seek to prepare money for needs and luxuries for future times that you are uncertain to reach and that are not assured to you. And, not only do you not render to Him service for the benefits you will receive in the future, but you don't even make an accounting with yourselves for the service to Him which you neglected to do in the past during which G-d has not neglected to provide for your livelihood in full."

ELUL 6

(4) One who takes a security pledge from his fellow does so for one of three reasons: One, maybe the fellow will become poor and won't be able to pay him. Two, maybe the fellow will close his hand [refuse to pay] and he may be unable to collect payment from him. Three, in case the fellow dies or won't be found. The security pledge is like a medicine

against these ailments that occur between people (i.e. if he takes a pledge he is immune from these ailments and worries - TL). But if men were assured of each other against these three mishaps, it would certainly be disgraceful to demand a security pledge. And the Creator for whom these three mishaps do not apply, how much more so is it a great disgrace to demand a security pledge from Him. And scripture already says "silver and gold is Mine" (Chagai 2:8), and "wealth and honor belong to You" (Divrei Hayamim 29:12).

(*Tov Halevanon*: It is not applicable to ask any kind of pledge from Him since everything is already by Him.)

ELUL 7

Pas Lechem: The latter two reasons do not need a proof [from scripture], because who is so foolish as to not know that He is living and among us, and that He has no trace of dishonesty or stinginess, ch'v. But on the first reason, perhaps a person will think "from where will G-d pay me, since He does not make coins?" On this he brought the verse "silver and gold is Mine", that nevertheless He has full capacity to give to whomever He wishes

Matanas Chelko: "disgrace to demand a security pledge from Him" - for G-d will not become poor or die. He can give whenever He wants. Only that a man doesn't believe in G-d and His ability. Therefore he seeks a pledge. But G-d already promised in His Torah that human beings should do the commandments and He will support them all of their days.)

ELUL 8

(5) One who obtains a security pledge from his fellow will be at peace with his pledge because he expects to collect from it and to derive benefit from it or its monetary value. But one who thinks that if the Creator will advance him future provisions he will have peace of mind regarding affairs of this world - his thinking is false and mistaken, because he cannot be sure the money will remain by him. It is possible that he will be struck by some mishap that parts him from the money, as written "in mid-life he will lose it" (Yirmiyahu 17:11).

And as for the claim that he will have peace of mind when he amasses wealth - this demonstrates falsehood and foolishness on his part. On the contrary this may well be the very cause that will cause him much mental pressure and anxiety as our sages said "more possessions, more worries" (Avos 2:7)..

ELUL 9

(*Pas Lechem*: "*this demonstrates falsehood and foolishness*" - either he is mistaken in this, or he himself knows this and deceives with this excuse.

Marpe Lenefesh: Even though it is a mistake to demand a pledge from G-d for many reasons, nevertheless, if he were assured that the money would stay by him and that he could do what he wants with it, his mistake would not be a falsehood. For example, let's say he took a pledge from someone who he did not realize that the man is an honorable and wealthy person. Even though he was mistaken in demanding a pledge, nevertheless, since he did not know the man, it is not falsehood, since nevertheless, he is assured by the pledge from many possible mishaps. But this that he took a pledge from G-d, not only was he mistaken in his outlook, but also his mistake will not yield any benefit, because he is still not assured that the money will be by him at a needy time, perhaps the money will be struck by a loss and nothing will remain or maybe he will die at midlife as [we see] happens every day. And even if we say that the wealth will stay by him, nevertheless it is uncertain whether he will serve G-d due to having wealth, because perhaps the money will bring him more mental pressure and anxiety than he had before he had it, since "more possessions, more worries")

ELUL 10

(6) If one who takes a security pledge from his fellow were certain that the fellow would pay him before the due time, and would out of pure kindness compensate him with an amount twice as much as was due for his waiting time, he would not seek a security pledge under any circumstances. Now, the blessed Creator, of who it is known to us of His benevolent conduct towards us, and of His great past and present favors

to us, and that He rewards acts of righteousness and service with reward that we cannot even imagine, as written "no eye had ever seen, O G-d, besides Yours, what He has prepared for those who wait (trust and hope - *TL*) to Him" (Yeshaya 64:3), certainly it is a great disgrace to ask for a security pledge.

(*Marpe Lenefesh*: "*reward that we cannot even imagine*" - that He bestows so much good reward for one mitzvah.

Pas Lechem: the hidden reward cannot be imagined by the human mind. All the more so, it cannot be described verbally.)

ELUL 11

(7) One who takes a security pledge from his fellow, is only justified in doing so if he is able to supply him with the merchandise purchased for which he takes the pledge. But one who seeks a security pledge from the Creator, in seeking advance favors, is not capable of paying for them in services. He is not even certain of paying back what he owes from past debts, all the more so for paying what he owes for future favors, because the righteous man cannot pay back the debts of gratitude of the Al-mighty on him except through the means of help which G-d renders him. And so, one of the pious in his praises of G-d said: "Even the thinking person who has knowledge of You, does not praise his own religious acts, but rather praises Your Name and mercy, for You have prepared his heart to know You. Through You (Your help - *ML*) the people of Israel will be found worthy and be praised saying: "We praised [ourselves] with G-d all day long, and we will forever thank Your name" (Tehillim 44:9).

ELUL 12

(*Marpe Lenefesh*: For example, if the lender takes a security pledge on condition that he will lend the borrower 1000 gold coins. Then, if the lender has the 1000 gold coins available, he can take the security pledge. If he does not [have the 1000 gold coins available], then he cannot take it. And a man knows that he does not have the ability to pay G-d in services and righteousness corresponding to all the benefits he gets from G-d. And especially, if he pays back a little bit, it is through G-d's help, as our sages expounded (Midrash Vayikra Rabba 27:2) on the verse: "Who has given Me anything beforehand, that I should repay him?" (Iyov 41:3) - Who put up a mezuzah before I gave him a house? [Who built a Sukkah before I gave him a place upon which to build it? Who performed the mitzvah of tzitzis before I gave him clothing?], likewise, even one's wisdom and praises is from Him, bb'h

ELUL 13

Matanas Chelko: even when a man praises G-d, the recognition itself that man has of G-d is from G-d, and the mouth with which he utters the praises is from G-d. Everything he does is using the tools which G-d has given him. This is what we say in the "Aleinu Leshabeach" prayer: "it is incumbent on us to praise the Master of the world... [and concludes] that we bow and praise the King of kings". What kind of praise is it to say that our portion is to praise Him? Rather, it is the exact same thing the author is saying; we are praising G-d for giving us the permission, ability, and opportunity to praise Him. Likewise, in the Modim prayer, it starts "we thank You..." and ends "on our thanking you"... The point is that a man does not do any "kindness" towards G-d. On the contrary, the kindness is from G-d who gave us the ability and possibility to come to the synagogue and pray to Him and praise Him. If one reflects on this, he will see it is the exact opposite of the outlook of the pledge-seeker who wants to receive everything before the service. But in truth, all the service they do - it is all from G-d.

ELUL 14

Chapter 7

Since we have completed in this gate, to the best of our ability, a fitting amount of discussion on the themes of trust, it is now proper to clarify the things detrimental to trust in the Al-mighty. I say that the detrimental things mentioned in the 3 preceding gates of this book are all likewise detrimental to trust [in G-d].

(*Marpe Lenefesh*: i.e. the Unity - to believe in the Creator of the world, as explained there [in Gate #1], and likewise on the [Gate of] examination, to examine His creations, and to assume the service of the Creator, as is fitting to Him. Whoever is far from the things mentioned in those gates and fell into the things detrimental to them as was explained earlier - he undoubtedly does not trust in G-d.

ELUL 15

Additional things which cause a loss of trust:

(1) Ignorance with regard to the Creator, and His good attributes, because one who does not realize the Creator's mercy towards His creations, His guidance, providence and rule over them, and that they are bound by His chains, under His total control - he will not be at peace (from mishaps - *PL*) and will not rely on Him (for providing his needs - *PL*).

(*Marpe Lenefesh*: *"Ignorance with regard to the Creator"* - he does not realize that G-d is a great and awesome King and that His reign is over everything.

"and His good traits" - how He guides His creations with kindness and mercy, and always gives them all their needs.

"that they are bound by His chains" - all the creations are truly bound by Him, that everything is from Him, all things that a human being does is completely from Him, and there is nobody who can change anything, except for yiras shamayim (moral choice) which G-d gave the free will in man's hands.

ELUL 16

Pas Lechem: (from the introduction) On the other things of the inner duties such as placing one's trust in G-d, giving over oneself to Him, and devoting one's acts to Him, and the like, *which stem from recognizing the greatness of G-d and of His beneficence.*)

(2) Another, ignorance of the Creator's commandments, namely His Torah, where He instructed us in it to rely on Him and trust in Him, as written "test Me in this..." (Malachi 3:10), and "trust in G-d forever" (Yeshaya 26:4).

ELUL 17

(*Tov Halevanon*: "*to rely on Him and trust in Him*" - in [performing] His service and guarding His commandments, and like our sages expounded: "take maaser so that you become rich", and [G-d] says: "test Me in this", i.e. in maaser, and likewise for all of the other mitzvot, and like the verse says (Tehillim 37:25): "yet I have not seen the righteous forsaken")

Another detriment to trust is to tend to rely on the means which one can see, without realizing that the nearer the causes are to the one affected by them, the less ability they have to help or harm him, and the further [up] they are, the stronger and the more power it has to help or harm him.

As an illustration, when a king decides to punish one of his servants, he commands his prime minister to take care of it, and the prime minister orders his chief of police, and the chief of police orders his sergeant, and the sergeant orders his officer, and the officer orders the policeman, and the policeman inflicts the punishment with the instruments (whip, stick, etc.) he has.

ELUL 18

The instruments have the least capability of all of them to reduce or increase his suffering because they have no will of their own. The policeman has greater capability than the instruments (to reduce the number of whippings - PL). Likewise, the officer has greater capability than the policeman, and the sergeant than the officer, and the chief of police than the sergeant, and the prime minister than the chief of police, and the king more than all of them, because if he wants, he can pardon the man (from everything - TL).

As you can see, the weakness and strength of the agents to affect the person are according to their remoteness from him or nearness to him. And the exalted Creator, who is the First Cause and infinitely remote from those affected by Him, is the One who it is proper to trust and rely on because of His infinite power to help or harm, as we explained.

ELUL 19

(*Marpe Lenefesh*: the thing near to him from which his livelihood comes has less power to provide his livelihood than the thing remote from him, which is the cause of this [near] thing, and this remote thing to another more remote thing, etc. All these agents from the man on are called causes and means, and G-d is the Means of all the means and the Cause of all the causes, and the man who receives from all the means is called "the affected". Understand this.)

The general principle in the matter of trust is that the degree of trust among those who trust in G-d increases according to the amount of knowledge of G-d, faith in His protection of them, and in His abundant providence to promote what is for their good.

ELUL 20

(*Tov Halevanon*: "*increases according to the amount of knowledge of G-d*" - knowing and understanding the extent of His reign on each and every act and cause - that everything depends on Him, bb'H. He will now bring an analogy to explain the matter.

Pas Lechem: The degree of level of trust among people, namely, the degree of trust which people differ in is "*according to the amount of knowledge of G-d, etc*"

Marpe Lenefesh: The proof of this is what he will mention shortly, that a baby at first trusts in his mother's breast, and afterwards on his mother, and afterwards on his father, and so on for the 10 levels he mentions. From this it is clear that the greater one's knowledge of G-d and of His providence on him, the more trust in G-d he will have.)

THE TEN LEVELS OF TRUST

(1) An infant, at the beginning of his existence, trusts in his mother's breast, as written "For You drew me from the womb; You made me trust on my mother's breasts" (Tehillim 22:10).

(*Matanas Chelko*: i.e. if the baby could speak and one would ask it how it lives, it would respond "from my mother's breast", not "from my mother". In his eyes, the breasts feed and sustain him. This is the outlook of a baby. He cannot grasp more than this.

ELUL 21

(**2**) When his perception strengthens, his trust moves to his mother, due to the great care she gives him, as written "I swear that I calmed and quieted my soul like a weaned child with his mother" (Tehillim 131:2).

(*Matanas Chelko*: when he grows a bit and his intellect opens a bit more, he recognizes that he receives several benefits from his mother, such as washing him, clothing him, etc. Hence, now he realizes that his sustenance comes from his mother. It is proper to add here the following analogy from the trust of a child to his mother and father. When a child stands on a table or chair and his father asks him to jump to his hands and the child does so. Certainly, without strong trust in his father, that his father worries for him and loves him, he would never have jumped thereby placing himself in danger of falling to the floor. His trust in his father is so great that he jumps to his hands. Likewise, for a man's trust in G-d, he must jump into the hands of G-d and trust in Him that He cares for him and loves him just like a father's love for his child.

ELUL 22

(**3**) When his understanding grows more, and he observes that his mother depends on his father, he moves his trust to his father due to the greater degree of protection he receives from him.

(*Tov Halevanon*: Her security and food through which she bestows on him - everything depends on the gift from the hand of the father.

Marpe Lenefesh: Even though his mother takes care of his needs, and not his father since he is not available, Nevertheless, he recognizes his father's protection, that sometimes his father saves him from things which cause him pain.)

ELUL 23

(4) When his body strengthens, and it becomes possible for him to earn for himself a livelihood through work or business, or the like, he moves his trust to his strength and resourcefulness, due to his ignorance that all the good that came before this was through the providence of G-d.

(*Tov Halevanon*: he is still boorish and does not realize that wealth does not come from the trade itself, and all the livelihood he received until now was from G-d.)

It is said of one of the pious, whose neighbor was a swift scribe and would earn his livelihood through his scribal skills. One day he inquired to the scribe: "how are things?" He answered "good, as long as my hand is still in good shape." Then, that evening his hand was crushed, and he could not write with it for the rest of his life. This was his punishment from G-d, in that he placed his trust in his hand. (to atone for him. Note that he must have been at a very high level of piety, therefore G-d paid him in this world even for minute sins so as to spare him from any punishments in the next world)

ELUL 24

(*Matanas Chelko*: "as long as my hand is still in good shape" - certainly it is permitted to speak like this. However, it all depends on one's intent. If he means "thank G-d, I still have the hand given to me to do my work", that he understands that the strength does not come from himself. Rather it is given to him by the grace of G-d, then his words are good and correct. However, it appears that the author's intent is that even words like this ascribe too much the ability and accomplishment to human power. If he thinks this is the way to his livelihood, that by G-d's giving him a hand, he is able to use it to work and earn a livelihood for himself, this is already considered shituf (association), G-d and himself. Since, what comes out of his words is that his intent is if he did not have a hand, he would not be able to provide for himself. This is not correct. For G-d can provide for him through other means. True, right now G-d gave him a hand through which he is providing for himself, but true trust is to recognize that even without his hand, G-d can still provide for him through his feet, his head or any other way. Hence, whenever a person ascribes excessive power and ability in the means itself, he already diminishes thereby his trust in G-d.

ELUL 25

Netziv commentary on Gen.40:23 - G-d punished Yosef for putting his trust in the Wine Master by causing the Wine Master to forget about Yosef for two years (midrash). From the fact that Yosef was punished for putting his trust in a person we learn about his greatness. The punishment indicates that Yosef had never before put his trust in man and was thus punished solely because he deviated from his high level of trust in G-d.

(5) If his livelihood comes through one of his fellow human beings, he will transfer his trust to them and rely on them.

(*Tov Halevanon*: The author returned to the previous matter, and said that there are those who do not rely on their own resourcefulness, and they recognize their own lackings. However, they trust in the salvation from human beings. He thinks that he does not need to trust in anything more, and even if he becomes disabled and unable to provide for himself, they will not abandon him.)

(6) But when his wisdom grows and he realizes their lacking and their need for the Creator, he will then move his trust to G-d, and rely on Him for things beyond his own control and which he cannot escape submitting to the decree of G-d, such as the falling of rainwater on the crops, or (safely) traveling through the sea, or crossing a barren desert, floods, outbreak of a plague among the living, or the like among matters which human beings have no plan whatsoever, as written "In the time of their trouble they will cry out: 'arise and save us'" (Yirmiyahu 2:27).

ELUL 26

(7) If his knowledge of G-d strengthens more, he will put his trust in G-d in matters where he has some plan, such as avoiding earning a livelihood through dangerous means or exhausting occupations that wear down the body, and trusts in G-d that He will provide for him through a lighter occupation.

(8) If his knowledge of G-d strengthens more, he will put his trust in G-d in all the means, whether difficult or easy, and while occupied in them, his intent will be directed to serve G-d and guard His commandments.

(*Tov Halevanon*: i.e. He will put to heart, that G-d has no limitations, and He can provide the livelihood of every person through any means. And that which he is occupied with a specific trade, this is in order to observe the service of G-d, which He commanded us to engage in matters that cause our livelihood to come, and as the author wrote earlier [in chapter 4])

(9) If his knowledge of G-d strengthens more regarding His mercy on the created beings, he will accept with heart and mind, outwardly and inwardly, the decrees of G-d. He will rejoice in whatever G-d does to him, be it death or life, poverty or wealth, health or sickness. He will not desire other than what G-d has chosen for him, and desire only what G-d has chosen for him.

(*Tov Halevanon*: i.e. he will acknowledge and bless G-d on the death of one of his relatives or children just like [he did] on their life, and likewise for poverty just like for wealth.

He will give himself over to G-d, and surrender his body and soul over to His judgment. He will not prefer one matter over another and will not choose anything other than his current situation, as one who trusts in G-d said "I never resolved to do a thing and desired something else".

(*Pas Lechem*: "*He will give himself over to G-d*" - regarding G-d's guidance of all of his needs.

"surrender his body and soul over to His judgment" - If some bad thing happens to him, he receives it and bears it with a good countenance.

ELUL 27

Manoach Halevavos: He does not trust in one matter more than another. He does not think one matter is more profitable than another. All the causes and means are equal to him, because he realizes that they all depend on the will of G-d. Therefore, he trusts only in G-d. Because of this, when he resolves to do something, he does not desire something else.

Matanas Chelko: this is the level of a true "baal bitachon" (truster in G-d). He does not trust in any means (even though he engages in them). Rather, he knows and believes that everything comes only from G-d. This level brings one to accept everything G-d decrees on him in all matters of life.)

(10) When his knowledge of G-d strengthens more than this and he understands the true intent why he was created and brought to this fleeting world, and he recognizes the exaltedness of the eternal, next world, he will think lightly of this world, and its means. With mind, soul, and body, he will flee from this world and surrender himself to the blessed Al-mighty, and delight in remembering Him in solitude. He will feel desolate when he is not (capable of - *MC*) meditating on His greatness.

(*Matanas Chelko*: this is an additional level of intensity of recognition and trust. Not only does he trust in G-d's ability and providence, but this recognition has brought him to strengthen his trust in the will of G-d. Now, he recognizes full well why he came to this world - not in order to work and make money, but only in order to do the will of G-d.

Manoach Halevavos: No thoughts come to his mind, except on the greatness of G-d. He is desolate and silent from other thoughts, and parts from them quickly if they enter his thoughts... He is astonished on those who do not contemplate. He thinks of the greatness of G-d always, and likewise he is amazed at himself if sometimes he does not meditate on the greatness of G-d, and he puts to heart that it is proper to think always of the greatness of G-d when sitting in his house, walking on the way, lying down, and rising up.

ELUL 28

Pas Lechem: When he is in solitude, away from people, and nothing distracts his thoughts, he will greatly delight in this because then he can remember Him with a focused mind.)

If he is among a crowd of people, he will long for nothing else than to do His will, and yearn only to come near to Him. His joy in his love of G-d will distract him from the pleasures worldly people have for this world, and even from the joy of souls in the next world.

(*Tov Halevanon*: His joy in love of G-d will distract him to such an extent that he will not be able to enter in his heart any joy of worldly people, namely, the worldly matters they rejoice in.

ELUL 29

Marpe Lenefesh: His joy in love of G-d is greater than the pleasure of the living in reaching their desires and even greater than the pleasures of the dead in the next world, as our sages said (Avot 4:17): "one hour of teshuva and good deeds in this world is better than all of the life of the next world")

This is the highest of the levels of those who trust in G-d, reached by the prophets, pious ones, and treasured, pure men of G-d, and this is what the verse refers to in saying "Even [for] the way of Your judgments, O L-ord, have we hoped for You; for Your Name and for Your remembrance is the desire of [our] soul directed." (Yeshaya 26:8), and "my soul thirsts to the Al-mighty, the living G-d; [when shall I come and appear before G-d?]" (Tehillim 42:3).

These are the ten levels of trust which one cannot escape belonging to one of them. We find the matter of trust in scripture expressed in 10 synonyms corresponding to these 10 levels. They are:

Mivtach (trust), *Mishan* (support), *Tikvah* (hope), *Machse* (protection), *Tochelet* (waiting), *Chikui* (expecting), *Semichah* (reliance), *Sever* (resting), *Misad* (confidence), and *Chesel* (assurance).

May G-d place us among those who trust in Him, who give themselves over to His judgment outwardly and inwardly, in His mercy, Amen.

The Gate of trust is Complete, to G-d the last and the first.

ENDNOTES

CHAPTER 1 -CHAPTER 6

1. Wehrenberg, Margaret (2014). "Cure or Control: Depression as a Chronic Condition," *Psychotherapy Networker*, November/December 2014.
Excerpt accessed Sept. 1, 2016 from https://www.psychotherapynetworker.org/blog/details/997/breaking-free-from-the-cure-myth .

2. Frankl, Viktor (1946). *Man's Search for Meaning*. Boston, MA: Beacon Press,pg. 110.

3. Ibid.,pg. 109.

4. Purdy, Matthew (1994). For Bullet's Victim, a Vigil Triumphs; Against Medical Odds, Yeshiva Student Emerges From Coma. S*New York Times*, May 28, 1994. Accessed Sept. 2, 2016 from http://www.nytimes.com/1994/05/28/nyregion/for-bullet-s-victim-vigil-triumphs-against-medical-odds-yeshiva-student-emerges.html?pagewanted=all .

5. Schneerson, Rabbi Menachem M. (2010) (Compiled by Uri Kaploun and Rabbi Eliyahu Touger), *As a Father Loves His Only Son*. Brooklyn, NY: Sichos In English.
Also accessed Feb. 11, 2017 from
http://www.chabad.org/therebbe/article_cdo/aid/2296496/jewish/Without-Fear-or-Worry.htm#footnoteRef39a2296496 .

6. Anxiety and Depression Association of America, "Facts & Statistics," Accessed

Oct. 16, 2016 from https://www.adaa.org/about-adaa/press-room/facts-sta-tistics .

7. National Institute of Mental Health. Depression: What You Need To Know, NIH Publication No. 15-3561, Accessed Oct. 17, 2016 from https://www.nimh.nih.gov/health/publications/depression-what-you-need-to-know/index.shtml .

8. Nord, Warren A. (1995). *Religion and American Education: Rethinking a National Dilemma.* University of North Carolina Press, pg. 284.

9. Freud, Sigmund (1927). *The Future of an Illusion* (New York NY: W.W. Norton and Company).

10. Pew Research Center (2015). *U.S. Public Becoming Less Religious: Modest Drop in Overall Rates of Belief and Practice, but Religiously Affiliated Americans Are as Observant as Before.* Accessed Sept. 1, 2016 from http://www.pewforum.org/2015/11/03/u-s-public-becoming-less-religious/ .

11. Alcoholics Anonymous. The Twelve Steps of Alcoholics Anonymous. Accessed on Oct. 6, 2016 from http://www.aa.org/assets/en_US/smf-121_en.pdf .

12. Letter from Dr. Carl Gustav Jung, Jan. 3, 1961. Accessed on Oct. 5, 2016 from http://www.barefootsworld.net/jungletter.html .

13. Ibid.

14. *Midrash Tanhuma*, Bereishit, pg. 222.

15. Rosmarin, David H.; Pargament, Kenneth I.; Pirutinsky, Steven;and Mahoney, Annette (2010) A randomized controlled evaluation of a spiritually-integrated treatment for subclinical anxiety in the Jewish community, delivered via the Internet. *Journal of Anxiety Disorders* 24 (2010) 799-808. Accessed on Feb. 27, 2017 from http://www.centerforanxiety.org/readings/JAD-Print.pdf .

16. Ibid.

17. Stein, Adam (2015). Student feedback from "Living in the Moment" course. Accessed on Jan. 22, 2016 from http://www.redefinetime.com/testimonials.html .

18. Ellison, Christopher G.; Boardman, Jason D.; Williams, David R.; and Jackson, James S. (2001). Religious Involvement, Stress, and Mental Health: Findings from the 1995 Detroit Area Study. *Social Forces* 80:1, September 2001. Accessed on Dec. 26, 2016 from http://www.colorado.edu/ibs/pop/boardman/articles/2001--Ellison,_etal_Social-Forces.pdf .

19. Good, Jennifer J. (2010). *Integration of Spirituality and Cognitive-behavioral Therapy for the Treatment of Depression.* Dissertation, Philadelphia College of Osteopathic Medicine Psychology Dissertations, pg. 15. Accessed Nov. 28, 2016 from http://digitalcommons.pcom.edu/cgi/viewcontent.cgi?article=1054&context=psychology_dissertations .

20. Ibid.,pg. 16.

21. Muelder, W. G. (1957). "The efficacy of prayer," In Simon Doniger (Ed.), *Healing: Human and divine: Man's search for health and wholeness through science, faith, and prayer.* New York: Association Press, pg. 131–143.

22. Excerpts of a letter from Rabbi Schneerson, M. to Israeli psychiatrist, Dr. S. Stern-Mirz in Haifa, concerning one of her patients. Letter dated June 19, 1969 (3rd Tammuz, 5729). Translation to English from Jacobson, Rabbi Y. Y., "Mrs. Mozart, Viktor Frankl & The Lubavitcher Rebbe: How a Chassidic Master Affected the Trend of Psychology in the 20th Century," Accessed on Feb. 26, 2017 fromhttps://www.theyeshiva.net/item/896 .

23. Ibid.

24. Miller, Rabbi Chaim (2014).*Turning Judaism Outward: A Biography of the Rebbe, Menachem Mendel Schneerson.* Brooklyn, NY: Kol Menachem,pg. 50.

25. Covey, Stephen R. (1989). *The Seven Habits of Highly Effective People.* New York, NY: Free Press, pg. 32.

26. Ibid.

27. Metcalfe, Janet. *Evolution of Metacognition.* Department of Psychology, Columbia University. Accessed Jan. 5, 2017 from http://www.columbia.edu/cu/psychology/metcalfe/PDFs/Metcalfe%20EvolMetacog.pdf

28. Beck, Judith S. (Author) and Aaron T. (Foreword) (1995). *Cognitive Behavior Therapy: Basics and Beyond.* New York, NY: The Guilford Press, pg. 179–180

29. *Man's Search for Meaning*, op. cit.,pg. 85.

30. Ibid. pg. 12.

31. Ibid. pg. 35.

32. Frankl, Viktor (1946. *The Doctor and the Soul: From Psychotherapy to Logotherapy.* New York, NY: Alfred A. Knopf Inc.,pg. 44.

33. Frankl, Victor (1967), *Psychotherapy and Existentialism* New York, NY: Washington Square Press.

34. Schneersohn, Rabbi Menachem M. (Tzemach Tzedek) (1828?). *Igeres Kodesh, Admor HaTzemach Tzedek*, Letter 15. Brooklyn, NY: Kehot Publication Society.

35. Schneerson, Rabbi Menachem M., *Likutei Sichos*, Vol. XXXVI, p.1. *Sichah.* Accessed 3/5/1 from http://www.chabad.org/therebbe/article_cdoaid/2295026/jewish/A-Knowing-Heart-Parshas-Shmos.htm .

36. Ibid.

37. Ibid.

38. Pinto Wagner, . *Worried No More: Help and Hope for Anxious Children.* Cary, North Carolina: Lighthouse Press, pg. 80.

39. Liebgold, Howard, M.D. (2004). *Freedom from Fear: Overcoming Anxiety, Phobias and Panic.* New York, NY: Kensington Publishing Corp., pg. 31.

40. Fredrickson, Barbara (2009). *Positivity: Top-Notch Research Reveals the Upward Spiral That Will Change Your Life.* New York, NY: Random House, pg. 129.

41. Ibid ,pg. 217.

42. Livehappy.com. *Make-A-Wish: Where Science and Hope Meet.* Accessed on Jan. 1, 2017 from http://www.livehappy.com/practice/giving/make-wish-where-science-and-hope-meet .

43. Mayo Clinic. *Positive thinking: Stop negative self-talk to reduce stress.* Accessed on Jan. 1, 2017 from http://www.mayoclinic.org/healthy-lifestyle/stress-management/in-depth/positive-thinking/art-20043950 .

44. Riken Research. *The power of positive memories.* Accessed on Dec. 24, 2016 from http://www.riken.jp/en/research/rikenresearch/highlights/8088/ .

45. Perreau-Linck Elisabeth; Beauregard, Mario; Gravel, Paul; Paquette, Vincent; Soucy, Jean-Paul; Diksic, Mirko; and Benkelfat, Chawki (2007). In vivo measurements of brain trapping of C-labelled alpha-methyl-L-tryptophan during acute changes in mood states. *Journal of Psychiatry and Neuroscience* 32 (6).

46. Kaplan, Aryeh (1982). *Meditation and Kabbalah.* York Beach, ME: Samuel Weiser, pp. 179–182.

47. Johns Hopkins Medicine. Forgiveness: Your Health Depends on It. Accessed Jan. 21, 2017 from http://www.hopkinsmedicine.org/health/healthy_aging/healthy_connections/forgiveness-your-health-depends-on-it .

48. Frankl, Viktor (1971), Video Lecture to Toronto Youth Corps. Accessed Jan. 21, 2017 from https://www.youtube.com/watch?v=fD1512_XJEw .

49. Nichols, Michael P. (2006). *Family Therapy Concepts and Methods*. Boston, MA: Pearson Educational Inc., pp. 327.

50. Ibid., pg. 327.

51. Ibid., pg. 330.

52. Ibid pg. 337.

53. Ibid., pg. 341.

54. Ibid., pg. 347.

55. Ibid., pg. 347.

56. Ibid., pg. 348.

57. Ibid., pg. 348.

58. Everydayhealth.com. "How Volunteering Can Lessen Depression and Extend Your Life." Accessed Jan. 22, 2017 from http://www.everydayhealth.com/depression/how-volunteering-can-lessen-depression-and-extend-your-life.aspx .

59. Smith, Jordan Michael (2014). Want to Be Happy? Stop Being So Cheap! Accessed Jan. 22, 2017 from https://newrepublic.com/article/119477/science-generosity-why-giving-makes-you-happy

60. Ibid.

61. Ilardi, Stephen (2009). Social Isolation: A Modern Plague. Accessed Jan. 15, 2017 from https://www.psychologytoday.com/blog/the-depression-cure/200907/social-isolation-modern-plague .

62. Glasser, William, M.D. (1998). *Choice Theory: A New Psychology of Human Freedom*. New York, NY: HarperCollins Publishers, pg. 14.

63. Schneerson, Rabbi Menachem M.; Kaploun, Uri (tr.) (2005), *In Good Hands: 100 Letters and Talks of the Lubavitcher Rebbe. Menachem M. Schneerson, on Bitachon: Trusting in G-d*. Brooklyn, NY: Sichos In English.
Accessed Feb. 1, 2017 from
http://www.chabad.org/therebbe/article_cdo/aid/2313473/jewish/12-People-study-and-study-but-when-it-comes-to-practical-application-wheres-the-trust.htm

ACKNOWLEDGMENTS

There are many people who I would like to thank for making this book possible. First and foremost is my wife, Daniela, who has always stood behind me in helping me launch great ideas for changing the world. I would also like to thank my children who put up with me during long hours of writing in preparation for making this book a reality. A special thank you to Rabbi Kadish Waldman who opened my eyes to the writings of the Mitteler Rebbe, Rabbi Simon Jacobson and Rabbi Michoel Seligson who reviewed the spiritual components of the manuscript, and finally my editor Mrs. Yedida Wolfe who brought my ideas and the text to life.

ABOUT THE AUTHOR

RABBI DANIEL SCHONBUCH, M.A., L.M.F.T. (Licensed Marriage and Family Therapist) is a renowned therapist whose warm and engaging approach has helped thousands of individuals and couples overcome depression, anxiety, OCD, and addiction, and enhance their relationships. He has trained in Cognitive Behavioral Therapy (CBT), Eye Movement Desensitization and Reprocessing (EMDR), and Emotionally-Focused Therapy.

81160009R00161

Made in the USA
Columbia, SC
16 November 2017